CSR, Sustainability, Ethics & Governance

Series editors

Samuel O. Idowu, London Metropolitan University, Calcutta House, London, UK
René Schmidpeter, Cologne Business School, Cologne, Germany

More information about this series at http://www.springer.com/series/11565

Mia Mahmudur Rahim
Editor

Code of Conduct on Transnational Corporations

Challenges and Opportunities

Springer

Editor
Mia Mahmudur Rahim
School of Law
University of South Australia
Adelaide, SA, Australia

ISSN 2196-7075 ISSN 2196-7083 (electronic)
CSR, Sustainability, Ethics & Governance
ISBN 978-3-030-10815-1 ISBN 978-3-030-10816-8 (eBook)
https://doi.org/10.1007/978-3-030-10816-8

Library of Congress Control Number: 2018965900

© Springer Nature Switzerland AG 2019, corrected publication 2019
This work is subject to copyright. All rights are reserved by the Publisher, whether the whole or part of the material is concerned, specifically the rights of translation, reprinting, reuse of illustrations, recitation, broadcasting, reproduction on microfilms or in any other physical way, and transmission or information storage and retrieval, electronic adaptation, computer software, or by similar or dissimilar methodology now known or hereafter developed.
The use of general descriptive names, registered names, trademarks, service marks, etc. in this publication does not imply, even in the absence of a specific statement, that such names are exempt from the relevant protective laws and regulations and therefore free for general use.
The publisher, the authors and the editors are safe to assume that the advice and information in this book are believed to be true and accurate at the date of publication. Neither the publisher nor the authors or the editors give a warranty, express or implied, with respect to the material contained herein or for any errors or omissions that may have been made. The publisher remains neutral with regard to jurisdictional claims in published maps and institutional affiliations.

This Springer imprint is published by the registered company Springer Nature Switzerland AG
The registered company address is: Gewerbestrasse 11, 6330 Cham, Switzerland

This book is dedicated to my wife Bipasha Haque.

Preface

Since World War II, there has been a great interest in a global code of conduct on Transnational Corporations (TNCs). This was more pronounced in the developing countries which seek equilibrium between the lures and the realities of globalisation, on the one hand, and a dream of a just and non-exploitative global order on the other. The United Nations initiated a process for such a code in the late 1970s. It proposed a draft Code of Conduct on Transnational Corporations (the Code). But the controversy over the form and provisions of the Code inhibited the consensus over it, despite over two decades of time and energy expended by the Working Group and other bodies within the UN system. The eventful but elongated codification process attested that the interests of the groups of the UN member countries are not only divergent, but also oft conflicting on TNCs' governance.

Although the precepts of globalisation have immensely transformed the global context, the 'protection versus interest' chase between the developed and developing countries is still prominent in any attempt for a global framework to ensure TNCs' social responsibility and accountability performance worldwide. Nonetheless, we now have plenty of alternatives to the framework, although none of them have been wholeheartedly accepted by all the stakeholders.

The recent resolution of the UN for a code of conduct therefore is noteworthy. Following this resolution, the UN framework would prepare an agenda for discussion on the issues around the social responsibilities and accountabilities of TNCs. Even if such forthcoming initiatives do not incarnate the doom days of the Code, this would certainly generate debates amongst the stakeholders on the rule that should govern TNC's accountability and responsibility, particularly in developing countries.

The theme of this book is to explore the intricacies to creating a global framework for TNCs. Thus, the first four chapters concentrate upon the major frameworks, including the Code, and postulates that (i) crafting a global code for TNCs in the present global context is challenging; (ii) the existing frameworks are with serious flaws, weak in implementation strategies and unable to meet a common ground on several vital issues; and (iii) there should be a framework that governs TNCs' social responsibility performance. The latter four chapters delineate the alternatives we may consider for/against an exhaustive global framework. They assert that in the absence of such a framework, stakeholders can seek for creating suitable approaches in the corporate self-regulation at the domestic level.

We hope this book contributes to the scholarship on the global framework for raising the social responsibilities of TNCs and serves as a platform for the progress of this scholarship.

Adelaide, Australia   Mia Mahmudur Rahim

Acknowledgements

I am deeply indebted to a number of individuals, without whose generous support I could not have completed this book project. Thanks are due first and foremost to the contributors for their excellent work; this book took more time than it was anticipated, but they were always supportive with utmost patience. Thanks are also due to Dr. Christian Rauscher and Dr. Sammuel O. Idowu who provided support and generosity.

Above all, I must thank my family—my daughters Raya and Rida, now old enough to spot the mistakes in my writings, and my wife Bipasha Haque, who has tolerated my endless kvetching about writing deadlines with nearly superhuman love and patience. As a researcher in her own right, Bipasha read and commented on my chapters in the book and shared ideas on a daily basis for enough years that I barely know whose are whose. Their love makes everything else possible.

Contents

Quest for a Global Code of Conduct for TNCs—A Grim Tale 1
Mia Mahmudur Rahim

An 'Instrument of Moral Persuasion'—Multinational Enterprises
and International Codes of Conduct in the 1970s. 23
Thomas Hajduk

TNC Code of Conduct or CSR? A Regulatory Systems
Perspective 45
Benedict Sheehy

Behavioral Dynamics and Regulation of Transnational
Corporations 63
Hervé Lado

The UN Global Compact for Transnational Business and Peace:
A Need for Orchestration? 89
Mariko Shoji

Transnational Corporations' Social License to Operate—The Third
Facet of Corporate Governance 111
Indrajit Dube

Enforcement of a Global Code of Conduct on TNC's Operations 131
Vicki Waye

Converged Approach in Regulation for Socializing Transnational
Corporations 155
Mia Mahmudur Rahim

Correction to: The UN Global Compact for Transnational Business
and Peace: A Need for Orchestration? C1
Mariko Shoji

Editor and Contributors

About the Editor

Dr. Mia Mahmudur Rahim is a Senior Lecturer in Law at the University of South Australia. Previously, he worked at the Queensland University of Technology and the Bangladesh Judiciary. He completed a Bachelor of Laws with Honours and Masters of Laws from Dhaka University, a master's in International Economic Law from Warwick University, a master's in Public Administration from the National University of Singapore and a Ph.D. from the School of Law at Macquarie University. His research interests lie in different forms of regulation and how this relates to legal structures that encourage social responsibility and accountability practice of regulatees. One of his recent books, *Legal Regulation of Corporate Social Responsibility*, has explained how a meta-regulation mode in laws can effectively raise social responsibility performance of corporations. He is the author of *Corporate Social Responsibility in Private Enterprises* and the lead editor of *Social Audit Regulation*.

Contributors

Indrajit Dube Rajiv Gandhi School of Intellectual Property Law, Indian Institute of Technology, Kharagpur, India

Thomas Hajduk University of St. Gallen, St. Gallen, Switzerland

Hervé Lado Asnieres sur Seine, France

Mia Mahmudur Rahim School of Law, University of South Australia, Adelaide, SA, Australia

Benedict Sheehy School of Law and Justice, University of Canberra, Bruce, ACT, Australia

Mariko Shoji Department of International Studies, Keiai University, Chiba, Japan

Vicki Waye School of Law, University of South Australia, Adelaide, SA, Australia

Quest for a Global Code of Conduct for TNCs—A Grim Tale

Mia Mahmudur Rahim

1 Introduction

The world has progressed in various areas—we now have access to a different planet, we have technologies for super-fast communication, we have successfully invented cures for many deadly diseases, and there are many more examples to add. In the meanwhile we have made some of our matters complicated too—number of countries with nuclear weapons are on the rise, internet is posing formidable challenges to the enjoinment of privacy, carbon emission has made its way to threaten the ecosystem of the Earth, and warfare and many more unforeseen happenings around the world keep challenging the humankind in many degrees. Happenings like these have been structuring and restructuring the balance and strategies of global governance. While countries alone were responsible for revising and creating global strategies, their capacities and stakes are less likely to complement the same of the private ordering system, in which transnational corporations (TNCs)[1] possess a major stake (Zerk 2006). Out of the top 100 economies in the world in 2015, 69 were

---

[1]The term 'Transnational Corporation' is used here in conformity with its definition provided the Intergovernmental Working Group. This group defines a TNC as 'an enterprise (a) comprising entities in two or more countries, regardless of the legal form and fields of activities in those entities; (b) which operates under a system of decision-making, permitting coherent policies and a common strategy through one or more decision-making centres; (c) in which the entities are so linked, by ownership or otherwise, that one or more of them may be able to exercise a significant influence over the activities of others and, in particular, to share knowledge, resources and responsibilities with the others' Report of the Secretariat on the Outstanding Issues in the Draft Code of Conduct on Transnational Corporations, U.N. Doc E/C. 10/1984/S/5. No distinction is intended from the term multinational enterprise' in this article. However, TNC and MNE are sometimes distinguished. For the purpose of this research the terms are used interchangeably.

M. M. Rahim (✉)
School of Law, University of South Australia,
GPO Box 2471, Adelaide, SA 5001, Australia
e-mail: mia.rahim@unisa.edu.au

© Springer Nature Switzerland AG 2019
M. M. Rahim (ed.), *Code of Conduct on Transnational Corporations*,
CSR, Sustainability, Ethics & Governance,
https://doi.org/10.1007/978-3-030-10816-8_1

TNCs (Inman 2016); they are now the hub of groundbreaking inventions and pioneers for fighting against threats to human wellbeing.

A way of improving the natural environment, human dignity, security and living conditions of the people worldwide could be through developing a sustainable governance within which all the stakeholders including the governments and TNCs work harmoniously together. In order to achieve this, it is critical to assess how TNCs interact and adapt to the social, economic, and environmental challenges in various countries. Prior studies reveal that many TNCs exploit local resources, particularly in developing countries. These countries have raised numerous concerns where they have been unable to encounter most of the TNCs strategies that go against their own interests. As Korten (1995) notes:

> The new corporate colonialism is no more a consequence of immutable historical forces than was the old state colonialism. It is a consequence of conscious choices based on the pursuit of elite interest. This elite interest has been closely aligned with the corporate interest in advancing deregulation and globalization. As a consequence, the largest transnational corporations and the global financial system have assumed ever greater power over the conduct of human affairs in the pursuit of interests that are increasingly at odds with the human interest. It is impossible to have healthy, equitable, and democratic societies when political and economic power is concentrated in a few gigantic corporations.

To avert the disaster foreseen by Korten (1995), it is important that countries and TNCs cooperate. This cooperation can be achieved with the creation of a core global regulatory framework. This chapter explores these issues, focusing on the interplay between such a framework and TNCs' social responsibility and accountability governance.

2 Major Global Frameworks

Several early attempts at an international framework were implemented in the 20th century (Rahman 1989), including the International Convention of Treatment of Foreigners (1920), the Havana Charter of the International Trade Organisation (1948), the International Code of Fair Treatment for Foreign Investments (1949), the International Association for the Promotion and Protection of Private Foreign Investment (1959), the Harvard Conventions on the International Responsibility of States for Injuries to Alien (1929, 1961). Ocran (1986) reports that these initiatives were: (a) sponsored by private organisations; (b) region or sub-region specific; and (c) narrowly focused on TNC issues. These frameworks invariably refer to investments, primarily in developing countries. Although these instruments failed to target the regulation of TNCs, these early attempts at maneuvering a relationship between developing countries and TNCs are illustrative examples of the intricacies involved in achieving consensus on the rules that govern the relationship between foreign investors and host countries (Ocran 1986). These initiatives have a significant emphasis on investor protection, a key factor that is observed over the course of the evolution of a global framework and bilateral investment treaties. Nevertheless, the practical impact of many of these frameworks is negligible.

These early attempts were superseded by international initiatives for minimizing conflicts between TNCs and developing countries implemented in the 1970s. This chapter does not discuss the initial frameworks developed in the 1970s; instead, it focuses on the following core post-1970s frameworks: the Draft Code of Conduct on Transnational Corporations, the International Labor Organization's Tripartite Declaration of Principles Concerning Multinational Enterprises and Social Policy, the OECD Guidelines for Multinational Enterprises, the UNCTAD Set of Multilaterally Agreed Equitable Principles and Rules for the Control of Restrictive Business Practices, the Draft Norms on the Responsibilities of TNCs and other Business Enterprises with Regard to Human Rights, the Bilateral Investment Treaty framework, the United Nations Global Compact, and the Guiding Principles on Business and Human Rights.

2.1 The Draft Code of Conduct on Transnational Corporations

During the 60s and early 70s, increasing inflation, protectionism, and food and oil crises revealed governance problems in Least Developed Countries (LDCs) and brought TNC issues to the forefront (Group of Eminent Persons 1974; Vernon and Vernon 1977).[2] This resulted in increased control of TNCs and the development of a New International Economic Order (NIEO). Meanwhile, the nationalisation of multinational companies and growing control of LDCs over TNCs invited developed countries to act on behalf of TNCs, as the majority of TNC owners during that time were citizens of developed countries. In juxtaposition, the Organisation of Economic Cooperation and Development (OECD) created the Committee for International Investment and Multinational Enterprises to remove the constraints on LDCs and influence the UN to pull away from its distinct regulatory position of TNC control. The OECD took steps to adapt a guideline for TNCs based on greater control over TNCs from Canada, the Netherlands, and some Scandinavian countries, while the trade unions demanded for control over TNCs through the Trade Unions Advisory Committee of the OECD. The business community representatives counteracted this via the Business and Industry Advisory Committee of the OECD (1994). On 21 June 1976 the OECD Guidelines on Multinational Enterprises was adopted as an Annex to the OECD Declaration on International Investment and Multinational Enterprises.

The newly independent colonies of the major European countries also took action to create TNC regulation, with several noteworthy political and economic

---

[2]Group of Eminent Persons, The Impact of Transnational Corporations on Development and on International Relations, UN Doc E/5500 Add.1. 1974.

implications. Firstly, this reduced the influence of colonizing nations, and secondly, most of these newly independent countries considered TNCs as an extension of prior colonial imperialism, albeit without colonial administrators (Muchlinski 2007). With their new sovereign authority and individual identity in the UN, these countries formed 'Group of 77', a new international pressure group with voting majority in the UN (Zerk 2006). This group of countries was supported by the then United Soviet Socialist Republic and thereby their developmental goals became the topmost priority in the UN's social and economic agendas, leading to the emergence of the concept of NIEO.[3]

The basis of NIEO was 'equity, sovereign equality, interdependence, common interest and cooperation among all countries…' (Preamble of the Declaration on the Establishment of a New International Economic Order 1974) to 'eliminate the widening gap between the developed and developing countries' (ibid). The NIEO's preamble committed to 'promote the economic advancement and social progress of all peoples' through safeguarding a 'steady, accelerating economic and social development and peace and justice for present and future generations (ibid).' This attempt necessitated the development of sustainable economic cooperation based on stable and equitable trade transactions. In the meantime, the developing countries established this economic cooperation through trade transactions and managed to set the core of the Charter of the United Nations, International Development Strategy for the Second United Nations Development Decade, and the Charter of Economic Rights and Duties of Countries at the core of NIEO.

During the development of NIEO, developing countries proclaimed their right to regulate and monitor TNC activities within their domain.[4] Although private transnational corporations were integral to the economic development of these newly independent countries, they failed to include TNCs in the development of any international economic policy frameworks. Developed countries vehemently opposed any global regulatory framework that would jeopardize the operation of TNCs in foreign lands. As result, the UN initiated a research project to assess the impact of multinational corporations on development and international relations under the administration of the Economic and Social Council in 1972, releasing a report in June 1974.[5] The key findings of this report are as follows:

> Some countries are concerned about the undesirable effects that foreign investment by multinational corporations may have on domestic employment and the balance of

---

[3] Res 3201 (S-VI) of 9 May 1974 of the UN General Assembly, Resolution on the New International Economic Order; Res 3202 (S-VI) of 16 May 1974 of the UN General Assembly, The Program of Action on the Establishment of a New International Economic Order. The Resolution on NIEO, however, did not achieve support from a number of countries, including Belgium, Denmark, Norway, United States, and the Federal Republic of Germany. Nine of the Western developed countries abstained from voting on this resolution.

[4] Article 4(e) of the Declaration on the Establishment of a New International Economic Order, Res 3201 (S-VI) of 1May 1974 of the UN General Assembly.

[5] Economic and Social Council Resolution 1721(LIII). For details, see UN Doc. E/5500/Rev. 1, ST/ESA/6 (New York: UN, 1974).

payments, and about the capacity of such corporations to alter the normal play of competition. Host countries are concerned about the ownership and control of key economic sectors by foreign enterprises, the excessive cost to the domestic economy which their operations may entail, the extent to which they may encroach upon political sovereignty and their possible adverse influence on socio-cultural values. Labour interests are concerned about the impact of multinational corporations on employment and workers' welfare and on the bargaining strength of trade unions. Consumer interests are concerned about the appropriateness, quality and price of the goods produced by multinational corporations. The multinational corporations themselves are concerned about the possible nationalization or expropriation of their assets without adequate compensation and about restrictive, unclear and frequently changing government policies (Impact of Multinational Corporations on Development and on International Relations, p. 26).

This research report also highlighted that TNCs and their home countries have a responsibility for the development of health and safety standards regarding workers working in their subsidiaries in developing countries (Impact of Multinational Corporations on Development and on International Relations, p. 79). It urged the UN to create a detailed policy framework such as a universal code of conduct to minimise conflicts and to maximise favourable conditions for TNCs and developing countries (Bondzi-Simpson 1990). This report found that a global framework is vital to harmonise the activities of developing countries and TNCs. Many international civil society groups, labour organisations, and developing countries proposed to codify TNCs activities in line with the development goals and objectives of host countries so that any detrimental effect of their operations in any particular country could be smoothly regulated. Thus, during the early 1970s the UNO formally initiated the Draft Code of Conduct for Transnational Corporations (the Code) aspiring that the Code would be instrumental for boosting world economic growth and wellbeing by harbouring a positive climate for international trade (International Chamber of Commerce 1983). In 1974, the Commission on Transnational Corporations was set up, and three years later the preparation of the draft text of the Code was presented to an Inter-governmental Working Group of the Commission.[6]

The Code's codification process caused significant conflicts amongst UNO member countries. The key conflict was the perceived need (or lack thereof) for standards of international legal norms capable of questioning the legitimacy of conduct by TNCs. The Group of 77 and the socialist countries doubted the validity of these standards, arguing that suitable standards had already been established through the practices of major capital exporting countries (Robinson 1986). They also argued that the national law of an individual country is sufficient to deal with these matters. These countries proposed a compromise in which the Code would form a set of guidelines rather than be enforceable by law: 'the principle of the

---

[6]On request of the Economic and Social Council through its 1982/68 of 27 October 1982 number resolution, the Inter Governmental Working Group prepared the draft code of conduct. This draft also considers a variety of resolutions adopted by the General Assembly and Economic and Social Council. It applies the ILO Tripartite Declaration of Principles concerning Multinational Enterprises.

fulfilment in good faith of international obligations will apply to the Code'.[7] Meanwhile, developing countries were unwilling to take undue risks, fearing exploitation by TNCs of Western European countries. In addition, developed countries began to doubt the operation of legal systems within the developing countries where their TNCs would eventually be operating.

Throughout these conflicts the purpose of both groups of UN member countries was to ascertain an amiable guiding norm (the Code) that would facilitate their individual group interests. For example, developing countries wanted a code that would allow them to effectively control TNCs, while socialist countries wished to keep their national enterprises away from the code's jurisdiction. Further, developed countries such as Canada concentrated specifically upon two dichotomous areas following the main underlying objectives of the OECD Guidelines: '(a) a requirement for national treatment of foreign controlled enterprises by a host country; and (b) an attempt to restrain the various incentives and disincentives to foreign investment which the various governments imposed' (Rahim 2010).

The main issues at the heart of these conflicts were related to (a) nationalization of TNC operation and compensation; (b) standards for the general treatment of TNCs in host countries; and (c) a forum for settling disputes between TNCs and countries (Ocran 1986).[8] On the basis of permanent sovereignty over natural resources, developing countries regarded expropriation as a 'legitimate means of recovering natural resources, transferring ownership of foreign-owned property and redistributing the world wealth' (Rahman 1989: 107).[9] Developed countries opposed such a wide scope of expropriation as they considered this right a source of discrimination to aliens. Developing countries, with the support of socialist countries, invoked the concept of 'equal treatment' to back their claim (Rahman 1989). As a result, seven provisions were included in the Code regarding treatment of TNCs in host countries. The developed country group demanded 'fair, equitable and non-discriminatory treatment in accordance with international law (obligation)'[10] as the basis of these provisions. The developing country group found it fair to differentiate between the host and alien enterprises (Rodriguez 1982 in Rahman 1989). Regarding the jurisdiction of settling disputes involving TNCs, the developing country group wanted to maintain that 'entities of transnational corporations are subject to the jurisdiction of the countries in which they operate' (Para 55 of the Code). The developed countries' stand on this matter was that the parties (including TNCs) in a dispute should be free to choose the forum or arbitrator for settling

---

[7]Official record of the Economic and Social Council, 1983, Supplement No.-7. Annex-II.

[8]For a detailed account of debate regarding these issues, see Report of the Secretariat on the Outstanding Issues in the Draft Code of Conduct on Transnational Corporations, U.N. Doc E/C.10/1984/S/5.

[9]Article 2(1) of the United Nations Charter of Economic Rights and Duties of States confirms this sovereignty; it reads: 'every state has and shall freely exercise full permanent sovereignty, including possession, use and disposal, over all its wealth, natural resources and economic activities.'

[10]Para 47 of the Code. E/C.101982/6.

disputes. All these disputes remained unsettled during negotiations of the Code, resulting in a 'voluntary' mode of implementation of its provisions.

The conceptual core of neo-liberalism was the basis of the arguments for the developed country group against the argument for a binding code for TNCs by the developing countries (Gilpin 2018). The developed countries contended that the output of transnational trade and investments would necessarily be market-driven so as to maximise welfare for all; and the interventionist policies, such as the draft Code, would contrarily be detrimental to global welfare in business and investment. Such contentions made the sole purpose of an international code of conduct for TNCs dubious. Further, lack of an equivalently influential opposition in the 1990s to challenge the developed countries' stand regarding codification of the Code was a significant factor that ultimately led to termination of the negotiation. As Rahman notes, 'the prolonged process of formulation of the [C]ode testifies to the fact that interest of different groups of states are not only divergent, but also often opposing. … The draft code in its present form is not only unacceptable to developing countries, but is also without any real perspective. Adoption of the code in its present form, it is concluded, would create additional threat to economic and political interest of the developing host countries' (Rahman 1989: 114).

Developed countries continued to oppose the idea of a global instrument for TNCs (Sagafi-Nejad and Dunning 2008). In fact, the United States of America 'remained lukewarm (if not directly hostile) to the [Code]' (Sagafi-Nejad and Dunning 2008: 119) throughout the negotiation. This country formally declared its intention to limit its participation in UNCTC initiatives related to the Code. The US administration during President Regan's second term blamed UNCTC as they found this organisation 'never given the Centre a clear mandate to include in its work the activities of state-owned enterprises from communist countries and MNCs from developing countries—a violation of the important UN principle of universality' (ibid: 119). Not only this, they also suggested that the US based business community should 'restrict its participation in the Centre's work' (State 1989 cited in Sagafi-Nejad and Dunning 2008: 120). The USA remained engaged in the Code negotiation, but silently crafted a consensus against any further negotiation on the Code. Later on September 1992, the President of the Forty-Sixth Session of the General Assembly reported:

> It was the view of delegations that no consensus was possible on the draft code at present. Delegations felt that the changed international economic environment and the importance attached to encouraging foreign investment required that a fresh approach should be examined, which could include the preparation of guidelines and/or any other international instrument on foreign investment at the next session of the Commission on Transnational Corporations (General Assembly Document A/47/446).

The codification initiatives were made redundant in 1992, after two decades of elaborate initiatives by the Working Group and other bodies within the UNO system. Thomas Hajduk, in Chap. 2 of this book provides a detailed account of the UNO initiatives for the Code. In this chapter he explicates how this initiative dragged on and why it had to be eventually abandoned.

2.2 Tripartite Declaration of Principles on Multinational Enterprises and Social Policy

The International Labour Organisation Governing Body issued a Tripartite Declaration of Principles on Multinational Enterprises and Social Policy (the Declaration) in 1977, widely viewed as a form of voluntary regulation of corporate behavior (Rudloph 2010). Through this Declaration, the ILO established a code of conduct on labour standards for TNCs, articulating the foremost concerns regarding labour rights and their protection (which are available in different ILO conventions). This Declaration was revised in 2000 so as to incorporate the ILO Declaration on Fundamental Principles and Rights at Work: (a) freedom of association and right to collective bargaining; (b) eliminating forced and mandatory labour; (c) banning child labour; and (d) eliminating workplace discrimination.

The ILO Tripartite Declaration provides guidelines on labour and employment matters that apply to governments, employers, workers organisations, and TNCs.[11] Its aim is to 'encourage the positive contribution which Multinational Enterprises can make to economic and social progress, and to minimise and resolve the difficulties to which their various operations may give rise.' To reach this goal the Declaration contains guidance principles and includes specific provisions for industrial relations.[12] This Declaration, unlike the Code, was successful as most of the stakeholders agreed upon its objectives.

The Declaration is a voluntary approach for regulating TNCs' behaviour (Rudloph 2010). Like the OECD guidelines, it does not provide a definition of a TNC, noting that 'to serve its purpose this Declaration does not require a precise definition of multinational enterprise' (ILO Declaration 2000: 189). Like the Guidelines, it does not require TNCs to maintain labour standards as per their home countries in the host countries (Muchlinski 2007).[13] There is no specific mechanism or monitoring process in the Declaration to implement the endorsed principles. The Declaration contains a co-regulatory approach or tri-party participation wherein the government, workers, and business enterprises actualise the principles. There is an

---

[11]The Declaration invites 'governments of state members of the ILO, the employers' and workers' organisations concerned and the multinational enterprises operating in their territories to observe the principles embodied therein' p. 423.

[12]Paragraph 10 of the Declaration notes: 'Multinational enterprises should take fully into account established general policy objectives of the countries in which they operate. Their activities should be in harmony with the development priorities and social aims and structure of the country in which they operate. To this effect, consultation should be held between multinational enterprises, the government and, wherever appropriate, the national employers' and workers' organisations concerned' p. 190.

[13]Paragraph 33 of the Declaration reads: 'Wages, benefits and conditions of work offered by multinational enterprises should not be less favourable to the workers than those offered by comparable employers in the country concerned' p. 192.

established bureaucracy inside the ILO to enable the Declaration. The ILO Secretariat, via the Committee on Multinational Enterprises, investigates and presents a report to the Board of Directors regarding the concerned business enterprise and government. This committee emphasises combined mediation of enterprises, their representatives and workers' organisations to resolve any disputes in order to maintain a healthy industrial environment and relationship amongst the industrial stakeholders. However, its role is limited to interpreting the provisions in the Declaration in case of disagreements over the meaning of the provisions (Deva 2012: 91). This committee is accessible only to governments; non-governmental organisations involved in a dispute cannot request this committee for any clarification and investigation. Deva (2012) summarises the impact of this as follows:

> [T]he ILO Declaration ends upping a merely aspirational declaration without any legal enforceability, or even the possibility of market correction in the absence of any process for publicly 'naming and shaming' delinquent companies. Apart from lacking of teeth to implement the provisions of the Declaration, it also fails to offer sound basis, rationale or strategy to encourage MNCs to observe best labour practices wherever they operate. The ILO Declaration thus fails the twin test of efficacy and could not be relied upon to promote labour rights against MNCs' continued drive for access to cheap labour in developing countries (p. 92).

2.3 The OECD Guidelines for Multinational Enterprises

One of the objectives in creating the OECD is to assist its member countries to protect and promote foreign direct investments worldwide. It first created the Declaration on International Investment and Multinational Enterprises as an umbrella framework to reach this goal. The OECD Guidelines for Multinational Enterprises (the Guideline), adopted in 1977, is particularly for TNCs operating in or from any of the OECD member countries. It had several subsequent amendments, of which the amendment in 2000 is significant as this amendment was based on significant research, negotiations with member countries, and deliberation with numerous NGOs (Hanakova 2005). The amended Guidelines delineate a comprehensive social responsibility code for TNCs by postulating non-binding principles and benchmarks for responsible business practice with the aspiration of advocating socioeconomic and environmental growth. The present text of the Guidelines is relatively detailed, comprising 38–54 definitive corporate responsibility issues.[14]

---

[14]The current text was enriched with the entirety of social responsibilities after a revision. The revision added a number of issues to the main text including an extension of labour rights, a direct referral to human rights assigning the multinational responsibilities, and a reference to their responsibility to the supply chain (i.e., business partners, suppliers and sub-contractors). More importantly, the applicability guidelines cover extraterritorial activities of TNCs.

The Guidelines, rationally enough, do not expect small and medium-sized enterprises to perform in a similar way to large businesses, and it does not intend to differentiate between transnational and domestic enterprises.[15]

The Guidelines' 'efficacy and utility have yet to be established' (Sagafi-Nejad and Dunning 2008: 112). OECD Watch analysed the cases filed by NGOs against corporations alleging violations of the OECD Guidelines in the last ten years. It revealed that the most common types of alleged violations of the Guidelines include environmental damages and human rights abuses in developing countries, and that the National Contact Points (NCPs) within the OECD rarely contributed to resolving the disputes related to these violations. "Only 5 of the 96 cases filed by NGOs have resulted in real improvements in corporate behaviour. In another 10 cases, NCPs have made useful recommendation to improve business conduct, but which have ultimately not materialised in concrete improvements. The remaining 84% of cases have failed to make any significant contribution to resolving the conflict" (Oldenziel et al. 2010). OECD Watch states that the NCPs can take steps for developing consensus amongst the disputing parties and pursue fact-finding activities related to a dispute raised by non-adhering countries, but it has not provided the NCPs any authority to take meaningful action against an enterprise that ignores their recommendations (Deva 2012). NCPs can arrange mediations, but they cannot take any determination on the basis of the merit of the disputes if the mediation fails. Whereas the Code was proposed as a legally effective instrument, the Guidelines embody a moderate approach to TNC matters.

The Guidelines represent an endeavour to harmonise the aims of regulating TNC activities and minimising obstacles to their operations (Hamilton 1984). It is a non-binding model for protecting investment treaties, with some incongruities remaining concerning the FDI's strategy and regulation matters amongst its affiliated countries. Most particularly, due to a lack of an effective enforcement mechanism, the voluntary nature of its compliance procedure, and provisions for exemptions on the grounds of business confidentiality, it has never been widely acknowledged as a model global framework for TNCs. After an assessment of the strengths, drawbacks, and development of this framework for TNCS, Deva (2012) states: 'although the OECD Guidelines offer some potential (especially after the 2011 update) they are hardly adequate—on account of offering very limited preventive and redressive efficacy—to ensure the [T]NCs respect their human rights responsibilities wherever they operate' (Deva 2012: 88).

---

[15]Chapter 1.4 of the OECD Guidelines states: "the Guidelines are not aimed at introducing differences of treatment between multinational and domestic enterprises; they reflect good practice for all. Accordingly, multinational and domestic enterprises are subject to same expectations in respect to their conduct wherever the Guidelines are relevant to both."

2.4 The Set of Multilaterally Agreed Equitable Principles, and Rules for the Control of Restrictive Business Practices

The United Nations Conference on Trade and Development initiated the Set of Multilaterally Agreed Equitable Principles, and Rules for the Control of Restrictive Business Practices (the Set), which aim 'to ensure that restrictive business practices do not impede or negate the realization of benefits that should arise from the liberalization of tariff and non-tariff barriers affecting international trade, particularly those affecting the trade and development of developing countries.' The Set's objective is therefore directed towards the progress of developing countries through reducing trade barriers among countries. It also establishes a comprehensive mechanism to endorse competition and dismiss prevalent anti-competitive attitudes of TNCs. However, like the Declaration and the Guidelines, it does not give any explicit definitions of TNCs.

2.5 The Bilateral Investment Treaty

TNC-related frameworks usually include customary international legal norms, which are typically laden with good faith and appropriate standards. However, these include significant levels of uncertainty and are generally unwelcome by developing countries. The increasing number of Bilateral Investment Treaties (BIT) means that the need for any universal framework has become largely redundant, especially for developing countries and TNCs. A bilateral arrangement means that both parties can mediate their interests openly without clinging to any fixed rules; they could even move beyond any international practice if they wished to. Consequently, the BIT has become a feasible alternative to the search for a universally accepted set of international legal standards for managing the relationships between TNCs and host countries (Muchlinski 2007).

Success of a BIT depends upon the capacities of the parties involved. If the economic capacity and negotiation skill of one party is inadequate, then there is a risk that the other party will exploit the weak party (Kollamparambil 2016). Hence, in most traditional BITs, host countries (particularly least developed countries) are at risk of exploitation by developed countries (Friedman and Verhoosel 2003).

As it transformed into a tool of exploitation, BIT as a framework that utilises TNCs began to lose its credibility. According to the UNCTAD, BIT related disputes reached 608 cases in 2014 compared to only 50 cases in 2000 (UNCTAD 2015). This disparity stems from developing countries' failures in international judicial or conciliation forums. For developing countries, international political, military and economic power structures become significant influencing agents rather than trade rationalities in shaping and maintaining BITs. This scenario is exacerbated for natural resource extracting TNCs and developing countries. The rise of termination of ongoing BIT by developing countries in recent years illustrates this situation; for example, Bolivia terminated its BIT with the Netherlands and the United States of America (Berger 2015), Ecuador and South Africa terminated nine and 11 BITs, respectively (Carim 2015), and Indonesia announced its intention to terminate 64 BITs with Western countries (Jailani 2015).

2.6 The Draft Norms on the Responsibilities of TNCs and Other Business Enterprises with Regard to Human Rights

Following the evolution of the Guideline, the Declarations, and the BIT frameworks, the need to clarify the role of TNCs in the international community has become increasingly urgent with the massive expansion of their business practices. In the early 2000s, the UN began to pay greater attention to the impact of corporate operations, especially on human rights issues. In August 2003, it created the UN Sub-Commission on the Promotion and Protection of Human Rights and adopted Draft Norms on the Responsibilities of TNCs and other Business Enterprises with Regard to Human Rights (the Norms). The Norms are unique in that they are widely considered to represent a significant international instrument with the potential to impose a wide range of accountabilities on both TNCs and countries.

The Norms clarify the general responsibilities of countries, TNCs, and other enterprises in upholding and securing human rights. It stipulates that countries are primarily responsible for promoting and protecting human rights, including their responsibility to ascertain if TNCs and business enterprises are respectful of human rights (Hillemanns 2003). The obligations fostered on business enterprises under these Norms at no stage decrease countries' obligations within the periphery of their own influence (ibid). These responsibilities, as the Norms reflects, can be enunciated as the right to equal opportunity and indiscriminate treatment; the right to security (of life); the right to work (including safe and healthy working environment); the right to collective bargaining; respect for national sovereignty and human rights; and consumer and environmental protection (ibid). In addition to these principles, the Norms refer to existent international principles and specify basic methods for implementing them in relevant contexts.

The Norms, as a framework for raising corporate responsibility in social and environmental spheres, propose three measures for manifesting its principles. Firstly, the Norms recommend adoption, dissemination, and application of internal rules of operation in accordance with the Norm principles. Secondly, reporting periodically on the implementation of the principles by all stakeholders, including the UN. Thirdly, monitoring of the corporate self-regulation performance by the UN and other national and/or international bodies (ibid). Accordingly, it necessitates collaboration to 'apply and incorporate these Norms in their contracts and other arrangements' for all individual parties, such as contractors, subcontractors, suppliers, licensees, distributors, and other natural or legal persons. Commentary on the Norms specifies that business enterprises must uphold human rights and if there is any persistent breach of the Norm principles, business enterprises must terminate their business contract. Business enterprises, in this case, are required to submit a periodical report on how they implement the Norms to all stakeholders and to the UNO (Blaikie 2004). Regarding monitoring, the commentaries note that companies shall be subject to periodic supervision; moreover, the UNO or other national and international mechanisms which already exist (or may be formed in future) will verify how the Norms are being applied (ibid).

The Norm stipulate that TNCs must comply with a very wide set of human rights and related obligations involving at least 56 international instruments (Baxi 2005). It mentions that the business enterprises shall contribute to peoples' right to 'development, adequate food and drinking water, the highest attainable standard of physical and mental health, adequate housing, privacy, education, freedom of thought, conscience, and religion and freedom of opinion and expression' (Paragraph 12 of the Norm). Quite often, due to such an overtly inclusive corporate human rights obligation, TNCs find it challenging to adhere to the Norm. To combat this, the Norm could provide a precise list of standard responsibilities applicable to TNCS. This would solve the conundrum related to the 'localisation of universality' of these universal rights viz a viz obligations (Hillemanns 2003; Nolan 2005a, b). Implementation of the Norms' provisions depends on mandatory and voluntary approaches. Unfortunately, the Norms remain unsuccessful in converging these approaches and also fail to utilise non-traditional means in its implementation mechanism (Commission on Human Rights 2005).

The Norms take a further step to define transnational and 'other business enterprises'. A transnational corporation is defined as 'an economic entity operating in more than one country or a cluster of economic entities operating in two or more countries whatever their legal form, whether in their home country or country of activity, and whether taken individually or collectively.' The definition of 'other business enterprises' (ibid) as mentioned in the Norms, includes any business, regardless of the nature of its activities (be it international or domestic, including transnational corporations; and a corporate partnership or other legal forms utilised to create the business entity. As such, this framework aims to cover a very wide spectrum, wherein the definition of domestic enterprises is yet to be clarified (Rangwaldh and Konopik 2010). It notes that the 'norms are presumed to apply, as a matter of practice, if the business enterprise has any relation with a transnational corporation, the impact of its activity is not entirely local, or the activities involve violation of the right to security.' However, its 'presumption of the application' is not transparent and therefore does not pinpoint the scope of the term 'other business enterprises'. In regard to the situation where corporations should take a role, it refers to the notion of 'sphere of influence', but does not provide any explanation of this notion and remains 'exceedingly vague' regarding the situations where corporations should play a role (Schutter 2013).

The definition of 'business enterprises' as regulatees is contentious. The definition of the regulatee determines the scope of any applicable regulatory framework, and in this scenario transnational corporations tend to stay beyond the scope of any such regulatory framework.

2.7 The Global Compact

The Global Compact (the Compact) is a flagship initiative of the United Nations in promoting social responsibility performance of TNCs. The Global Compact aims to increase the number of agreements between the UN and world business communities on social responsibility and ethical operations of large business entities. It was initiated by the then UN Secretary-General Kofi Annan in his speech at the World Economic Forum in Switzerland in 1999, and subsequently implemented in July 2000. Initially, the Compact comprised nine principles of good corporate citizenship, including human rights, labour standards, and the environment. In 2004, upon a revision, an additional principle concerning bribery and corruption was included.[16] The principles covered in the Compact initiatives are based upon the Universal Declaration of Human Rights (1948), the ILO's Tripartite Declaration of Principles Concerning Multinational Enterprises and Social Policy (1977), and the Rio Declaration for Environment and Sustainable Development (1992).

The Compact is arguably the largest integrated approach for raising corporate social responsibility performance (Rasche 2009; Hemphill 2005). As of 2 August 2018, 10,806 business corporations are actively involved in its various programs. Its programs aim to create a 'global framework to promote sustainable growth and good corporate citizenship through committed and creative corporate leadership'. In addition, it endeavours to explicate its principles informatively. Hans Corell opines that the Compact attempts to achieve two kinds of goals which are reciprocal in nature: firstly, to make the Compact and its principles integral to a business' internal strategies and operations; and secondly, to interconnect stakeholders and corporations and assist them to settle general problems. To reach these goals within the Global Compact's organisational forum, four mechanisms have been set up, namely: dialogue, learning, local networks, and project partnerships. With these

---

[16]The principles of the Compact are: (i) businesses should support and respect the protection of internationally proclaimed human rights; (ii) make sure that they are not complicit in human rights abuses; (iii) businesses should uphold the freedom of association and the effective recognition of the right to collective bargaining; (iv) the elimination of all forms of forced and compulsory labour; (v) the effective abolition of child labour; (vi) the elimination of discrimination in respect of employment and occupation; (vii) businesses should support a precautionary approach to environmental challenges; (viii) undertake initiatives to promote greater environmental responsibility; (ix) encourage the development and diffusion of environmentally friendly technologies; and (x) businesses should work against corruption in all its forms, including extortion and bribery. For a detailed description of each of these principles, visit the Global Compact at https://www.unglobalcompact.org/what-is-gc/mission/principles, accessed on 23 July 2018.

initiatives the Compact aims to have negotiations to reach mutual ground and carry out combined efforts among businesses, labour and non-governmental organisations in facing the challenges of globalisation. As a facilitative forum for promoting CSR and working for a sustainable future, the Compact engages private sectors to work with the UN, in collaboration with the ILO and NGOs, and to identify and promote good corporate practices which are based on universal principles. The Compact, as a global platform, aspires to motivate business sectors to be strategic partners for development by bringing business, labour and civil societies together to seek solutions to contemporary challenges.

In Chap. 5 of this book, Mariko Shoji explains the core approach in implementing the aims of the Compact initiatives. She argues that communication through a transnational network is a vital pathway for effective orchestration of the soft-law based strategies for raising TNCs' social responsibility performance.

However, some critics argue that the Compact lacks sound monitoring and enforcement procedures, opining that companies' participation in the Compact is largely opportunistic: 'many corporations would like nothing better than to wrap themselves in the flag of the UNO in order to "blue wash" their public image, while at the same time avoiding significant changes to their behaviour' (Nolan 2005a, b; Knudsen 2011). The UN's decision to adopt a 'facilitative approach rather than enforcement' has raised skepticism that the Compact offers these companies a 'free ride'. Sethis and Schepers (2014) even argue that 'all credible and publicly available data and documentation conclusively demonstrate that the [Compact] has failed to induce its signatory companies to enhance their CSR reports and integrate the 10 principles in their policies and operations' (p. 193). Drawing on insights from stakeholder, network, and institutional theory, Schembera (2018) although found positive impact in the companies as long as they are involved in Compact programs, he noted that the effect of the Compact programs on the companies is much smaller than previous practitioner studies revealed; his study also noted flaws in the Compact initiatives' accountability structure. The Compact programs heavily rely on 'continuous stakeholder dialogue' for implementing its principles (Maon et al. 2010); many scholars and studies, however, marked this implementation strategy insufficient for creating incentives towards the Compact objective (Berliner and Prakash 2015; Deva 2006; Rasche et al. 2013).

Despite this criticism, the fact remains that the Compact has launched initiatives that undeniably showcase the recent prominence of corporate social responsibility (CSR) on the international agenda, mainly through minimizing the gap between two dominant perceptions in socialising business enterprises: 'one focused on human rights compliance and developed under the supervision of an inter-governmental body (i.e. the Human Rights Council), and another addressing broader areas of corporate social responsibility, led by the private sector and facilitated by the United Nations Secretariat but without any direct role for government' (Schutter 2013: xviii).

2.8 The Guiding Principles on Business and Human Rights

The Guiding Principles on Business and Human Rights (the UNGPs), adopted in June 2011, is considered the most authoritative UN framework for raising human rights responsibilities of state and corporate enterprises. With the aim of involving the business community in restoring human rights, it denotes several core responsibilities for corporations and urges corporations to act with 'due diligence' to 'avoid infringing on the rights of others and to address adverse impacts with which they are involved' (Para 6, the UNGP). Chap. 6 of this book explicates the problems with the normative status of the UNGPs on Business and Human Rights. It discusses concerns related to the lack of specific responsibility for remediation and measures governing access to justice, as well as the failure of UNGPs to address extraterritorial reach. This chapter further highlights criticism of these principles, including the different approaches toward the attribution of fault between parent and subsidiary companies, challenges to jurisdiction on forum non-convenience grounds, and lack of effective machinery to enforce foreign judgments among states. Deva and Bilchitz (2013) also question the integrity of the implementation mechanism for the principles contained in the UNGPs. They argue that this framework places too much emphasis on building a consensus in its implementation mechanism, which devalues the currency of its principles, and thus facilitates a 'consensus without content'. Nolan contends that 'the language adopted in the [UNGPs] is weak and non-authoritative' and it 'prizes dialogue and consensus over ambition' (Nolan 2013).

The dominant international frameworks have thus far been unable to lessen the primary dichotomous conflicts; namely to curtail the strife between TNCs and developing countries, or to agree upon a universal framework that could diminish animosities amongst TNCs and developing countries in order to cultivate a tenable trade atmosphere (Hopkins 2004). Their approaches to minimise conflicts between non-state actors, private regimes, TNCs, and countries for the development of a sustainable trade environment are continuing to evolve. As discussed, the initiatives through the NIEO were entirely country-centric and also underestimated the capacity of TNCs regarding the progression of international economic conditions. Thereafter, the UN drive for the Code, even though it incorporated the implications of the participation of TNCs in international trade, also fell short of becoming a final framework. Although the Code initiatives remained unsuccessful, it succeeded in identifying some of the prime indecisive issues defining the relationship between countries and TNCs as well as the conflicting interests amongst different groups of countries.

The Declaration and the Set are related only regarding international commercial and economic issues. These frameworks had specific objectives and refrained from incorporating general conflicting issues amongst TNCs and developing countries. The Guideline does not constitute a universal framework (even after its modification) as it does not serve as a substitute for national laws and only embodies supplementary principles and standards of behaviour of a non-legal character. For example, the latest instrument of OECD, that is, the Multilateral Agreement on Investment, has a different motive, although its underlying principles do not include the interests of developing countries. Essentially, the Norm focused on human rights issues and created misunderstanding with its scope of application rather than settling the ambiguities in the issues of corporate coverage.

The dominant frameworks discussed above share one collective goal—to build a sustainable trade atmosphere—although they approach this goal in diversified ways. Unfortunately, a suitable standard remains to be created. One of the key reasons for the failure of these frameworks is that they could not formulate any ubiquitous and effective administering groups to cater for their implementation. It can be contended that due to the absence of effective administrative bodies within these frameworks, the frameworks can be viewed as voluntary in nature. A further salient cause for their inability to separate overlapping interests between developing countries and TNCs is their failure to define and incorporate 'international law'. As such, these frameworks actually raise a variety of issues that could be considered as root causes for creating conflicts amongst TNCs and countries. These frameworks reveal that the relationship of these two international actors is contingent upon several key issues: (a) historical traits and the theoretical basis for such traits; (b) the voluntary or mandatory nature of the universal framework; (c) the need for an international platform for regulating such relationship; and (d) the call for settling disputes on globally accepted norms and definitions.

Indeed, the success of a global framework for TNCs depends upon the economic strength, impact, and role of the parties involved in global political order. In Chap. 4 of this book, Harvey Lado explains how TNCs get involved in political and economic games in national and international arenas in order to sustain their competitiveness. This chapter explicates that powerful countries—be they from the western world, Asia or Latin America—support their TNCs through economic diplomacy mechanisms, especially when they operate overseas in weak institutional environments, mainly to secure their political goals and economic rents. Such relationships between TNCs and their country of origin is therefore likely to nurture predatory practices such as human rights violations or inflict damage to the natural environment. Effective regulation against predation depends not only on their intrinsic quality but also on the institutional environment and the behavior of parties involved in their implementation. Drawing on North et al. (2009, 2013) taxonomy of social orders, and building on Greif and Tadelis' (2010) concept of crypto-morality, this chapter shows that TNCs adjust their behavior to adapt to their institutional environments, and they make a cost-benefit assessment to arbitrate between a responsible or a predatory behavior.

Benedict Sheehy provides a detailed account of the progress of different global initiatives to govern TNCs' social and ethical performance and accountability in Chap. 3. This chapter argues that while from an institutional perspective, codes may be of some use for driving changes to the norms of the institutional environment (Sahlin-Andersson 2006), from a legal point of view, they are but one piece of a regulatory system (Feaver and Sheehy 2015; Sheehy and Feaver 2015). This chapter describes how and to what extent codes set out applicable norms and as such provides a foundation for a suitable regulatory system. To be effective, as this chapter further describes, any global framework needs to be integrated into a coherent regulatory system that is facilitative of the necessary administrative and institutional infrastructure, otherwise it will likely end up as a stand-alone solution and destined for obscurity and non-implementation.

3 Conclusion

Over the last few decades, a variety of global initiatives for governing both financial and non-financial performance of TNCs have been proposed. The objectives of these initiatives share a similar purpose: to minimise conflicts towards developing a sustainable trade environment. However, most of these initiatives have been only partially successful. Some of these initiatives failed to reach completion, some are obsolete, and one was abandoned. The initiatives that are currently in operation have never been accepted by all stakeholders. A poignant reason for their poor performance is their lack of capacity to include the dynamics of governance beyond government, regulation beyond law, and responsiveness beyond responsibility. Ruggie (2003: 303) observes:

> [The] probability of the General Assembly's adopting a meaningful code anytime soon approximates zero…any UN attempt to impose a code of conduct not only would be opposed by the business community, but also would drive progressive business leaders, who are willing to engage with the Compact, into a more uniform anti-code coalition.

The UN initiatives for the Code were a major attempt for a global binding instrument for TNCs. This chapter describes the core reasons for its failure. However, as Chap. 2 of this book underscores, the debate during the negotiation on the Code was far from fruitless. The spectrum of opinions voiced during this debate established the very idea that TNCs have moral responsibilities vis-à-vis government and society to human society, while revealing that crafting a global code or binding framework for TNCs is extremely challenging. In this kaleidoscope, it would be costly and risky to jump-start the long-forsaken negotiation of the Code. Rather, we should seek other feasible options as alternatives to a global binding code or framework. Harvey Lado in Chap. 4 of this book narrates how legal regulation can impose dissuasive sanctions when social responsibility needs are not met. He argues that such sanctions are necessary to ensure that TNCs behave ethically and responsibly. Like Lado, Benedict Sheehy in Chap. 3 narrates that the principles in CSR should be comprehensive and upheld through adequate and suitable regulatory arrangements. Indrajit Dube in Chap. 7 explains the concept of 'social license to operate' and suggest the use of the currency of this concept to urge corporations to employ self-regulatory strategies in order to be more sensitive to their social responsibility needs. Vicki Waye further explicates this concept in Chap. 6 of this book. She critically assesses the alignment between the international instrument developed by the open-ended intergovernmental working group and domestic enforcement methods. In this chapter she highlights that the development of the international mediation and arbitration forum and creation of an international court solely for dealing with TNC issues can complement the meta-regulatory frameworks at the country level.

The drafting of 'guidelines', 'codes of conduct' and 'multi-stakeholder' approaches continue to serve at a modest level in the void of an exhaustive, mandatory, and universal framework for TNCs and developing countries. The guidelines are confined to specific issues for specific actors and do not consider general aspects that arise from conflicts of interest amongst TNCs and countries. TNC-initiated guidelines ultimately benefit the worldwide capitalist economy, and thus development of a universal standard of social responsibilities of TNCs through an effective inclusion of the main CSR principles in corporations is necessary. CSR is a non-binding framework for TNCs since it contains the essence of a multi-stakeholder approach. CSR is based on the spontaneous participation of TNCs in developing milder forms of self-regulation and self-monitoring. In Chap. 8 of this book, Mia Mahmudur Rahim elaborates on the principles of CSR and suggests that in the absence of any accepted global framework for regulating TNCs' social responsibility and accountability performance, a feasible approach is to converge regulatory approaches and include CSR principles at the centre of corporate self-regulation. He argues that legal regulation of TNCs—which are linked with their business operations in host countries in multifaceted ways, including the buyer driven global supply chain—is costly and unsuitable. He presents the 'converged approach', a relatively new approach in regulatory practice, that does not solely rely either on laws or on private ordering systems to oblige TNCs to be more socially responsible, and instill accountability to benefit stakeholders. This book ends in Chap. 8, with a call for further research on this regulatory approach.

References

Baxi, U. (2005). Market fundamentalisms: Business ethics at the Altar of human rights. *Human Rights Law Review, 5*(1), 1–26.

Berger, A. (2015). *Developing countries and the future of the international investment regime.* Retrieved from https://www.die-gdi.de/uploads/media/giz2015-en-Study_Developing_countries_and_the_future_of_the_international_investment_regime.pdf.

Berliner, D., & Prakash, A. (2015). "Bluewashing" the firm? Voluntary regulations, program design and member compliance with the United Nations Global Compact. *Policy Studies Journal, 43,* 115–138.

Blaikie, H. (2004). *Corporate social responsibility and codes of conduct: The privatisation of international labour law.* Paper presented at the Canadian Council on International Law Conference.

Bondzi-Simpson, P. E. (1990). *Legal relationships between transnational corporations and host states.* Praeger Pub Text.

Carim, X. (2015). *International investment agreements and Africa's structural transformation: A perspective from South Africa.* Retrieved from https://www.southcentre.int/wp-content/uploads/2015/08/IPB4_IIAs-and-Africa%E2%80%99s-Structural-Transformation-Perspective-from-South-Africa_EN.pdf.

Commission on Human Rights. (2005). Report of the United Nations high commissioner on human rights on the responsibilities of transnational corporations and related business enterprises with regard to human rights, UN doc. e/CN.4/2005/91. February 15, 2005.

Deva, S. (2006). The UN global compact for responsible corporate citizenship: Is it still too compact to be global. *Corporate Governance Law Review*, *2*, 145.

Deva, S. (2012). *Regulating corporate human rights violations: Humanizing business*. Abingdon: Routledge.

Deva, S., & Bilchitz, D. (2013). The human rights obligations of business: A critical framework for the future. In S. Deva & D. Bilchitz (Eds.), *Human rights obligations of business: Beyond the corporate responsibility to respect?* Cambridge: Cambridge University Press.

Feaver, D., & Sheehy, B. (2015). A positive theory of effective regulation. *UNSW Law Journal, 35* (3), 961–994.

Friedman, M., & Verhoosel, G. (2003). Global litigation-arbitrating over BIT claims. *National Law Journal, 15*(78).

Gilpin, R. (2018). *The challenge of global capitalism: The world economy in the 21st century*. Princeton: Princeton University Press.

Hamilton, G. (1984). *The control of multinationals: What future for international codes of conduct in the 1980s?* Institute for Research and Information on Multinationals.

Hanakova, L. (2005). *Accountability of transnational corporations under international standards*. (LLM), University of Georgia. Retrieved from http://digitalcommons.law.uga.edu/stu_llm/17.

Hemphill, T. A. (2005). The United Nations global compact: The business implementation and accountability challenge. *International Journal of Business Governance and Ethics, 1*, 303–316.

Hillemanns, C. (2003). UN Norms on the responsibilities of transnational corporations and other business enterprises with regard to human rights. *German Law Journal, 4*(10).

Hopkins, M. (2004). *Corporate social responsibility: An issues paper*. Retrieved from https://www.ilo.org/legacy/english/integration/download/publicat/4_3_285_wcsdg-wp-27.pdf.

Inman, P. (2016, September 13). Study: Big corporations dominate list of world's top economic entities. *The Guardian*. Retrieved from https://www.theguardian.com/business/2016/sep/12/global-justice-now-study-multinational-businesses-walmart-apple-shell.

Jailani, A. (2015). *Indonesia's perspective on review of international investment agreements*. Retrieved from http://igj.or.id/indonesias-perspective-on-investment-agreement-review/.

Kollamparambil, U. (2016). *Bilateral investment treaties and investor state disputes*. ERSA working paper 589.

Korten, D. (1995). *When corporations rule the world*. San Francisco, CA: Berrett-Koehler Publishers.

Knudsen, J. (2011). Company delisting from the UN Global Compact: Limited business demand or domestic governance failure? *Journal of Business Ethics, 103*, 331–349.

Maon, F., Lindgreen, A., & Swaen, V. (2010). Organizational stages and cultural phases: A critical review and a consolidative model of corporate social responsibility development. *International Journal of Management Reviews*, *12*(1), 20–38.

Muchlinski, P. (2007). *Multinational enterprises and the law*. Oxford: Oxford University Press.

Nolan, J. (2005a). With power comes responsibility: Human rights and corporate accountability. *UNSW Law Journal, 28*, 581.

Nolan, J. (2005b). United Nations' Compact with business: Hindering or helping the protection of human rights. *University of Queensland Law Journal, 24*(2), 445.

Nolan, J. (2013). The corporate responsibility to respect human rights: Soft law or not law. In S. Deva & D. Bilchitz (Eds.), *Human rights obligations of business: Beyond the corporate responsibility to respect?* Cambridge: Cambridge University Press.

North, D., Wallis, J. J., Webb, S. B., & Weingast., B. R. (2009). *Violence and social orders. A conceptual framework for interpreting recorded human history*. Cambridge: Cambridge University Press.

North, D., Wallis, J. J., Webb, S. B., & Weingast., B. R. (2013). *In the shadow of violence: Politics, economics and the problem of violence*. Cambridge: Cambridge University Press.

Ocran, T. (1986). Interregional codes of conduct for transnational corporations. *Connecticut Journal of International Law, 2,* 121.

OECD. (1994). *The OECD guidelines for multinational enterprises.* Paris: OECD.

Oldenziel, J., Wilde-Ramsing, J., & Feeney, P. (2010). *10 years on: Assessing the contribution of the OECD guidelines for multinational enterprises to responsible business conduct.* Retrieved from https://papers.ssrn.com/sol3/papers.cfm?abstract_id=1641036.

Rahman, M. (1989). United Nations Code of conduct on transnational corporation (TNCs) in the aspect of private international law. *Dhaka University Studies Part F, 1*(1), 101–116.

Rahim, M. (2010). Who's who: Transnational corporations and nation states interface over the theoretical shift into their relationship.

Rangwaldh, J., & Konopik, P. (2010). The UN Norms on the responsibilities of transnational corporations and other business enterprises with regard to human rights. In R. Mulleart (Ed.), *Corporate social responsibility: The corporate governance of the 21st century.* Chapman: Kluwer Law International.

Rasche, A. (2009). "A necessary supplement": What the United Nations global compact is and is not. *Business and Society, 48,* 511–537.

Rasche, A., Waddock, S., & McIntosh, M. (2013). The united nations global compact: Retrospect and prospect. *Business & Society, 52*(1), 6–30.

Robinson, P. (1986). The question of a reference to international law in the United Nations code of conduct on transnational corporations.

Rodriguez, M. M. (1982). The negotiations on the United Nations' code of conduct on transnational corporations: Some issues. *The CTC Reporter, 12.*

Rudloph, P. H. (2010). The tripartite declaration of principles concerning multinational enterprises. In R. Mullerat (Ed.), *Corporate social responsibility: The corporate governance of the 21st century*: Kluwer Publisher.

Ruggie, J. (2003). Trade sustainability and global governance: Keynote address. *Colombia Journal of Environmental Law, 27,* 297.

Sagafi-Nejad, T., & Dunning, J. H. (2008). *The UN and transnational corporations: From code of conduct to global compact.* Bloomington: Indiana University Press.

Sahlin-Andersson, K. (2006). Corporate social responsibility: A trend and a movement, but of what and for what? *Corporate Governance, 6*(5), 595–608.

Schembera, S. (2018). Implementing corporate social responsibility: Empirical insights on the impact of the UN Global compact on its business participants. *Business & Society, 57*(5), 783–825.

Schutter O. D. (2013). Forward: Beyond the guiding principles. In S. Deva & D. Bilchitz (Eds.), *Human rights obligations of business: Beyond the corporate responsibility to respect?* Cambridge: Cambridge University Press.

Sethi, S. P. & Schepers, D. H. (2014). United Nations global compact: The promise -performance gap. *Journal of Business Ethics, 122,* 193–208.

Sheehy, B., & Feaver, D. (2015). A normative theory of effective regulation. *UNSW Law Journal, 35*(1), 392–425.

UNCTAD. (2015). *IIA Monitor.* Retrieved from Geneva: http://unctad.org/en/Pages/DIAE/International%20Investment%20Agreements%20(IIA)/IIA-Monitor.aspx.

US Department of State. (1989). Multinational Corporations' GIST: A quick reference aid on U.S Foreign Relations. In B. o. P. Affairs (Ed.). Washington D.C: U.S Department of State.

Vernon, R., & Vernon, H. (1977). *Storm over the multinationals: The real issues.* Harvard University Press.

Zerk, J. A. (2006). *Multinationals and corporate social responsibility: Limitations and opportunities in international law* (Vol. 48). Cambridge: Cambridge University Press.

Dr. Mia Mahmudur Rahim is a Senior Lecturer in Law at the University of South Australia. Previously he worked at the Queensland University of Technology and the Bangladesh Judiciary. He completed a Bachelor of Laws with Honours and Masters of Laws from Dhaka University, a Masters in International Economic Law from Warwick University, a Masters in Public Administration from the National University of Singapore and a Ph.D. from the School of Law at Macquarie University. His research interests lie in different forms of regulation and how this relates to legal structures that encourage social responsibility and accountability practice of regulatees. One of his recent books *Legal Regulation of Corporate Social Responsibility* has explained how a meta-regulation mode in laws can effectively raise social responsibility performance of corporations. He is one of the authors of *Corporate Social Responsibility in Private Enterprises* and the lead editor of *Social Audit Regulation*.

An 'Instrument of Moral Persuasion'—Multinational Enterprises and International Codes of Conduct in the 1970s

Thomas Hajduk

1 Introduction

On July 4, 1974, the debate about multinational enterprises (MNEs) had finally hit TV screens. In this day's episode of the high-brow talk show 'The Open Mind', historian and host Richard Heffner discussed 'Multinationals and the Public Interest'.

> This evening, my guests and I are going to examine a subject that could not, would not have surfaced a generation ago, when this program series first began. For our concern now is with the extraordinary rise over the past two decades of the multinational [...]. Here, in the multinational, we have an institution [...] that may be about more profound change in our own economic lives, and ultimately in the very structure and conduct of national and international political affairs than any other development in the history of modern man.[1]

Heffner's introduction indicates that something has indeed changed between the late 1950s—Open Mind was first broadcast in 1956—and the mid-1970s. In this time, a seemingly new phenomenon called the multinational enterprise (MNE) or transnational corporation (TNC) grasped the attention and imagination first of economists and later of politicians, diplomats, journalists, and activists. Although agreed facts on MNEs as well as basic statistics had yet to be generated, it was obvious for many observers that the rise of the post-war MNEs in the United States and Western Europe marked a new era in international business. Given the initial paucity of agreed MNE concepts, their nature and effects on society were contested

---

[1]The views, thoughts, and opinions expressed in the text belong solely to the author, and not necessarily to the author's employer. The Open Mind 1974, *The Multinationals and the Public Interest*. Available online: https://archive.org/details/openmind_ep356. Last access on 11 January 2017.

T. Hajduk (✉)
University of St. Gallen, St. Gallen, Switzerland
e-mail: thomas.hajduk@unisg.ch

© Springer Nature Switzerland AG 2019
M. M. Rahim (ed.), *Code of Conduct on Transnational Corporations*,
CSR, Sustainability, Ethics & Governance,
https://doi.org/10.1007/978-3-030-10816-8_2

and at best seen as ambiguous. On the one hand, they were considered the harbingers of wealth and development, as champions of the efficient management of capital, technology and people. On the other hand, they were deemed a threat to organised labour and even sovereign governments, particularly in the developing world. This ambiguity, or what I call the 'multinational dilemma', was at the centre of a political debate about MNEs in the early and mid-1970s and the question how to deal with these entities. Given their 'global reach', a large portion of the MNE debate took place in international organisations, where in the mid-1970s governments reacted to the MNE dilemma by arguing over rules for multinationals. It was here that in the course of political and ideological confrontation the first norms of behaviour or so called 'codes of conduct' were adopted by governments and thereby the idea of 'corporate responsibility' (CR) was codified on the intergovernmental level.

In this chapter, I will trace the global origin of CR in three steps. I will first explain the 'MNE dilemma' by means of two central UN reports on the nature and role of MNEs. The reaction to these reports took the form of international codes of conduct. The two most eminent and antagonist codes were drafted at the United Nation Economic and Social Council (ECOSOC) and at the Organisation of Economic Co-operation and Development (OECD); I will analyse the development and substance of these codes in the third section of this paper. Finally, I will conclude with a few observations on the legacy of the codes and link my historical insights with today's debate on global norms for business. Yet before I turn to the MNE dilemma, it is necessary to describe my approach and the historical source material on which my narrative is based.

In their pioneering history of CR in the United States, Archie B. Carroll, Kenneth E. Goodpaster, Kenneth J. Lipartito, James E. Post and Patricia H. Werhane state that CR 'is not a unitary idea. Corporate responsibility is, in fact, a *concept*, a *challenge to business*, a *field of practice*, and an area of *academic study*' (Carroll et al. 2012, p. 6). Ideas (or concepts) and practice go hand in hand and both of them need to be reconstructed in order to understand CR and its history. In this chapter I focus on *ideas* about MNEs and their responsibilities and, in doing so, draw on Mark Bevir's interpretative approach, one of the more recent contributions to the history of ideas (see below). The reason lies in the very nature of the debate from which the first CR norms emerged: MNEs are abstract and complex businesses, which are not easy to understand and were even less so when a wider public became aware of them for the first time. In the 1970s there were not many agreed facts about MNEs. So the debate on their characteristics and their role in society was primarily one involving contesting ideas. To give a basic example: not even the definition of MNE or terminology per se (MNE, MNC, TNC etc.)[2] was clear and agreed upon, let alone normative ideas about 'corporate responsibility'. Such

---

[2]There were other terms such as 'multinational corporation', 'supranational firm', 'cosmocorp' etc. (see UNDESA 1973, pp. 118–121). However, 'MNE' and 'TNC' became the preferred notions at the OECD and the UN, respectively.

concepts were conceived and put forward in the socio-economic and political context of the 1970s. This context with its international business operations, its ideological front lines, its North-South divisions and critical attitudes towards 'development' informed the ideas about MNEs and codes of conduct. So despite the emphasis on ideas, my research does not ignore the significance of practices; on the contrary, I understand ideas and practices as mutually constitutive.

This theoretical assumption rests on the interpretative approach and Mark Bevir's (1999) 'logic of the history of ideas', which is based on four concepts: practice, belief,[3] tradition and dilemma. In a nutshell, Bevir argues that practice without meaning is not possible and that there is no pure experience, but only perceptions that 'always incorporate elements of our theoretical understanding of the world' (ibid., p. 90). People hold and express beliefs in order to ascribe meaning to their perceptions of themselves and the world; scholars refer to such beliefs in order to account for people's actions. '[B]eliefs and practices are constitutive of each other' (Bevir and Rhodes 2006, p. 2).

Beliefs are informed and explained by traditions and dilemmas. A tradition is 'a set of understandings someone receives during socialization', as a 'social heritage' it is the 'necessary background to the beliefs we adopt and the actions we perform' (Bevir et al. 2003, pp. 6–7). This background accounts for the status quo of the beliefs held by an individual and thereby for continuity in beliefs. Traditions are developed by 'relevant beliefs and practices' that are 'passed from generation to generation' and the 'continuity lies in the themes developed and passed on over time, rather than any self-conscious sense of continuity' (Bevir and Rhodes 2006, p. 8). By contrast, change and thus the possibility of 'individual agency' is conceptualised by the term 'dilemma' (Bevir et al. 2003, p. 10). A dilemma is given 'when a new idea stands in opposition to existing beliefs or practices and so forces a reconsideration of these existing beliefs and associated traditions' (Bevir and Rhodes 2006, p. 36). In other words, a dilemma is a problem which questions existing ideas and traditions and prompts individuals to consider new ideas (and practices) and modify traditions.

The emergence of the multinational enterprise and the code debate illustrate how traditional ideas are challenged by a dilemma and how new ideas, and with them new practices, emerge in response. In the post-war period, MNEs were a new phenomenon which could not be understood with traditional ideas about international business and investment, but required fresh concepts and new data (see Sect. 2). The codes of conduct were meant to reflect these new ideas and to impose normative concepts on the behaviour of MNEs (see Sect. 3). Although the immediate results of the codes were modest, they contributed to an emerging tradition of international CR norms (see Sect. 4).

---

[3]The terms belief, idea and concept are used synonymously.

My research rests mainly on archival documents from international organisations which had a stake in the multinational dilemma and the code debate.[4] The material can be distinguished into publicly available records like reports and unpublished archival documents like drafts, correspondence and working papers. Usually I was able to request declassification of documents that have been created before 1981. While declassification for this period was no problem, the availability and organisation of the material was sometimes challenging.[5] For this reason, this paper also draws on contemporary publications like books and press articles. Moreover, I analysed the 'Kissinger cables', when they had been made available online by Wikileaks in April 2013.[6] The cables from the US State Department give insights behind the scenes of negotiating the codes.

2 The Multinational Dilemma

One of the guests of the Open Mind episode on MNEs was Philippe de Seynes, the Undersecretary General of the United Nations for Economic and Social Affairs. Inviting a senior bureaucrat may appear a strange choice when discussing MNEs, but made perfect sense. For de Seynes was the spiritus rector behind two seminal UN reports on MNEs and world development. The second of these reports, devoted to the 'impact of multinational corporations on development and international relations' (UNDESA 1974a) had just been published, marking a culminating point of several years of intense debate.

At the beginning of the debate stood economists like Charles Kindleberger, Edith Penrose and Raymond Vernon. At Harvard Business School, Vernon directed the Multinational Enterprise Project, which began to study the different dimensions of US MNEs. This type of company with huge revenue streams and operations abroad had significantly proliferated since World War II. The research group studied 187 companies of the Fortune 500 list, which ranks the largest US enterprises by revenues. The whole sample came from manufacturing and extractive industries and was 'distinct in many respects from the rest of the US corporate economy' with regard to their revenues, number of foreign subsidiaries and the number of people they employed, for instance (Vernon 1971, p. 11). In the first

---

[4]These were the UN, the OECD, the International Labour Organization (ILO), the European Parliament, the European Commission (EC), and the Council of Europe. Archival material is cited in footnotes.

[5]The archival management of the UN is still evolving. When the official United Nations Intellectual History Project started, its lead authors noted that the UN records deserved better management (Emmerji et al. 2001, p. XX).

[6]Wikileaks obtained over 1.7 million diplomatic cables dating back to the period between 1973 and 1976 from the National Archives and Record Administration. Wikileaks uploaded them on its own servers and developed a comprehensive search engine: https://wikileaks.org/plusd/.

major book emanating from the project ('Sovereignty at Bay') Vernon's introducing sentences became iconic:

> Suddenly, it seems, the sovereign states are feeling naked. Concepts such as national sovereignty and national economic strength appear curiously drained of meaning. [...] Though the sense of nakedness and dependence has produced only inhibited responses so far, it has focused the world's interest on the institutions that are thought to be the main agents of the change. One of these is the multinational enterprise (Vernon 1971, p. 3).

By the end of the 1960s, the rising number of large US-based and ever more European and later Japanese companies with international operations raised fears both in the developed and the developing world. MNEs were criticised by governments, trade unions, and journalists. Whereas their proponents—mainly in the West—saw them as bastions of free market capitalism, even their mere existence had become questionable in some corners of the world, predominantly in the developing countries. Their perceived size and power combined with the lack of reliable data resulted in debates which were fuelled by rational as well as emotional concerns. Multiple editions of popular books like 'Le Défi Américain' (Servan-Schreiber 1967) and 'Global Reach' (Barnet and Müller 1974) captured the mood of critics as well as their concerned readers. Such fears about the rise of MNEs reflected a period which can be generally characterised by 'a widespread perception of crisis' (Ferguson 2010, pp. 14–15) on a global scale.

This is not to say that such anxieties were merely products of vivid imagination. Scepticism concerning MNEs was warranted for several reasons. First, scholarly work like Vernon's Harvard project showed that MNE numbers were rising, even though data collection was just at its beginning and the required statistics from many different countries were not yet fully available. Second, trade unions, in particular their international secretariats, were the first stakeholders to demand binding rules for MNEs (ICFTU 1971, pp. 21–22; Petrini 2011). Unionists were early witnesses to the mobility of MNEs and their ability to circumvent industrial relations. The third reason was a corporate scandal which was often referred to in the MNE debate. The International Telephone and Telegraph (ITT) affair embodied all concerns about corporate power. In 1972 the American columnist Jack Anderson had revealed 80 pages of internal documents created at ITT, a large US-based conglomerate. According to these 'secret memoranda', ITT had planned to destabilise the Chilean economy in 1970, when the Marxist Salvador Allende was poised to become president and threatened to nationalise ITT's Chilean subsidiaries (Sampson 1973, pp. 13, 232, 235, 245–252).

The ITT scandal became a cause célèbre in international affairs. At the UN General Assembly, the Chilean delegation demanded the creation of a 'group of eminent persons' to study MNEs and their impact on international relations (ECOSOC Resolution 1721 LIII). This resolution was the starting point for comprehensive studies conducted by the UN, or more precisely the ECOSOC, and later by other international organisations and some national parliaments.

The two UN studies were the first official, large-scale attempts of taking stock of MNEs across the globe. To get the broader picture, the UN Secretariat tested a new instrument: a 'Group of Eminent Persons' (GEP) was established in order to hold public hearings, discuss the findings and prepare a report. The UN Secretariat listed candidates from government, business, trade unions and economics and invited 20 of them to join the group. As these were the days of the Cold War and open conflicts between developing and developed world, the UN staff was anxious to maintain a balance. Among the more prominent members were the economist John H. Dunning, US Senator Jacob Javits, the former president of the European Commission Sicco Mansholt, J. Irwin Miller, chairman of Cummins Engine Co. Inc., and the Chilean diplomat Juan Somavía, who in 1998 would become Director-General of the ILO.

To facilitate the deliberations of the GEP, the UN Secretariat compiled a report which was meant to provide conceptual clarification and basic statistical data (size, geographical distribution, industrial structure and ownership patterns) (UNDESA 1973, p. vi). Although the report was the first of its kind and to some extent served as a role model for similar reports, it was limited. For a start, the authors warned their readers that 'figures must be treated with caution and their interpretation is subject to a considerable margin of uncertainty' (UNDESA 1973, p. 4). Moreover, to meet the broad ECOSOC mandate the authors adopted a simple definition: 'In the broadest sense, any corporation with one or more foreign branches or affiliates engaged in any of the activities mentioned may qualify as multinational' (UNDESA 1973, p. 5). This definition of a 'multinational corporation', as the UN called MNEs at first, could cover a broad range of enterprises at the cost of glossing over more specific and contentious details such as the ownership of a company (private, public, mixed), questions that would later bedevil the UN code negotiations.

According to the report, MNEs shared a few characteristics. They usually made more than $100 million in sales, were 'predominantly oligopolistic', had 'sizeable clusters of foreign branches and affiliates' which were further growing; MNEs were 'in general a product of developed countries', with MNEs from the US, the UK, the Federal Republic of Germany, and France alone accounting for three quarters of the total number of foreign affiliates (UNDESA 1973, pp. 6–8). In 1966, MNEs in manufacturing generated 40% of total foreign direct investment (FDI), petroleum 29%, mining seven per cent and other industries 24% (UNDESA 1973, pp. 10–11). As MNEs were considered an integral part of the world economy, the report scrutinised a fairly broad scope of issues. The authors studied the impact of MNEs on international relations (i.e., relations between the MNEs' home and host countries), technology transfer, employment, labour standards, the balance of payments in developing countries, socio-cultural considerations (i.e., threat to local traditions), effects on the monetary system and international trade, and taxation. However, the focus was often on MNE-state relations in those areas and less frequent about MNE-society relations.

Throughout the report, the authors arrived at the conclusion that the effect of MNEs on a specific issue was either uncertain or mixed. As the report was largely written for developing countries, the UN's main constituency (at least in membership numbers), the multinational dilemma was explicitly stated:

When considering economic costs and benefits, governments are sometimes faced with a dilemma. On the one hand, they judge that multinational corporations can contribute to the rate of increase of income and exports, and can raise the level of technology, employment and managerial know-how. On the other hand, they recognize that multinational corporations can also undermine governmental priorities, fiscal and monetary policies, and income distribution policies, and may have an unfavourable effect on the balance of payments (UNDESA 1973, pp. 44–45).

Thus, the report affirmed some alleged problems associated with MNEs—for example, their 'oligopolistic nature' and their challenge to state sovereignty—while acknowledging the advantages of FDI inflows. In terms of practical conclusions, this excluded drastic solutions like (the rights to) the dismantling or general expropriation of MNEs. Instead, the report suggested solutions on the part of companies, trade unions, home and host countries and the international system. On the business level, the authors claimed that MNEs could adopt 'standards of good citizenship' and the 'recognition of the concept of corporate social responsibility', but warned that their efficacy was 'likely to be limited' since they were subject to varying interpretations of 'responsibility', if not window-dressing (UNDESA 1973, pp. 78–79). Emanating from the UN, the recommendations regarding international organisations were most concrete. The authors suggested establishing an international forum for MNE-related affairs and an information centre at the UN, and to provide technical cooperation and training to developing countries (UNDESA 1973, pp. 87–88). The negative impact of MNE activities could be remedied by a 'General Agreement on Multinational Corporations', which would lay down a limited set of universally accepted principles, the authors claimed. Because such an agreement would take some time to be established, a code of conduct could be negotiated first and through its 'educational value' serve as a 'guide to the [UN] review and appraisal of the activities of host and home countries as well as of the multinational corporations' (UNDESA 1973, pp. 92–93, 102). For the latter purpose, the authors recommended a UN 'registry of MNCs', which would monitor MNEs and could document good corporate behaviour.

In its public hearings in New York and then Geneva in 1973, the GEP had ample opportunity to further explore the report's themes and theses. In total, 47 experts from MNEs, developing countries, trade unions, international organisations, academia, think tanks and civil society presented their statement before the group and gave answers to their questions (UNDESA 1974b). Many of these experts were senior executives and ministers. Business leaders in particular were eager to state their views, perhaps in order to put right the accusations they were faced with. Jaques Maisonrouge (IBM), Irving Shapiro (DuPont) and Giovanni Agnelli (Fiat) were among the most prominent executives presenting before the group. The participation of such senior executives demonstrates the importance which business representative attached to the whole exercise.

Given the scale of the GEP hearings and the sheer amount of statements and verbatims documenting both hearings and (a part of) the internal deliberations, it is impossible to summarise them at this point.[7] Suffice it to say that the GEP hearings did little to resolve the idea of the multinational dilemma. On the contrary, the statements highlighted the complexity of the MNE phenomenon and the diversity of professional and political perspectives on it. As a result, the GEP was confronted with contradicting or incompatible statements. It was no help that the GEP members themselves were a diverse lot with their own divergent views. A compromise to resolve the multinational dilemma was nigh impossible under these circumstances.

This plethora of ideas partly translated into the group's final report which was submitted to the UN General Secretary in May 1974 (UNDESA 1974a). It was remarkable for two reasons. First, it actually made recommendations to the UN, host and home countries and MNEs despite disagreement in the GEP. The recommendations to the UN were the most serious ones, because they had an immediate impact and were largely adopted by the UN Secretary General. The GEP recommended setting up a UN commission on multinational corporations to deal with MNEs on a regular basis and to establish an information and research centre, which would gather reliable information and provide technical co-operation (UNDESA 1974a, pp. 52–54). The GEP also proposed a work programme for the commission which assigned highest priority to the development of a code of conduct understood as a 'consistent set of recommendations which are gradually evolved' and which are 'not compulsory in character' but 'act as an instrument of moral persuasion, strengthened by the authority of international organisations and the support of public opinion' (UNDESA 1974a, p. 55).

The second remarkable feature of the report was its appendix. It contained comments by nine individual members of the group who wished to contradict the text of the official report. The longest and most critical comment was made by Hans Schaffner, a former Swiss President and vice-chairman of Sandoz, a Swiss chemical company (UNDESA 1974a, pp. 140–162). Schaffner's detailed criticism is noteworthy, because a few years later a Swiss NGO found out that he had met regularly with a secretive group of senior Swiss executives during his mandate as GEP member (Erklärung von Bern 1978).[8] In hindsight, the efforts taken by his Swiss supporters are further evidence of how important business leaders considered the UN hearings. Notwithstanding, the comments of the nine dissenters made clear how difficult compromise on the multinational dilemma was. This boded ill for the work ahead.

The multinational dilemma was not confined to the many-voiced UN. The ILO and the Council of Europe held their own consultations. So did national bodies such as the German Bundestag, the US Congress or the Labour Party in the United Kingdom. However, one international organisation kept a relatively low profile

---

[7]The majority of verbatims, statements and drafts created during the GEP hearings are kept by the United Nations Archives and Records Management Section (UNARMS) in New York: see UNARMS, Box: S-089-148-01; UNARMS, Box: S-089-148-02.

[8]Schaffner passed on internal documents and was briefed by the group in order to influence the GEP's work. He was indeed a vocal advocate of MNEs during the hearings, but was neither able to convince his opponents nor the group as a whole.

regarding MNEs, at least in its publications. As a club of industrialised countries (with the exception of Turkey) the OECD did welcome MNEs, the majority of which were headquartered in the OECD area. Despite saying little about MNEs in public,[9] the OECD members held meetings on the MNE dilemma and possible codes of conduct as early as in 1973.[10] Their interest in the subject grew significantly, after the UN reports had been published and negotiations on a UN code of conduct were imminent.

3 Codes of Conduct

Despite the diverging views on the nature of MNEs, there was a widespread belief in the necessary regulation of MNE behaviour, sparking work on codes of conduct in several international organisations. I will focus on two of them, which can be considered as the opposite poles in the codification of business norms—the UN Code of Conduct and the OECD Guidelines.[11]

The UN was first to officially announce code negotiations. The GEP's recommendation to start negotiating a code of conduct was welcomed by the ECOSOC and included into the terms of reference of the new Commission on Transnational Corporations (ECOSOC Resolution 1913 LVII). Apart from work on the code, the Commission was to contribute to intergovernmental arrangements and agreements on different aspects of MNEs (ECOSOC Resolution 1913). The Commission was to be supported by the UN Centre on Transnational Corporations (UNCTC), which was also established in 1974 and was meant to provide studies and support services to the code negations.[12]

The creation of the Commission and the Centre coincided with another development at the UN. On May 1, International Worker's Day, the General Assembly at its Sixth Special Session adopted two resolutions which combined the political agenda of the developing world: the Declaration on the Establishment of a New International Economic Order and the Programme of Action on the Establishment of a New International Economic Order (reproduced in Ahmia 2009, pp. 206–210, 210–228). These documents represented the developing world's demand for structural changes in global economic relations which, as the Declaration put it,

---

[9]The so called 'Rey report' is an exception (OECD 1972).

[10]OECD Archives, Ad hoc Meeting of Experts on Guidelines and Consultation Procedures in Matters Pertaining to International Investment, Paris 1973, document code: CES/73.88.

[11]There were two other codes relevant to the code debate in the 1970s. First, there was the Draft Code of Principles on Multinational Enterprises and Governments, elaborated in 1976 in a joint session of the US Congress and the European Parliament (EP 1977, pp. 7–17). This 'Lange-Gibbons code', named after its two sponsors, never materialised. Second, foreign ministers of the EEC adopted a Code of Conduct for European Firms Operating in South Africa in 1977.

[12]ECOSOC Resolution 1913. Moreover, the UNCTC advised developing countries in their dealings with MNEs.

would be based on 'equity, sovereign equality, interdependence, common interest and cooperation among all States' (Ahmia 2009, p. 206). The proclamation of the New International Economic Order (NIEO) was a result of the growing clout of developing countries at the UN, which have become ever more numerous in the wake of decolonization. Although the Security Council remained under control of the Permanent Five, the rest of the UN system, which dealt with social and economic issues, was dominated by the developing countries. They coordinated their policy and voting behaviour under the umbrella of the Group of 77 (G-77). Borrowing conceptually from dependency theory, the NIEO sought an alternative to both the Capitalist and Socialist ideas of development by modernization. MNEs were to serve this overall purpose rather than to seek profits for their owners. According to the NIEO Programme of Action, 'all efforts should be made to formulate, adopt and implement an international code of conduct for transnational corporations'; the code should prevent domestic interference and collaboration with 'racist regimes and colonial administrations', regulate MNE operations, restrictive business practices and bring them in line with national development plans (Ahmia 2009, pp. 218–219).

This—and the mutual suspicion between the Eastern and the Western blocs—was the climate in which the UN set out to formulate a code. However, the actual negotiations did not start before the Commission's second meeting in March 1976, when it established an intergovernmental working group, which started its work only in January 1977. In the meantime, the OECD saw the potential threat emanating from a code or even an international agreement on MNEs drafted in the spirit of the NIEO. When investment experts met at the executive committee in special session, a political governance body at the OECD, to discuss the GEP report, the US delegate noted that 'most delegates expressed dissatisfaction in varying degrees to quality and tone of report'.[13] At this point, the OECD had already been working on a code or guidelines on national treatment[14] and the governmental use of investment incentives and disincentives. This work was in line with its market-liberal Code on Liberalization of Capital Movements (1960). However, some OECD members were sceptical about the possibly binding nature of the investment guidelines, and France, supported by Italy, Australia and Canada, argued for a 'balanced movement' by linking investment with MNE issues.[15] The idea of a 'package' of investor rights and obligations was controversial and initially objected by the US, UK, Dutch and German representatives. However, a few months later the US and UK delegations, which were the most active players in the negotiations, gave in and the UK delegate proposed a 'package deal' in order to

---

[13]Public Library of US Diplomacy (PLUSD), Fifth XCSS Experts Meeting On Investment, July 8–9, 1974, document code: 1974OECDP16779_b, para. 17. Last access on 11 January 2017.

[14]The principle of 'national treatment' implies that OECD member countries should treat investments and MNE subsidiaries controlled by nationals of another member country according to international law and not less favourable than domestic companies.

[15]PLUSD, Fourth XCSS Experts' Meeting on Investment, April 29–30, 1974, document code: 1974OECDP10631_b, para. 5. Last access on 11 January 2017.

assuage investment-sceptical delegations.[16] Addressing the sceptics, the delegate made clear that the MNE code would be the 'prime objective' and national treatment and incentives/disincentives 'were to be played down'—privately he told his US colleague that the Labour government back home would not agree to any proposal unless it also 'laid obligations on MNEs as well as governments'.[17]

With this political background the OECD negotiations on a MNE code began in earnest in March 1975. The newly created Committee on Investment and Multinational Enterprises (CIME) held its first meeting to elaborate an OECD declaration on investment which would also cover MNE obligations. Despite earlier misgivings about the balance between investor and government responsibilities, there was 'broad support for [a] concept of non-binding OECD standards of behaviour',[18] the US delegate cabled to Washington. Only Canada and the US were still sceptical about the code. The US delegation was not in favour of any standards for MNEs, it had to make this concession because it was faced with a 'clear reaffirmation by most members that [the] political decision on them [i.e. national treatment and investment incentives and disincentives] cannot be taken before MNE standards [are] completed'.[19] Therefore, the OECD Guidelines were an unintended consequence of the organisation's work on investment liberalisation. It was a quid pro quo: give investors—including MNEs—rights vis-à-vis host governments, and MNEs will be officially asked to behave.[20]

This was the original idea behind the Guidelines. Its second raison d'être was what commentators called a 'counter-attack' (Robinson 1983, pp. 117–118; Muchlinski 2007, p. 659). If the OECD would manage to produce a code agreeable to the industrialised countries before a UN code was concluded, it would set a precedent and possibly steal the UN's (and G-77's) thunder. This thinking was present in the first CIME meeting, as was evinced by a comment of the German delegation which chaired the committee until 1979 and stressed the 'desirability of developing OECD standards for use in UN bodies which consider MNE codes of conduct'.[21] This reasoning probably increased the code's appeal. Yet first and foremost it was the majority's desire for a balanced investment 'package' which placed a MNE code on the OECD agenda.

The following months of drafting and negotiations were relatively efficient and smooth when compared to the UN negotiations. It took the OECD only 14 months

---

[16]PLUSD, Executive Committee in Special Session (XCSS) Meeting Nov. 25–26: Investment Issues and Date of Next XCSS, document code: 1974OECDP28560_b, para. 2.

[17]PLUSD (XCSS Nov. 25–26), para. 3. Last access on 11 January 2017.

[18]PLUSD, First Meeting of Investment Committee (IME) March 3–4, 1975, document code: 1975OECDP05832_b, para. 5. Last access on 11 January 2017.

[19]PLUSD (IME March 3–4), para. 1.

[20]This reasoning did not go unnoticed. For example, a UNCTC staff member explicitly referred to quid-pro-quo deal at the OECD (Sauvant 1977, p. 384).

[21]PLUSD (IME March 3–4), para. 6. This idea was reiterated in the State Department's 1975 annual policy assessment; cf. PLUSD, Annual Policy Assessment, 1975, document code: 1975OECDP16403_b, para. 16. Last access on 11 January 2017.

to reach an internal agreement which was adopted by the Ministerial Meeting in June 1976. To be sure, there were a few major points of divergence which pitted some European delegations against the US delegation and its supporters. For example, the Nordic countries pushed for a more detailed, country-by-country disclosure of information, while Norway, Denmark and the Netherlands were in favour of a stronger section on industrial relations and more influence for trade unions.[22] However, this could not obscure the fundamental agreement on the 'package deal'. Moreover, the OECD group was homogenous enough to find agreement and have similar ideas and interests, as the final text shows.

The Declaration on International Investment and Multinational Enterprises (OECD 1976) consisted of five interconnected parts: the Declaration, the annexed Guidelines and three Council Decisions on the implementation of the Declaration, national treatment and international investment incentives and disincentives. The form of a 'declaration' was not only a new instrument but also peculiar, because there were no official provisions for it in the OECD Convention.[23] In fact, the organisation could only take Decisions binding for all members, make non-binding recommendations to members or enter into agreements with members and third parties. But as the Guidelines were addressed to MNEs—a novelty at the OECD—they could not be promulgated by the OECD Council, but only by the member countries within the OECD framework. Moreover, declarations do not imply any legal obligations for their originators or their addressees and cannot be vetoed by other member countries. By contrast, the three decisions were binding for OECD members and made up an odd instrument: governments voluntarily abided by the Declaration, but were obliged to engage in its implementation and follow-up procedure (like promoting the Guidelines in their country and reporting on progress) and comply with the national treatment principle and coordinate investment incentives and disincentives. This gave the OECD some flexibility, for example by dealing with dissenting member countries,[24] and at the same time strengthened the investment-related principles and weakened the legal status of the Guidelines.[25]

The text of the Guidelines was about seven pages and, after an introduction, was divided into seven sections: general policies, disclosure of information, competition, financing, taxation, employment and industrial relations, and science and technology. These sections reflected the main issues of the multinational dilemma and the overall theme of the debate, namely the lack of governmental control vis-à-vis MNEs. The preamble described the importance of MNEs, but also claimed that

---

[22]PLUSD, CIME meeting, November 19–20, 1975, paras. 16, 21.

[23]The instrument was first used for the Trade Pledge in May 1974, see OECD Archives, Folder 229334, Draft of a Manual on the Declaration by the Governments of OECD Countries […], 29. VIII. 1976, p. 5, fn. 1.

[24]The Declaration was adopted by consensus except Turkey's abstention. Reaching agreement on a Convention would have proved trickier.

[25]The decision to avoid legal language was made early in the negotiations, after the UK delegation had proposed the use of 'straight prose' at the beginning of the negotiations, see OECD Archives, Folder 230614, Drafting group, 30/4/75.

concerns might arise due to their complex structure and that 'their operations beyond the national framework may lead to abuse of concentrations of economic power and to conflicts with national policy objectives' (OECD 1976, p. 11). The aim of the OECD governments was 'to encourage the positive contributions which MNEs can make to economic and social progress and to minimise and resolve the difficulties' (ibid.). This should be achieved by cooperation between OECD governments and non-member countries, the mode of which would be 'continuing, pragmatic and balanced' (ibid.).

The reference to a pragmatic approach was essential for the Guidelines, since it helped the OECD countries to avoid conceptual pitfalls and legal debates which plagued the UN code negotiations. For example, the preamble stated that a 'precise legal definition of multinational enterprises is not required for the purposes of the guidelines' (OECD 1976, p. 12). Instead of a legal definition, a pragmatic definition was given, saying that MNEs 'usually comprise companies or other entities whose ownership is private, state or mixed, established in different countries and so linked that one or more of them may be able to exercise a significant influence over the activities of others' (ibid.).[26] The actual recommendations were fairly abstract and modest at the same time. The 'general policies' section is a good example. MNEs were asked among other things to consider the policy objectives of their host state, observe local laws, cooperate with local community and business, not to bribe officials and abstain from 'improper involvement in local political activities' (OECD 1976, pp. 13–14). These norms reflected conventions, laws and regulations that were already in force in most OECD countries. Where the recommendations were not rooted in laws and regulations, the wording was explicitly ambiguous and conditional. For example, the Guidelines asked MNEs to 'supply their entities [i.e., subsidiaries] with supplementary information the latter may need in order to meet requests by the authorities of the countries in which those entities are located for information relevant to the activities of those entities, *taking into account legitimate requirements of business confidentiality*' (OECD 1976, p. 13; emphasis added by author). The text does neither clarify the meaning and scope of 'supplementary information' or 'legitimate requirements of business confidentiality' nor does it support any criteria or references to determine it. As a consequence, the 'pragmatic approach' in drafting the OECD code resulted in a liberal, light-touch understanding of CR, which restated existing business conduct and regulations and, where it went beyond convention, counterbalanced such norms with conditional rescue clauses. In fact, the abstruse, non-committing character of the text worked so well that numerous requests for clarifications were made to CIME in the following years (see Sect. 4).

Back at the UN, code negotiations took a slow start. The Commission on Transnational Corporations met in March 1975 for the first time. Three factions emerged at this meeting and submitted their demands (ECOSOC-CTC 1975):

---

[26]This definition was appropriately called a '(non) definition' by Blanpain (1979, p. 58).

delegations from the G77, the Western OECD countries and the Socialist countries. In a nutshell, the G77 delegations formulated numerous demands in line with the NIEO. They stressed the sovereignty of host states, including the right to nationalise foreign property without compensation, and wanted a binding code. The Western delegations by contrast did not want any obligations for MNEs. They proposed voluntary principles like those created by the OECD: while MNEs would have certain responsibilities towards the host states in which they operated, the latter would have responsibilities towards MNEs as well, especially such regarding national treatment and security of investments. The Socialist delegations pointed out some negative impacts of MNEs, which they deemed agents of capitalism, and left the field otherwise to the G77. They were conspicuously silent about their own state-controlled enterprises with operations abroad. A year later the Commission met for its second session. The work programme was presented and discussed (ECOSOC-CTC 1976). With view to the Code, it was decided to form an intergovernmental working group for its formulation. The working group would consist of at least four representatives of each of the three factions in the Commission and be supported by the different UN bodies. As was to be expected in light of the three factions' differing views, the formulation of the code proved difficult. It was not until the end of 1978 that a first 'annotated outline' could be presented by the chairman of the group (ECOSOC-CTC 1978).

The 1978 code draft was structured into two main sections: the activities of transnational corporations and the treatment of transnational corporations. Like the OECD Guidelines, the UN draft thus focused on the relationship between MNEs and host countries. Yet the emphasis was clearly on the behaviour of MNEs; the corresponding sections accounted for about three quarters of the draft. Since the UN Code was pushed by the G-77, the responsibilities of MNEs were drafted with an eye on the concerns of developing countries. The draft asked MNEs to respect national sovereignty, observe domestic laws, regulations and administrative practices and to adhere to economic goals and development objectives as well as socio-cultural objectives and values (ECOSOC-CTC 1978, pp. 4–5). Similar but less clear and detailed demands could also be found in the preamble and the general policies of the OECD Guidelines.

However, the UN Code differed considerably from the Guidelines in having sections on human rights and fundamental freedoms. The code asked MNEs to respect the latter two, not discriminate on the basis of 'race, colour, sex, religion, language, social origin, or political and other opinions' (ECOSOC-CTC 1978, p. 5) and not to collaborate with the apartheid regime in South Africa. The UN Code had also sections devoted to environmental protection, an issue only very briefly referred to in the Guidelines, and consumer protection, which had no equivalent in the OECD text. Likewise, the two sections on non-interference in internal political affairs and in intergovernmental affairs were more elaborate than the corresponding norms in the 'general policy' section of the OECD code. Apart from these agreed draft sections, there were also a few headings without text, because the working group still had not reached agreement on them. They were the abstention from corrupt practices, taxation, restrictive business practices, transfer of technology, and employment and labour. On the one hand this was due to pragmatic reasons; the group waited for parallel developments at other UN organisations. For example, the UN Conference on Trade and Development (UNCTAD) was working on a code on restrictive business practices[27] (adopted in 1980) and a code on the transfer of technology (never adopted). On the other hand, the empty sections indicated how difficult the UN negotiations were.

The most controversial part of the draft code was its section dealing with the general treatment of MNEs by host countries. It differed most significantly from the spirit of the OECD Guidelines. The provisions under this heading reiterated the sovereignty of (host) states and ascribed great importance to governmental rights rather than their responsibilities towards MNEs. Countries 'determine the role that such corporations may be called to play in economic and social development' (ECOSOC-CTC 1978, p. 11). This did not preclude the principle of national treatment, 'fair and equitable treatment' of MNEs which 'should be accorded the same treatment under national laws, regulations and administrative practices […] as that accorded to domestic enterprises, *in situations where the operations of transnational corporations are comparable to those of domestic enterprises*' (ECOSOC-CTC 1978, p. 11; emphasis added by author). This conditional clause introduced a basis for treating MNEs differently, because developing countries had always stressed that MNEs were different from domestic companies and therefore needed appropriate regulation (whereas the OECD upheld the principle of 'national treatment'). This bias towards host states continued in the provisions on jurisdiction and nationalization and compensation. In general, MNEs were subject to the jurisdiction of their host state (ECOSOC-CTC 1978, p. 12). International arbitration was possible, if agreed to by the state. Only if two jurisdictions clashed over a MNE-related dispute and governments agreed to international intermediation, the draft code recommended 'adoption by the States concerned of mutually accepted principles and procedures, bilaterally or multilaterally' (ECOSOC-CTC 1978, p. 13). This possibility was far away from the OECD Declaration which preferred international cooperation to domestic action.

In a similar vein, the provision under the headline of 'nationalization and compensation' was very different from the Guidelines. It held that 'States have the right, acting in the public interest, to nationalize property in their territory', provided that it was done under 'due process of law, in accordance with international laws, regulations and administrative practices' and 'payment of just compensation' to the MNE affected (ECOSOC-CTC 1978, p. 12). This provision clearly addressed and meant to legitimise the nationalisation policies of developing countries like Chile's expropriation of the foreign-held copper industry in 1972 or Venezuela's nationalisation of its oil-extracting sector. To OECD countries this was anathema,

---

[27]Adopted by General Assembly Resolution 35/63 and officially known as Set of Multilaterally Agreed Equitable Principles and Rules for the Control of Restrictive Business Practices.

although instances of nationalisation did also occur in Europe, albeit within more predictable legal frameworks than in some developing countries. The controversy around the nationalisation and compensation section was stressed by the annex to the draft, which tried to find some common grounds in this political minefield.

The influence of the OECD Guidelines on the UN negotiations was limited, as differences between developed and developing countries were already deeply entrenched. However, they were instrumental in negotiating the ILO Tripartite Declaration of Principles Concerning Multinational Enterprises and Social Policy, which were adopted in 1977 (ILO 1977). With its narrower mandate and unique tripartite structure, the ILO looked better prepared for fruitful negotiations. But the tripartite meeting in 1972 had made visible disagreements between trade union and employer representatives, which were further complicated by the adoption of the NIEO in 1974 and its implementation throughout the UN. In this constellation the ILO tripartite drafting group had limited room for manoeuvre.[28] The code did not become a binding ILO convention, as trade union representatives and G77 representatives had demanded, but a non-binding 'Declaration'. This was not the only striking resemblance with the Guidelines. The ILO Declaration also eschewed a MNE definition, preferring a non-legal, practical 'understanding' of the subject (ILO 1977, p. 6). Although it was more detailed on the sections it covered—employment, training, work and life conditions, and industrial relations—it did not substantially go beyond the OECD Guidelines. In fact, an ILO representative called the Declaration and the Guidelines 'completely compatible texts' (Günter 1980, p. 175). This was the public version endorsed by both organisations. Within the ILO, however, there were reservations about the OECD influence. The World Confederation of Labour, the international secretariat of the Socialist trade unions, regarded the 'affinities between the OECD code of conduct and the declaration of principles as extremely serious' because thereby characteristics of the 'Capitalist countries' were projected on the 'entire Third World'.[29] Whether this was true or not, the OECD hallmark was recognisable. This may be the reason why the ILO Declaration did not play a major role in the code debate (when compared to the ILO's original mission of contributing to 'social justice') and has not made any deeper impact on today's CR debate.[30]

---

[28]On the development of the Declaration, see ILO Archives, File Series: GB, File Number: 203-100-6, report of the reconvened tripartite advisory meeting on the relationship of multinational enterprises and social policy, document code: MNE/1977/D.8, pp. 1–2.

[29]ILO Archives, File Series: GB, File Number: 203-100-6, Statement by the representative of the World Confederation of Labour, May-June 1977, document code: GB.203/6/20.

[30]The ILO representative cited earlier called it a 'technical contribution to the work of the UN' (Günter 1980, p. 175).

4 Aftermath

The code debate lost steam by the late 1970s and had little practical consequences after the OECD and ILO codes had been published. Apart from human rights in apartheid South Africa[31] and the 1981 WHO code of marketing breast milk substitutes (Post 2013, pp. 53–63), there was not much talk or action about codes during the 1980s and early 1990s. The UN code negotiations dragged on with a few minor breakthroughs like the Socialist countries' acceptance of considering state-owned companies with foreign subsidiaries as MNEs (Dell 1990, pp. 87, 118–120, 122–123). However, this did not help the UN code to withstand changes in the 1980s world economy and international relations. The global recession in the late 1970s and early 1980s and rising unemployment numbers in the OECD area had weakened trade unions. The developing countries which had stood more or less united behind the NIEO and demanded control of Western MNEs, now were craving for FDI inflows. By the early 1980s, countries in South America were beset by a debt crisis, which made them turn to the International Monetary Fund for help and assume more investment-friendly economic policies in return. In such an environment the UN code lost appeal and political support.

The OECD and ILO codes were also affected by these economic and political changes. At the beginning, trade unions and labour governments used the possibility to demand clarification of the Guidelines in specific cases in which MNEs had allegedly 'breached' the Guidelines. The cases mostly involved the industrial relations section.[32] However, the consequences of the interpretation were negligible, since they carried no legal weight and the interest of the public in bureaucratic proceedings was low.[33] The ILO was even less prepared to deal with specific cases.[34] The code area finally ended with the demise of the UN code in 1992, when a UN General Assembly report stated that it was 'the view of delegations that no consensus was possible on the draft code at present' and a 'fresh approach should be examined' (UN General Assembly, A/47/446). In 1993, the remainders of UNCTC (which had been

---

[31]The nine foreign ministers of the EEC drafted a Code of Conduct for European firms operating in South Africa in 1977. The code was implemented in each country differently and updated in 1985. For more information, including a reprint of the code, see Wiebalck (1992). Another, non-governmental approach was taken by the Sullivan Principles, a set of norms created by human rights activist Leon Sullivan in 1977. The Sullivan Principles were recommended to all US MNEs with operations in South Africa.

[32]An overview of the cases can be found in Blanpain (1979). The author was a member of the Belgian delegation to CIME and acted as an advisor to a case which was opened by his government ('Badger case').

[33]An article about the OECD Guidelines was accompanied by a cartoon showing the devil visiting 'Multinational Inc.' and being told by the receptionist: 'You are wasting your time—we're following the new OECD Code of Conduct now!'; see accompanying article by Kransdorff (1980).

[34]The mere possibility was discussed in the Governing Body only in 1980, see GB 214/PV (Rev.), IV/5-IV/11. The first request was transmitted to the ILO in 1984, see ILO Archives, File Series: GB, File Number: 228-MNE-101-123, "Follow-up at the Tripartite Declaration of Principles Concerning Multinational Enterprises and Social Policy" (GB.288/MNE/1/3), pp. 8–9.

moved to the UN Department of Economic and Social Development) was merged with UNCTAD and thus abolished as an independent body.

However, the very idea that MNEs had some responsibilities due to their size and global reach has survived until today. It has assumed other forms and was taken up by other organisations. In 1992, when the UN code was buried, global business presented itself as a partner in the pursuit of 'sustainable development', as it was now called, at the UN Conference on Environment and Development or the 'Earth summit'. Stephan Schmidheiny, a Swiss entrepreneur, advised the UN on how to involve business and for this purpose founded the Business Council for Sustainable Development (BCSD).[35] The Council and Schmidheiny introduced the idea of 'eco-efficiency' to the business community; this concept related the economic value of production to its impact on the environment (Schmidheiny 1992). The Earth summit ushered in a new climate of cooperation and reached its climax in 1999 when UN Secretary-General Kofi Annan proposed a 'Global Compact' to business leaders around the world. In a speech before the International Chamber of Commerce, which was instrumental in mobilising the first MNEs for participation, Annan claimed that '[c]onfrontation has taken a back seat to cooperation. Polemics have given way to partnerships' (UN 1999). A year later the UN Global Compact became operational and invited companies and their stakeholders to join the network and to learn about 'corporate responsibility', which has a widely used term by now. In exchange, business participants were asked to commit to nine, later ten general principles and to report on their activities to implement the principles (Rasche 2012). The Global Compact deliberately refrained from control mechanisms, stressing the voluntary commitment of the participants. Over the following decade the Global Compact became the largest international CR initiative with over 6000 business participants in 135 countries at the end of 2010 (UNGC 2011, p. 6).

Apart from the development of new CR initiatives, existing instruments were adapted to new circumstances: the OECD Guidelines and the ILO Tripartite Declaration were substantially updated in 2000. The OECD text received another major update in 2011. At the Ministerial Meeting in May 2011, US Secretary of State Hillary Clinton lauded the text: 'For over 35 years, these guidelines have occupied a unique space within the world of corporate social responsibility. They are the only ones formally endorsed by governments, 42 at last count' (US DoS 2011).

When compared to the MNE responsibilities discussed in the late 1970s, the new business norms are focussed much more on company behaviour than on the mutual rights and responsibilities of business and host states. What is more, the new norms are no longer primarily addressed to MNEs, but to business at large, including small and medium-sized enterprises. This was a late, yet ironic victory of the code critics who rejected norms for MNEs on the grounds that they did not differ from other companies. In fact, the extension of CR went so far as to include all organisations.

---

[35]In 1995 the BCSD and the World Industry Council became the World Business Council for Sustainable Development, which promotes business-friendly concepts for sustainable development.

The idea of the 'social responsibility of organizations' was the most striking conceptual innovation of the ISO 26000 norm, which was published by the International Organization for Standardization in 2010 after ten years of negotiation (ISO 2010). The adoption of this norm was a remarkable feat in itself, when the diversity of its creators—experts from different backgrounds and more than 90 countries—is taken into account and compared to with the UN code project.

The latest developments suggest that the era of partnership and co-operation might come to a close. Human rights have re-entered the international CR agenda. This time business and human rights is not limited to questions regarding investments and the treatment of black employees in apartheid South Africa. By contrast, the debate has become much more general and is largely about 'business and human rights'. After the failure of the legalistic approach of the UN Draft Norms on the Responsibilities of Transnational Corporations and Other Business Enterprises with Regard to Human Rights in 2003 (Weissbrodt 2005), Kofi Annan appointed a UN Special Representative for Business and Human Rights, John Ruggie, who developed a conceptual 'UN framework'. This was a political rather than legal concept which proposed a government duty to protect human rights, a business responsibility to respect human rights, and access to remedy in case of violations (UNHARC 2008). The UN 'Guiding Principles' were endorsed by the Council three years later and gave recommendations to businesses and states how to implement the UN framework, particularly with regard to their 'human rights due diligence' (UNHRC 2011).

Although the current debate is much further developed and more explicit about 'corporate responsibility', it still echoes the multinational dilemma and the first attempt to codify norms for global business in the 1970s. In this period the idea that companies had responsibilities vis-à-vis states (and therefore to society at large) was conceived and delivered. The OECD and ILO codes fell considerably behind what proponents had hoped for. Yet they also went beyond what critics of the code debate were willing to concede, which is nothing less than a common understanding that there is something like 'corporate responsibility' and that businesses should respond to such claims. The moment the world's governments decided to discuss norms of responsible business behaviour, they passed a point of no return. Today, CR critics cannot undo the tradition of the code era, the basic idea that, to contradict Friedman's (1970) famous quote, the responsibility of business is more than to increase its profits, much more than that.

References

Ahmia, M. (2009). *The collected documents of the group of 77. The North-South dialogue, 1963–2008*. New York, Oceana.
Barnet, R. J. & Müller, R. E. (1974). *Global reach: The power of the multinational corporations*. New York: Simon & Schuster.
Bevir, M. (1999). *The logic of the history of ideas*. Cambridge: Cambridge University Press.
Bevir, M., & Rhodes, R. A. W. (2006). *Governance stories*. London: Routledge.

Bevir, M., Rhodes, R. A. W., & Weller, P. (2003). Traditions of governance: Interpreting the changing role of the public sector in comparative and historical perspective. *Public Administration, 81*, 1–17.

Blanpain, R. (1979). *The OECD guidelines for multinational enterprises and labour relations 1976–1979: Experience and review*. Deventer: Kluwer.

Carroll, A. B., Goodpaster, K. E., Lipartito, K. J., Post, J. E., & Werhane, P. H. (2012). *Corporate responsibility: The American experience*. Cambridge: Cambridge University Press.

Dell, S. S. (1990). *The United Nations and international business*. Durham: Duke University Press.

Economic and Social Council Commission on Transnational Corporations (ECOSOC-CTC). (1975). *Report on the first session, official records of the economic and social council, Fifty-ninth Session, supplement No. 12*. New York, document code: E./C.10/6.

ECOSOC-CTC. (1976). *Report on the second session*. New York, document code: E./C.10/16.

ECOSOC-CTC. (1978). *Report on the sixth session*. New York, document code: E./C.10/AC.2/8.

Erklärung von Bern (Ed.). *Die Unterwanderung des UNO-Systems durch multinationale Konzerne: Auszüge aus internen Protokollen*, Zurich.

Emmerij, L., Jolly, R., & Weiss, T. G. (2001). *Ahead of the curve? UN ideas and global challenges*. Bloomington: Indiana University Press.

European Parliament (EP). (1977). *Report on the principles to be observed by enterprises and governments in international economic activity*. Strasbourg/Brussels, document code: PE 47.701/fin/Annex.

Ferguson, N. (2010). Crisis, what crisis? The 1970s and the shock of the global. In N. Ferguson (Ed.), *The shock of the global. The 1970s in perspective* (pp. 1–24). Cambridge, Cambridge University Press.

Friedman, M. (1970). A Friedman doctrine—The social responsibility of business is to increase its profits. *The New York Times Magazine*. September 13, pp. 32–33, 122–124.

Günter, H. (1980). The tripartite declaration of principles (ILO): Standards and follow-up. In N. Horn (Ed.), *Legal problems of codes of conduct for multinational enterprises* (pp. 155–176). Deventer: Kluwer.

International Confederation of Free Trade Unions (ICFTU). (1971). Resolution on freedom of association and multinational companies. *ICFTU Economic and Social Bulletin*, Jan-Feb, pp. 21–22.

International Labour Organisation (ILO). (1977). *Tripartite declaration of principles concerning multinational enterprises and social policy*. Geneva.

International Organization for Standardization (ISO). (2010). *ISO 26000: Guidance on social responsibility*. Geneva.

Kransdorff, A. (1980). The curious case of the reluctant multinationals. *Financial Times*. April 22, p. 13.

Muchlinski, P. T. (2007). *Multinational enterprises and the Law*. Oxford: Oxford University Press.

Organisation for Economic Co-Operation and Development (OECD). (1972). *Policy perspectives for international trade and economic relations*. Paris.

Organisation for Economic Co-Operation and Development (OECD). (1976). *International investment and multinational enterprises*. Paris.

Petrini, F. (2011). *'Who'll stop the runaway shop? The battle to regulate multinationals' activities inside the EEC at the dawn of globalization*. Paper presented at the EUSA Twelfth Biennial International Conference, Boston, 3–5 March.

Post, J. E. (2013). The United Nations global compact: A CSR milestone. *Business and Society, 52* (1), 53–63.

Rasche, A. (2012). The United Nations and transnational corporations. How the UN global compact has changed the debate. In J. T. Lawrence & P. W. Beamish (Eds.), *Globally responsible leadership. Managing according to the UN global compact* (pp. 33–49). Los Angeles: Sage.

Robinson, J. (1983). *Multinationals and political control*. New York: St. Martin's Press.

Sampson, A. (1973). *The sovereign state of ITT* (3rd ed.). New York: Stein & Day.

Sauvant, K. P. (1977). Controlling transnational enterprises: A review and some further thoughts. In K. P. Sauvant & H. Hasenpflug (Eds.), *The new international economic order. Confrontation or cooperation between North and South?* (pp. 356–434). Boulder Colorado: Westview Press.

Schmidheiny, S. (1992). *Changing course: A global business perspective on development and the environment.* Cambridge MA: MIT Press.

Servan-Schreiber, J. J. (1967). *Le défi américain.* Paris: Denoël.

United Nations Department of Economic and Social Affairs (UNDESA). (1973). *Multinational corporations in world development.* New York.

United Nations Department of Economic and Social Affairs (UNDESA). (1974a). *The impact of multinational corporations on development and international relations.* New York.

United Nations Department of Economic and Social Affairs (UNDESA). (1974b). *Summary of the hearings before the group of eminent persons to study the impact of multinational corporations on development and on international relations.* New York.

United Nations. (1999). *Press release SG/SM/7022: Secretary-general, addressing United States chamber of commerce, highlights fundamental shift of attitude towards private sector, 8 June.* Available from: http://www.un.org/News/Press/docs/1999/19990608.SGSM7022.html. (11 January 2017).

United Nations Global Compact (UNGC). (2011). *Annual review.* New York.

United Nations Human Rights Council (UNHRC). (2008). *Protect, respect and remedy: A framework for business and human rights.* Geneva.

United Nations Human Rights Council (UNHRC). (2011). *Guiding principles on business and human rights: Implementing the United Nations "Protect, respect and remedy" Framework.* Geneva.

United States Department of State (US DoS). (2011). *Commemoration of the 50th anniversary of the OECD on guidelines for multinational enterprises, May 25, 2011.* Available from: http://www.state.gov/secretary/20092013clinton/rm/2011/05/164340.htm. (11 January 2017).

Vernon, R. (1971). *Sovereignty at Bay.* Harlow: Longman.

Weissbrodt, D. (2005). Corporate human rights responsibilities. *Zeitschrift für Wirtschafts- und Unternehmensethik, 6*(3), 279–297.

Wiebalck, A. (1992). *The European economic community code of conduct for companies with interests in South Africa.* Roderer: Regensburg.

Thomas Hajduk studied history, political science, and philosophy in Münster, Potsdam, and Berlin and graduated at the University of Durham. Thomas is currently CR manager at a large media company in Germany and visiting lecturer at the University of St. Gallen. Before his current affiliation, he worked on CR and sustainbility in various positions in government, academia and consulting.

TNC Code of Conduct or CSR? A Regulatory Systems Perspective

Benedict Sheehy

1 Introduction

There is an increasing emphasis on codes in both international private law and specifically in efforts to encourage businesses to take on a greater share of the social costs of their activity. This chapter argues in the first instance the view that codes by themselves are inadequate to the task. While from an institutional perspective, they may be of some use driving changes to the norms of the institutional environment (Sahlin-Andersson 2006), from a legal point of view, they are but one piece of a regulatory system (Sheehy and Feaver 2015; Feaver and Sheehy 2015). Codes set out the norms and as such provide a foundation upon which a regulatory system stands. And, as all regulatory systems are aimed at guiding behaviour to achieve certain desired ends they are norm based. Codes that are not integrated into a coherent regulatory system suffer from their status as a stand-alone solution, are orphaned and destined for obscurity. Thus for codes to be effective, they must be embedded within a regulatory system that includes the necessary administrative and institutional infrastructure.

The chapter develops a second line of argument that CSR can be best understood as form of international private business regulation (Sheehy 2015, 2017b). As such, CSR requires a coherent set of norms and appropriate complementary regulatory system components including some form of code. The chapter proceeds by first examining codes and taking an example of a code-only approach through an analysis of ISO 26000. It then turns to examine the design of regulatory systems and the place of codes within such systems. Next it lays out the landscape of CSR (problems of politics) and provides a well-justified definition. Finally it concludes with a summary of issues to be addressed in moving ahead with effective TNC conduct regulation.

B. Sheehy (✉)
School of Law and Justice, University of Canberra, Bruce, ACT 2617, Australia
e-mail: Benedict.Sheehy@canberra.edu.au

2 Background

One of the core challenges for governments at least since the time of Plato's *Republic* has been balancing the competing interests of public good and its governance on the one hand with appropriate advancement of private and related commercial interests on the other. This is one of the core regulatory challenges faced by government. What an appropriate balance looks like depends on the government of the day, the society which it governs and the place and time in history under consideration. In other words, far from being a static balance, a once for all time, all actors and all industries type solution, the balance must be a dynamic one. It must be dynamic in order to respond to the needs of the society which is to be served by government and in which private commercial interests are being pursued.

While the basic concepts of the challenge of governance as set out above remain valid, two significant changes have occurred in the interim as a result of globalisation (Scholte 2005; Osterhammel and Petersson 2005). Together, they fundamentally alter the challenge faced by government. First, the core unit of analysis has changed. The core commercial unit is no longer a local manufacturer of goods or provider of services but an enormous transnational actor—the transnational corporation ("TNC"). Further, this actor when considered as a whole not subject to any particular law (de Jonge 2011). Finally, this actor generates very significant social costs.

Second, the economic environment has changed. It is not a local economy but a globalized economy resting on a volatile financialized footing in which the new actor acts. The new actor within this globalized economic context poses a significant challenge for governments of all types seeking to execute their task of balancing those competing interests (Stiglitz 2002). The two core challenges are harnessing the contribution of the TNC locally while exerting appropriate power to achieve local ends.

Two major responses to these changes in actors and environment are the development of codes of conduct and the inception and subsequent growth of CSR. The chapter next turns to examine and evaluate the approaches of each response.

3 Codes

Although much has been made of codes of conduct in recent decades, the whole concept of a global code of conduct is not new. The Roman emperor Justinian is famous for his sixth century code and at the international level, codes of conduct have been around since Grotius first came to conceptualise international law in the seventeenth century. Codes have been developed for actors of all types on a wide range of issues from the conduct of war to conventions on ozone in the environment.

In the context of corporate law, a variety of codes have been developed. For example, corporate governance codes have been developed over the last few decades to deal with a continuum of matters initially addressing matters of business ethics, to more technical matters such as minority shareholder rights, refinement of roles of officers and other gap filling. Other codes of conduct deal with matters such as internal organisational issues unrelated to social responsibility—and scholars need to be cautious in the assumption that codes necessarily deal with such matters (Bondy et al. 2008). In the in related socially responsible investment industry, a range of codes exist, from normative frameworks with broad and substantive guidance to process focused codes used to develop measurable standards against which performance can be evaluated (Richardson 2015).

3.1 What Is a Code of Conduct?

Codes of conduct are ubiquitous for all sorts of organization, from tiny service businesses and small autonomous non-profits to enormous private enterprises and global public institutions like the UN. Further, they may be categorised as supra-organisation, organisational or sub-organisational, industry focused (Preuss 2010), issue focused such as child labour or product focused such as blood diamonds. Within different contexts, codes may function together in what has been described as "a cascade of codes' to [form] a lattice-work of intermeshing documents" (Preuss 2010).

What their function is and what precise problem they solve is open for debate (Jenkins 2001). Richardson observes that codes can work as coordinating, standardising and facilitating tools (Richardson 2015). Some argue that such codes are externally focused and may be understood as solving any one of a number of problem from legitimacy by adding window dressing and generating a social license (Howard-Grenville et al. 2008). Others, emphasising organisational codes, argue that codes of conduct are internally focused and may function as anything from solving problems such as providing clear standards for employee performance and dismissal, to standing as organizational aspirational statements drawing attention to and loyalty from the members of the organization with the aim of helping members to collaborate as a team supporting the organization in achieving its mission as first noted in an article on codes of conduct (White and Montgomery 1980). Still others, taking a non-organisational focus and argue that codes have a coordinating role, helping a set of organizations collaborate using the same norms. Regardless of the orientation, codes of conduct all function to a greater or lesser degree as a guide for acceptable behaviour, and so have a regulatory effect on the conduct and activities of all members and the organization itself (Jenkins 2001).

The discussion leads to the basic question: What are codes? Codes are an organised collection of norms used to communicate behavioural norms which are accepted or rejected within a specific institutional context. They identify which behaviours will be rewarded and which will be punished. As noted above, the outcome or effect of such a communication is regulatory parties subject to the code will find their behaviour re-enforced or challenged in line with the norms set out in the code.

3.2 Codes and Law

Broadly speaking, codes are directly related to law. While code writers are in the business of codification—i.e. identifying, classifying, ordering norms and then specifying them as derived rules—in other words, creating rule frameworks, a clear understanding of the relationship between these codes and law is often lacking. While these tasks of identification of norms, classification, norm ordering and specifying rules are core tasks of law, there remains a wide domain of law beyond this simple understanding of law (Hart 1994).

The broader relationship between codes and law in not well represented in the recent history of industrial codes. The lack of that connection is reflected in what appear to be the assumptions underlying code creation and promulgation. To a greater or lesser degree, the common understanding of codes mirrors the positivist understanding of law, black letter law, namely, that law is no more than the printed words of the legal text, the statute or case judgement. In this understanding of law, neither legislator, nor judge, nor citizen has any role in law through performance or otherwise acting out the law. This minimalist vision of law lacks the basic concepts of institutions and of legal system necessary to animate the law beyond mere text. Following this minimalist path, some advocates of codes focus exclusively or almost exclusively on the creation of a text. This narrow focus constrains the potential for advancing a regulatory agenda or ensuring the desired conduct or objective is achieved, in the case at hand, the regulation of industrial behaviour.

An alternative view of codes and law comes from a broader understanding of law in two senses. First, if one accepts that not all law emanates from authoritative state bodies, one can look elsewhere for law. For example, law can come into existence through customary practice or usage. This process has produced much of the globe's commercial law or *lex mercatoria*. (Webb 2015) At pp. 484–490. It is reflected in the development of private international business sustainability regulation, namely, CSR (Sheehy 2015)—a type of self-regulation (Mares 2010). Thus, law need not come from an authoritative governmental body and can readily be made by any organisation deemed to hold some form of legitimate rule making power.

Second, the broader view of law draws attention to the conundrum that in terms of formal legal systems, no law goes into the statute books unless done by law makers who themselves are the creation of prior law based constitutional arrangements. Thus the right and authority to make laws comes from the constitution, itself the product of a group of people who have been successful in gaining power. In other words, laws embody the political wishes of those with power to make things happen.

This broader understanding of law makes it clear that the law on the books only becomes effective when put into play by lawyers, judges and by citizens interacting with the system. Applying this broader thinking to codes leads to a critical insight: a code of conduct that is embedded in an appropriate institutional environment has a much greater probability of being effective (Loconto et al. 2012), and the corollary is equally true: a code that is merely text is a powerless, largely meaningless exercise in print.

4 Understanding Regulation

Codes are regulation—an effort to regulate behaviour. They set forth principles and standards which are both to guide or regulate organisations' behaviour and to create a measure against which organisations agree to have their behaviour judged. Indeed, CSR and its codes can be best defined as a form of "international private business self-regulation" (Sheehy 2015; Mares 2010). Yet, regulation itself is a much maligned and poorly understood creature. Lawyers understand it primarily as "delegated legislation" while businesses often regard it as "red tape" and an unavoidable obstacle to making money. Neither of these approaches appreciates the necessity and sophistication of contemporary regulation nor the important coordination solutions it provides. Finally, these views do not reflect recent advances in regulatory theory (Sheehy and Feaver 2015; Feaver and Sheehy 2015).

Contemporary thinking about regulation draws insights from psychology, political science, economics, organizational theory among others (See for example, (Baldwin and Cave 1999; Ogus 1994; Black 2002; Braithwaite and Drahos 2000; Moran 2002; Morgan and Yeung 2007; Sparrow 2000).

Recent work drawing on systems theory has developed a framework to facilitate the design, evaluation and reform of regulation (Sheehy and Feaver 2015; Feaver and Sheehy 2015). Following this framework, the Theory of Coherent Regulation ("TCR"), facilitates an analysis of the code-only approach to regulation that illuminates its defects clearly.

TCR posits that for a regulatory system to be effective, it must be coherently designed beginning with the problem it attempts to address (Sheehy and Feaver 2015), through developing policy and constructing appropriate structures for regulatees or regulated parties, to the establishment of reasonable administrative arrangements for the administration of the system (Feaver and Sheehy 2015). In the case of CSR, there are issues all of these broad systemic issues. The issue or problem that CSR attempts to address is for many conceptually unclear (Sheehy 2017a). It is complex because it has a threefold agenda: law reform, organizational change and the politics of addressing social costs (Sheehy 2017a). While there is contest about the two former, there is reasonable consensus on the latter. Such social costs may include matters such as precarious employment, under pay, unsafe labour conditions, environmental damage, community nuisance and corruption (Sheehy 2004). While addressing any one of these objectives is not necessarily incoherent with the rest, addressing them all at once creates diverse demands on organisations. As such, developing a focus for CSR as regulation requires a careful balance and alignment of issues as well as proposed solutions. TCR analysis makes clear the wide array of objectives being pursued under the single acronym.

In terms of institutional infrastructures, TCR draws attention to the necessity for regulatees to be correctly motivated to engage in and respond to the regulation. Appropriate motivation must be tailored to the actor and environment. (Sheehy and Feaver 2015). For such structures to exist, some type of investment—whether public or private or both—needs to be made. For example, if a voluntary CSR code is to attract interest from business, such a code must be well advertised to business and the benefits at least equally well advertised if business is to be expected to adopt it widely. If CSR is to be mandatory, some type of public investment, whether penalty or incentive, will be necessary to gain compliance. Again, for example, if government mandates CSR it will need to implement a fine or taxation system which penalizes non-compliant businesses or create an incentive scheme to encourage business to take up CSR. In this over-simplified mandatory-voluntary binary example, the absence of such institutional infrastructure leads TCR scholars to suggest that, significant uptake of meaningful CSR is unlikely to occur (Mares 2010).

Finally, in terms of administration, TCR emphasises that no regulatory system is self-executing/self-operating. In other words, some body or organization must take responsibility for the oversight, implementation and maintenance of the regulatory system. This administration is necessarily a costly exercise and few businesses are enthusiastic about the outlay required to maintain an appropriately funded, administrative organization charged with monitoring, adjudication and enforcement. As the UN Global Compact is exclusively a norm consolidating norm generator not further involved in compliance monitoring or enforcement—it has no such mandate—CSR globally has no executive or administrative body. Although a number of particular private schemes do have some institutional infrastructure (See, for example, (Loconto and Fouilleux 2013) discussion of ISEAL bodies.) they are clearly limited to their respective industries, regions or specific social, environmental or other concern.

5 CSR as Regulation

All codes are regulatory in nature in that they provide a prescription for behaviour. That is, they aim to regulate behaviour by providing a guide for acceptable behaviour and/or a benchmark against which parties are able to test or measure their conduct as acceptable/compliant or unacceptable/non-compliant. Yet, as noted, codes require more than drafting and publication to have effect. Before turning to discuss the regulatory aspects of CSR, however, a clearer understanding of CSR itself is necessary.

5.1 Understanding CSR

Most of the research and discussion about CSR is in the fields of management, economics and political science (Sheehy 2015). These disciplines focus on organisations and individual consumers rather than institutions and systems. Accordingly, they view CSR first and foremost from the point of view of the firm. From the perspective of the firm, CSR is an intra-firm strategic decision, a policy framework implemented through an internal management system. This firm focus in CSR scholarship leads to definition of the term along the lines of Carroll and others who look to classify and prioritise firm behaviours (Carroll 1991). From an inter-firm systemic perspective, however, CSR is best understood more broadly. CSR can be considered as an effort to regulate industrial activity (Sheehy 2015). I have defined it elsewhere as:

> a type of international private law [that]… can be defined as a socio-political movement which generates private self-regulatory initiatives, incorporating public and private international law norms seeking to ameliorate and mitigate the social harms of and to promote public good by industrial organisations. (Sheehy 2015)

A more workable, shortened version of that definition would be "international private business self-regulation." (Sheehy 2015). It is a type of transnational law (Mares 2010).

CSR's goal broadly stated is to reduce the social costs of industrial activity and improve public goods (Sheehy 2017b). In the voluntary context, it may be driven either by strategic considerations such as differentiation or response to external pressures such as boycott, or as a reflection of the ethics of insiders. Social or environmentally related activities that are not part of organizational policy but are communictions strategies managed by a PR or marketing department cannot be called CSR. Such activities are properly called "greenwash" (Laufer 2003) and they expose an organization to legal and reputational risks for false and misleading advertising, deceptive conduct among other risks [See for example discussion in (Monsma and Buckley 2003–2004) pp. 182 ff and (Webb 2015)]. When CSR is an organizational response to protest, it forces the organization to focus on issues with its policy, products or safety (Soule 2009) pp. 54–59. Taking this last example of protest, one can readily see how CSR is about regulating the conduct of an organization or industry.

Given the extremely broad scope of activity that can be included in the term "industrial activity" it is clear that CSR must address a very wide range of activities and potentially actors. There is good reason to limit CSR to those actors whose socio-ecological footprint is significant within a particular community. Doing so allows CSR to be more focused on those actors. CSR then is a type of regulation which focuses primarily on the larger actors within the community.

What then does CSR address? At a practical level, it addresses all aspects of the organization, from procurement, to workplace practices, to environmental impacts, community impacts and customer knowledge and safety. Conceptually, it addresses a broader set of issues including political issues concerning industrial organization

(Sheehy 2017a). Nevertheless, from a regulatory perspective, the focus of CSR is on the conduct of business operations around the globe.

Bringing together the previous two sections on TCR and CSR it can be stated that to function effectively as a regulatory system, CSR requires appropriate institutional infrastructure, from a well-defined problem it seeks to address, to appropriate institutional structures and well-designed administrative machinery. Among the most well-known and widely disseminated CSR initiatives, the ISO 26000. The section which follows is a case study of that CSR code developed by the well-respected global standards organization.

6 Stand-Alone Code: ISO 26000 Case Study

An international private law code dealing with CSR was created by one of the preeminent international standards body, the International Standards Organisation ("ISO") [See discussions in (Ward 2011; Webb 2015)]. That code took much longer to produce than the other ISO standards: it was stymied by political stalemate, and ultimately generated a code of questionable value. The story of the code demonstrates a number of failings of the restricted code approach, namely, problems with the difficult processes engaged for purposes of addressing core political issues and underlying political conflict; challenges arising from a non-systemic approach to regulation, and ultimately, a document of contestable value in terms of achieving the desired change.

6.1 Background

The ISO, is a non-governmental body located in Geneva. It was established in 1947 and has representatives from 161 countries (http://www.iso.org/iso/home/about.htm). Recognising the need for international standards in all range of issues, from transport to food safety, the ISO provides over 21,000 technical standards across a wide spectrum of industrial activity countries (http://www.iso.org/iso/home/about.htm).

The ISO works through Advisory Groups and Working Groups that develop standards in consultation with relevant stakeholders and professional advisors (Balzarova and Castka 2012). Given both growing interest and growing pressure in the area of social responsibility, the ISO took the decision to step away from its core expertise, that is to say, the development of technical standards to step into the gap it perceived in the social standards arena (Ward 2011). In September 2002, ISO Council established a Strategic Advisory Group on Corporate Social Responsibility. The Group was assigned responsibility to determine the feasibility of ISO venturing into CSR, or more accurately, "SR", as the standard was to be applicable to all types of organisations and not solely corporations. The Group's recommendations were submitted in February 2003, and a Technical Report was to be drawn up examining the global context (http://www.iisd.org/pdf/2003/standards_csr_conference_call_1.pdf). This step was taken and a working group established which in turn established a further Six Task Groups. The six tasks and groups were established:

1. A funding and stakeholder engagement group to provide funds to less advantaged but interested groups such as consumer organizations and developing countries.
2. A communication group to assist the various participants contribute and understand the process despite being located in all part of the globe. As well it was responsible for disseminating information about the standard.
3. An operating procedures group to revise and develop processes for the Working Group.
4. A task group to manage stakeholder identification, engagement and communication.
5. A task group to examine SR issues, definitions, principles, and the interaction with society.
6. A task group to examine how and what language would be useful in providing guidance about SR to organizations in general and what would be appropriate for specific organizations (www.iso.org/iso/home/standards/iso26000.htm?archive=all).

As noted, the ISO sought to include a wide range of stakeholders particularly for this standard because of the broad scope of the proposed standard. It established six formal stakeholder categories and sought representation in each. The six categories were: consumers, government, industry, labour, NGO's and a general experts group "Service, Support, Research and Others (SSRO)" (Schmiedeknecht 2008).

The task groups worked together to develop the standard. The task groups themselves were formed two years later at an ISO meeting in Bangkok in September of 2005. This slow progress marked the first of many problems and associated delays dealing with the social standard. Why? Social standards, unlike mechanical standards, engage politics to a much greater degree. They include not only politics of whose process or substantive outputs are to be preferred, but penetrate more deeply into the normative worldview of the parties. It extends to understandings of what a society should look like, what values are to be preferred and which ones are to be left alone. Regulatory objectives can be unclear or even in conflict as a result of the politics involved in the development of an instrument—a particular problem in the CSR space (Zerk 2006; Sheehy 2015). Successfully managing these differences to have any positive outcome at all requires implicit and ultimately explicit determinations about whose interests will be preferred, advanced and protected and whose interests will be neglected (Sheehy 2017a). In other words, for social standards and social regulation generally, significant political work is required (Slob and Oonk 2007; Hohnen 2005; Schmiedeknecht 2008). This work was new to ISO.

The areas addressed by the ISO 26000 standard are: organisational governance, human rights, labour practices, environmental matters, fair operating procedures, consumer issues and community involvement and development (See overview of standard at http://www.iso.org/iso/discovering_iso_26000.pdf). While this standard provides a fairly broad coverage of issues, it could be argued that it places minimal importance on significant areas of CSR activity such as supply chain issues—although its sphere of influence principle does create opportunity to address such matters.

6.2 Analysis and Critique of the ISO 26000

Considering the long-term benefits that ISO 26000 promises to deliver, and also the complexity of environment and operations faced by commercial and non-commercial entities, it may prove to be a significant tool to address a host of concerns important to organizations and societies around the world. Nevertheless, it is not unidirectional. Indeed, as Ward, an active participant in several of the plenary sessions notes:

> An ISO social responsibility standard could potentially matter a great deal to the uptake of social responsibility. But if organizations consider it irrelevant, inapplicable or obtuse, it might turn out not to matter at all. Worse, there are fears that it could inadvertently further the global squeeze on small producers if they are unable to meet the aspirations of its guidance (Ward 2011) 667.

In a similar vein, the ISO's efforts to develop strong stakeholder engagement is noteworthy. Although cumbersome and time consuming, its stakeholder engagement process has been suggested as a model for similar exercises. To the extent that the ISO's development of this standard it has been a success "owes much to the innovative procedural inter-actor bridging function performed by the ISO 26000 standards development approach." (Webb 2015). The ISO's stakeholder process has been described as allowing "norm conversation's to take place among diverse state (and inter-governmental) and non-state parties. …[such that] a credible transposition of concepts and obligations found in intergovernmental and non-state SR instruments occurred." (Webb 2015).

Despite significant efforts to include a range of stakeholders, some still argue that the code suffers from a legitimacy deficit (Ward 2011, p. 718. See also, Hahn and Weidtmann 2016). In fact, the deep and well-known political problems of CSR (Sheehy 2015) were encountered early on. The Advisory Group, which provided a state of the art report on Social Responsibility, noted the existence of a diverse range of views concerning the substantive obligations to be included in SR (*iso26000.jsa.or.jp/_files/doc/2004/sagreport_eng.pdf*) pp. 25–31. Thus while there was a general agreement that a social standard was desirable, the lack of consensus on the substantive issues led to a serious disagreement and subsequent breakdown in the development of the standard. It was a matter of concern to the Working Group early on in the process that this standard, rather than merely adding yet another standard to an already crowded field would make a substantive contribution to defining CSR and specifically the issues to be addressed (Ward 2011).

Although there is the long standing attack on the legitimacy of privately developed standards, others argue that the concern about a legitimacy deficit is unfounded. A more sophisticated analysis of legitimacy in rule making leads to the suggestion that there are a variety of legitimacies—pragmatic, moral and cognitive —and that the ISO was not lacking in any regard (Webb 2015, pp. 471–475). In addition to using a multi-stakeholder approach—stakeholders included a wide array of interests as noted (Schwartz and Tilling 2009)—and its "transparent, deliberative, consensus-based participatory process" (Webb 2015) 476 the ISO explicitly developed processes to engender legitimacy (Tamm Hallstrom 2008) and in addition, avoided creating new norms of its own. Rather, the ISO 26000 was to be consistent with existing standards and draw from international and transnational instruments which contain norms and standards. It was not to operate as a substitute for government, but a supplement or aggregation of norms (Webb 2005). Finally, recognising the changing global environment, a post-national approach to legitimacy is emerging for such codes (Mueckenberger and Jastram 2010). Thus, from a TCR perspective, the standard meets a basic level of coherence in drawing together an appropriate set of norms that address the non-financial, insider concerns of parties effected by business operations.

A second issue with the ISO 26000 from a TCR perspective it the result of its status. The standard is guidance standard and not a certification—a necessary political compromise among its divergent stakeholder groups. As such, there are no compliance or enforcement mechanisms. Without some certification available, no party is able to determine compliance and so to check and assure external parties. As a result, the utility of the standard is significantly limited (Balzarova and Castka 2012). It is unable to produce a clear indication to any constituency either internal or external that a particular organization is in fact fulfilling its social responsibilities. This status has a further consequence for supply chains. Without certification it becomes impossible to create or identify a coherent group of businesses along a supply chain so as to determine their compliance with any particular social standard and so lack the ability to assure suppliers, customers, governments and communities alike that the goods and services supplied are produced, delivered or conducted in a socially responsible manner (Hirschland 2006).

A corollary of ISO 26000's status as guidance is that it needs no institutional infrastructure to deal with monitoring and enforcement. There is no need for compliance institutions such as inspectorates or disclosure regimes which would allow both internal and external parties to determine compliance. Further, as a corollary to the absence of compliance institutions, there are no enforcement institutions, whether reputation opprobrium, de-certification or penalty, nor positively, incentives such as certification to be promoted to the public. Thus, quite logically, with ISO 26000 as simply guidance lacking certification, there is no need for additional infrastructure. Problematically, however, this status allows the charge to be levelled that far from supporting improved social responsibility, the standard may actually contribute to greenwash because it fails to demarcate organisations with legitimate claims to socially responsible behaviour from those without such legitimacy. By being mere guidance, ISO 26000 may add to the murkiness that already threatens to overwhelm the space of socially responsible enterprises. Indeed some parties argue that the creation of any standards at all, such as the ISO 26000, provide institutional opportunities for de-coupling organizational practices from compliance with standards (Schwartz and Tilling 2009) at 296.

Although these issues of legitimacy and guidance are arguably significant weaknesses, it is not that the ISO 26000 is without value. It has been described as "proto-law", (noted earlier by (Selznick 1969 in Sheehy 2017b), and provides a "novel construction of global SR custom" which could find utility in the courts in private litigation (Webb 2015). Nevertheless, without the institutional infrastructure, it harbours a distinct weakness for exploitation and possibly failure (Parker and Howe 2011; O'Brien 2011).

7 Codes in Context: Success and Failure

Codes are regularly and simultaneously hailed as champions and disparaged as failures. While there are a range of reasons for these claims, this section briefly surveys a few critical issues for those claims. A significant challenge for industrial codes arises from the method of their creation. Codes purport to put forth community standards of some sort. Yet, as self-regulation they are usually developed or at least finalized, behind closed doors. In this aspect, many codes suffer from a legitimacy deficit, (Cashore 2002. See also Ward 2011, p. 669; Bernstein and Cashore 2007; Sheehy 2012). With only the people at the table granted voice and the others/outsiders, regardless of numbers or the significance of their effected interests, are excluded (Ward 2011, p. 711). While often outside stakeholders are consulted on aspects of codes, the selection and appointment of such stakeholders may be criticized as arbitrary and/or random at best. As a regulatory institution, codes will have an effect to the extent that they have some level of credibility or legitimacy. Where codes reflect the interests of an industry, they are likely to promote the norms accepted by the industry rather than the norms deemed appropriate by the broader community. It has been said that "The wolf pack has never been known to organize for the benefit of the deer." (Vogt 2001). If industry is the wolf pack organising around a code, it is hard to make the case that the code is for the benefit of the broader community.

Codes have seen different levels and types of success. Success in this context depends very much upon how one sees it: to some, success is the achievement of the agreement and drafting of a code in itself. To others, success is measured by the extent to which parties have achieved their regulatory objectives through compliance with a code. Still others count success as thwarting the development of an effective code, or successfully derailing alternative, tougher public regulatory measures. Finally there are those for whom being able to divert the regulatory objective in order to achieve their individual distinct divergent political aims counts as success (see Slob and Oonk 2007).

For purposes of the argument, success will be referenced in terms of developing a system for achieving the regulatory objective, namely, the regulation of TNC's conduct to achieve reduced social costs and improved public goods. In terms of success, there is a significant line of research which questions the effectiveness of codes in achieving stated objectives. Such research demonstrates that in some instances, the mere presence of the code appears to shield a whole of the industry from critique. Or even less promising, the presence of a code actually detracts from overall social performance (King and Lennox 2000; Haufler 2009, 2010). Such outcomes support an argument for seeing a code critically from a TCR perspective which sees it as destined to fail as a mere code is an orphan or mere a part of an incomplete or improperly designed regulatory system.

Yet, codes may be considered successful in other ways. Rather than focusing directly on organisations' immediate internal workings and behaviours, considering the effect of codes more widely in the institutional environment is important. Codes have been used in courts to establish acceptable standards and subsequently become significant benchmarks in risk management strategies (Webb 2015, pp. 491–496). In the context of social responsibility, codes have been understood by institutionalist scholars as signifying membership in an elite club of sorts, putting social pressure on industry participants to collaborate and comply (Sahlin-Andersson 2006). Success may be a longer term measure where over several decades a slow but definite progression may be observed from internal organisational discussions, to soft-law and finally to hard law offering greater protections to a wider range of actors (Sheehy 2017b). See case extensive case studies in Mares (2010)

8 A New Code?

There is no shortage of codes for business behaviour. Indeed, there is a plethora of such codes (Zerk 2006) pp. 242–263. From international codes such as the UN's Global Compact (Some would argue that the Code idea has moved on and been transformed into the Global Compact (Sagafi-nejad and Dunning 2008) OECD Guidelines and the ISO 26000 to narrower industry focused, regional and issue specific codes, in addition of course, to the millions of individual corporate codes of conduct, the world is not lacking in codes. Codes have come in and out of fashion for a host of political and economic reasons (Hirschland 2006, pp. 117–122).

But to achieve behavioural change, it is insufficient to merely create a code "as an instrument of moral persuasion" as the UN described its earlier TNC work (cited in Zerk 2006) 245. Such an approach, from a TCR perspective, not only lacks appropriate motivation but is also lacking coherent, effective compliance and enforcement mechanisms. Further, with the proliferation of codes, many of which are incoherent both within themselves and with others in addition to lacking the institutional infrastructure for compliance monitoring and enforcement, a confused, counterproductive array of apparent options (Zerk 2006) 282–284 becomes the institutional landscape for CSR. Thus from the perspective of TCR and regulatory success (being the achievement of regulatory objects), the challenge is not to write another code, a better code, with the hope that "this time we'll get it right." Rather, challenge is one of thinking more systemically about the problems of TNC regulation for purposes of broader social public good.

TCR makes it clear that in problematizing an area of social activity for potential regulation requires connection with existing institutional arrangements and norms (Sheehy and Feaver 2015). In the case of CSR regulation, there is a clear need for identifying the issues associated with different regional, national and industrial contexts (Matten and Moon 2008), as well as coordination of existing standards, norms and codes to identify and clarify coherence among them. Such work is both political in the coordination and conceptual in the identification tasks. To fail to address these issues is to fail to appreciate both the complexity of the arena of ideas as well as that of the industries and actors involved (Rubin 1995, pp. 1281–1282). As noted by the Chair of the Working Group of the United Nations Code of Conduct: "Never launch an initiative of this complexity and magnitude without sufficiently long and thorough preparations." (Quoted in Sauvant 2015, p. 76) If the UN is to make a further attempt in this area, it would do well to take account of the ISO 26000 which has been well described as a significant and indeed unique "framework rule instrument in the global SR rule architecture." (Webb 2015, p. 479). That is, although the ISO 26000 provides an effective framework for SR rules and does so by its linking functions across different levels and entities of stakeholders bridging governments, inter-governmental actors, private sector and NGO's (Webb 2015, pp. 479–480) it needs to go further.

The TCR posits that regulation must address a clearly conceived issue (Sheehy and Feaver 2015). While some parties may be focused on specific objectives, as noted, other parties may be focused on political goals such as excluding competitors or dissenting voices. The complexity today is greater and poses a more substantial hurdle today than the efforts some 40 years ago (Sauvant 2015, p 78). The result of such conflicts may not only be procedural and political, but are likely to lead to substantively different outcomes. As noted above, this unclear and conflicting agenda has been an issue with the ISO 26000 negotiations and development (Schwartz and Tilling 2009).

In terms of global CSR, TCR indicates that beyond a code, a positive institutional infrastructure needs to be developed for regulation to be effectively implemented, monitored and enforced (Feaver and Sheehy 2015). It is not that a single international or set of national governments need to create command-and-control style regulation (Mares 2010). Rather, that these additional elements need to be included, for it has been weakness in this aspect of regulation that has impaired success in prior efforts (Sauvant 2015, pp. 79–81). Thus in the case of proposed CSR regulation, there is a clear need to reconsider the development of international institutional infrastructure to address monitoring of compliance and enforcement, or some form of coordination for such among regulating parties. The lack of such infrastructure has been noted in the past and been a matter of scholarly consideration as well as political debate (Zerk 2006, pp. 274–276, 282).

9 Conclusion

This chapter has argued following TCR that a strict code approach to TNC's is an incomplete solution to a very complex problem. The approach fails to address the underlying issues associated with the regulation of behaviour. Particularly in the complex arena of global industrial regulation, sophisticated regulatory design and development are called for. Further the chapter has used TCR to set out in broad terms what issues need to be addressed and it has provided a glimpse of what such a framework might include. It is to be hoped that at a global level, bodies such as the ISO and other code producing bodies continue their work and expands beyond code production to include additional elements of a coherent regulatory system to achieve the substantive ends their codes were designed to achieve.

References

Baldwin, R., & Cave, M. (1999). *Understanding regulation: Theory, strategy, and practice,* Oxford: Oxford University Press.
Balzarova, M. A., & Castka, P. (2012). Stakeholders' influence and contribution to social standards development: The case of multiple stakeholder approach to ISO 26000 Development. *Journal of Business Ethics.*
Bernstein, S., & Cashore, B. (2007). Can non-state global governance be legitimate? An analytical framework. *Regulation & Governance, 1,* 347–371.
Black, J. (2002). *Critical reflections on regulation.* Esrc Centre for Analysis of Risk and Regulation.
Bondy, K., Matten, D., & Moon, J. (2008). Multinational corporation codes of conduct: governance tools for corporate social responsibility? *Corporate Governance: An International Review, 16,* 294–311.
Braithwaite, J., & Drahos, P. (2000). *Global business regulation.* Cambridge, UK: Cambridge University Press.
Carroll, A. B. (1991). The pyramid of social corporate responsibility. *Business Horizons,* July-August, 39–50.
Cashore, B. (2002). Legitimacy and the privatization of environmental governance. *Governance, 15,* 503–529.
De Jonge, A. (2011). Transnational corporations and international law: Bringing TNCS out of the accountability vacuum. *Critical Perspectives on International Business, 7,* 66–89.
Feaver, D., & Sheehy, B. (2015). A positive theory of effective regulation. *Unsw Law Journal, 35,* 961–994.
Hahn, R., & Weidtmann, C. (2016). Transnational governance, deliberative democracy, and the legitimacy of ISO 26000. *Business & Society, 55,* 90–129.
Hart, H. L. (1994). *The concept of law, with a postscript edited by Penelope A. Bulloch and Joseph Raz.* Oxford: Clarendon Press.
Haufler, V. (2009). The Kimberley process certification scheme: An innovation in global governance and conflict prevention. *Journal of Business Ethics, 89,* 403–416.
Haufler, V. (2010). Disclosure as governance: The extractive industries transparency initiative and resource management in the developing world. *Global Environmental Politics,* 10.
Hirschland, M. (2006). *Corporate social responsibility and the shaping of global public policy.* New York and Basingstoke, Palgrave Macmillan.

Hohnen, P. (2005). The ISO and social responsibility: Breakdown or breakthrough in Bangkok. *Ethical Corporation* (Online). Available: Http://Www.Hohnen.Net/Articles/20050909_Ethicalcorp. Html.

Howard-Grenville, J., Nash, J., & Coglianese, C. (2008). Constructing the license to operate: Internal factors and their influence on corporate environmental decisions. *Law & Policy, 30*, 73–107.

Jenkins, R. (2001). *Corporate codes of conduct: Self-regulation in a global economy*. Geneva: United Nations Research Institute for Social Development.

King, A. & Lennox, M. (2000). Industry self-regulation without sanctions: The chemical industry's responsible care program. *Academy Of Management Journal, 43*, 698.

Laufer, W. S. (2003). Social accountability and corporate greenwashing. *Journal of Business Ethics, 43*, 253–261.

Loconto, A., & Fouilleux, E. (2013). Politics of private regulation: Iseal and the shaping of transnational sustainability governance. *Regulation & Governance*, N/A–N/A.

Loconto, A., Stone, J. V., & Busch, L. (2012). Tripartite standards regime. *The Wiley-Blackwell encyclopedia of globalization*. New York: John Wiley & Sons Ltd.

Mares, R. (2010). Global corporate social responsibility, human rights and law: an interactive regulatory perspective on the voluntary-mandatory dichotomy. *Transnational Legal Theory, 1* (2), 221–285.

Matten, D., & Moon, J. (2008). Implicit and explicit Csr: A conceptual framework for a comparative understanding of corporate social responsibility. *The Academy of Management Review, 33*, 404–424.

Monsma, D., & Buckley, J. (2003–2004). Non-financial corporate performance: The material edges of social and environmental disclosure. *University of Baltimore Journal. Environmental Law, 11*.

Moran, M. (2002). Understanding the regulatory state. *British Journal of Political Science, 32*, 391–413.

Morgan, B., & Yeung, K. (2007). *An introduction to law and regulation: Text and materials*. Cambridge: Cambridge University Press.

Mueckenberger, U., & Jastram, S. (2010). Transnational norm-building networks and the legitimacy of corporate social responsibility standards. *Journal of Business Ethics, 97*, 223–239.

O'brien, C. (2011). The un special representative on business and human rights: Re-embedding or dis-embedding transnational markets. In C. Joerges & J. Falke (Eds.), *Karl Polanyi, globalisation and the potential of law in transnational markets*. Oxford: Hart Publishing Ltd.

Ogus, A. (1994). *Regulation: Legal form and economic theory*. Oxford: Clarendon Press.

Osterhammel, J., & Petersson, N. P. (2005). *Globalization: A short history*. Princeton, NJ: Princeton University Press.

Parker, C., & Howe, J. (2011). Ruggie's diplomatic project and its missing regulatory infrastructure. In R. Mares (Ed.), *The un guiding principles on business and human rights: Foundations and implementation*. Leiden: Martinus Nijhoff Publishers.

Preuss, L. (2010). Codes of conduct in organisational context: From cascade to lattice-work of codes. *Journal of Business Ethics, 94*, 471–487.

Richardson, B. J. (2015). Financial markets and socially responsible investing. In B. Sjåfjell & B. Richardson (Eds.), *Company law and sustainability*. Cambridge, Uk: Cambridge University Press.

Rubin, E. S. (1995). Transnational corporations and international codes of conduct: A study of the relationship between international legal cooperation and economic development. *American University International Lr, 10*, 1275–1289.

Sagafi-Nejad, T., & Dunning, J. H. (2008). *The Un and transnational corporations: From code of conduct to global compact*. Bloomington, In: Indiana University Press.

Sahlin-Andersson, K. (2006). Corporate social responsibility: A trend and a movement, but of what and for what? *Corporate Governance, 6*, 595–608.

Sauvant, K. P. (2015). The negotiations of the United Nations code of conduct on transnational corporations: Experience and lessons learned. *The Journal Of World Investment & Trade, 16*, 11–87.

Schmiedeknecht, M. (2008). *ISO 26000—reflecting the process of a multi-stakeholder dialogue: An empirical study*. Konstanz: Kiem. Working Paper Series. Konstanz: Htwg Konstanz, University of Applied Sciences, Kiem Institute for Intercultural Management, Values and Communication.

Scholte, J. A. (2005). *Globalization: A critical introduction*. New York, Uk: Basingstoke, Palgrave Macmillan.

Schwartz, B., & Tilling, K. (2009). 'Iso-Lating' corporate social responsibility in the organizational context: A dissenting interpretation of ISO 26000. *Corporate Social Responsibility and Environmental Management, 16*, 289–299.

Selznick, P. (1969). *Law, society and industrial justice*. New York: Russell Sage Foundation.

Sheehy, B. (2004). Corporations and social costs: The Wal-Mart case study. *Journal of Law & Commerce, 24*, 1–55.

Sheehy, B. (2012). Understanding Csr: An empirical study of private self-regulation. *Monash University Law Review, 38*, 103–127.

Sheehy, B. (2015). Defining CSR: Problems and solutions. *Journal of Business Ethics, 131*, 625–648.

Sheehy, B. (2017a). Conceptual and institutional interfaces between CSR, corporate law and the problem of social costs. *Virginia Law & Business Journal, 12*, 93.

Sheehy, B. (2017b). Private and public corporate regulatory systems: Does Csr provide a systemic alternative to public law? *Uc Davis Business Law Journal, 17*, 1–55.

Sheehy, B., & Feaver, D. (2015). A normative theory of effective regulation. *Unsw Law Journal, 35*, 392–425.

Slob, B., & Oonk, G. (2007). *The ISO working group on social responsibility: Developing the future Iso Sr 26000 standard*. Amsterdam: Somo Centre for Research on Multinational Corporations.

Soule, S. (2009). *Contention and corporate social responsibility*. Cambridge, UK: Cambridge University Press.

Sparrow, M. K. (2000). *The regulatory craft: Controlling risks, solving problems and managing compliance*. Washington: Brookings Institution Press.

Stiglitz, J. E. (2002). *Globalization and its discontents*. New York: W. W. Norton.

Tamm Hallstrom, K. (2008). ISO expands its business into social responsibility. In M. Bostrom & C. Garsten (Eds.), *Tamm Hallstrom, Kristina. "ISO expands its business into social responsibility." In organizing transnational accountability, edited By Magnus Bostrom and Christina Garsten* (46–60). Cheltenham, UK, Northampton, USA: Edward Elgar.

Vogt, C. (2001). On not letting the wolves watch out for the deer. *It World* (Online). Available: Http://Www.Itworld.Com/Article/2797623/Data-Center/On-Not-Letting-The-Wolves-Watch-Out-For-The-Deer.Html. Accessed 13/02/2017.

Ward, H. (2011). The ISO 26000 International guidance standard on social responsibility: Implications for public policy and transnational democracy. *Theoretical Inquire is Into Law, 12*, 664.

Webb, K. (2005). *The ISO 26000 social responsibility guidance standard—Progress so far. Les Cahiers De La Chaire—Collection Recherche*. Montreal: Uqam.

Webb, K. (2015). Iso 26000 social responsibility standard as 'Proto Law' and a new form of global custom: Positioning ISO 26000 in the emerging transnational regulatory governance rule instrument architecture. *Transnational Legal Theory, 6*, 466–500.

White, B. J., & Montgomery, B. R. (1980). Corporate codes of conduct. *California Management Review, 23*, 80–87.

Zerk, J. (2006). *Multinationals and corporate responsibility: Limitations and opportunities in international law*. Cambridge, UK: Cambridge University Press.

Associate Professor Benedict Sheehy is the Head of the School of Law and Justice at the University of Canberra, Australia. He holds the JD (Windsor), LLM (Queensland) and Ph.D. in Law (Australian National University) as well as masters degrees in humanities and social science from Canadian universities. He was called to the bar and practiced law in Canada for several years prior to entering the academy. His academic work explores the interactions among law, commerce and society and he has published major works in both leading law and business journals around the world. He has delivered lectures in Canada, Mexico, Australia, Hong Kong and Singapore.

Behavioral Dynamics and Regulation of Transnational Corporations

Hervé Lado

1 Introduction

North et al. (2009, 2013) have developed a conceptual framework in which they describe development as a slow maturation of institutions from limited access social orders (developing countries) to open access social orders (developed countries). In limited access orders (or natural States), access to political and economic activities is reserved for elites and violence is widespread. Institutions and organizations are typically not sophisticated and they perform on a custom basis dependent on the social status of individuals. Stability is ensured by a dominant coalition made of powerful elites who manipulate rents and privileges. In open access orders, access is open to all; the State controls violence through a Weberian monopoly of legitimate force. Institutions and organizations are numerous and sophisticated, and they operate on an impersonal basis. Stability is ensured by the Schumpeterian creative destruction mechanism through free political and economic competition.

North et al.'s framework has provided an outstanding decryption of behavior patterns of parties involved in rent-seeking activities that shape the development path of a social order. How do parties behave and interact in the international scene where there is no global State, and where players come from different social orders? Do transnational corporations (TNCs) behave the same way in any social order? To better inform regulatory choices aimed at mandating global conduct related to the activities of TNCs, it is crucial to understand their behavioral dynamics. In this chapter I develop an analytical framework that reveals the development of

H. Lado (✉)
16 Rue Gilbert Rousset, Asnieres sur Seine 92600, France
e-mail: herve.lado@yahoo.fr

© Springer Nature Switzerland AG 2019
M. M. Rahim (ed.), *Code of Conduct on Transnational Corporations*,
CSR, Sustainability, Ethics & Governance,
https://doi.org/10.1007/978-3-030-10816-8_4

predator-prey dynamics[1] by TNCs and States in the international social order due to the diversity of national regulations and the limited sophistication of international institutions. I focus on the analysis of institutional environments and not on the content of a global code of conduct per se. Basically, effective regulations depend not only on their intrinsic quality but also on the institutional environment in which they are applied and the behavior of parties involved in their implementation.

The international social order is comprised of States, TNCs, and other actors such as intergovernmental organizations and non-governmental organizations. This work focuses on States and TNCs, as they are pivotal players in the production and redistribution of rents in the international arena. Further, this work explores the specific configuration in which TNCs and States act as predator and prey, respectively. Drawing on North et al.'s terminology and categorization of social orders, this analytical framework explains the behavior of TNCs dependent on the institutional environment (open access or limited access). It appears that free political and economic competition prevailing in the international social order enables what I term an international order of predation.

In the first section of this chapter, the characteristics of this international social order are analyzed and its predatory nature explained: in the search for economic and geostrategic rents, powerful actors of the international social order may dominate the weak and confiscate their rights, due to the insufficient sophistication of international institutions. This sophistication is largely related to the number of organizations and institutions, and also involves their ability to regulate the increasingly complex interactions between actors whose powers are obviously asymmetric. TNCs play a pivotal role in this global trend.

The second, third and fourth sections are dedicated to the actual construction of the framework. This leads to the assessment of the risk of predation; that is, the risk for a TNC to develop predatory behaviors vis-à-vis the host social order. The assessment is based on the 'Predatory Potential' of the TNC (its propensity to behave as a predator) and on the 'Prey Potential' of the host social order (its propensity to behave as prey). A high predatory potential of a TNC and a high prey potential of a social order does not automatically define a predator-prey relationship, although this behavior is likely.

As the sustainable development (SD) and corporate social responsibility (CSR) movements aim at combating predation and promoting more responsible behaviors, I assume that a global code of conduct should be based on well-designed SD and CSR tools. Therefore, in the fifth section, building on Greif and Tadelis (2010)'s concept of crypto-morality, I demonstrate that responsible behaviors based on SD and CSR strategies require an institutional environment where predatory behaviors are highly detectable and heavily sanctioned.

---

[1]My concept of "predator-prey dynamics" does not refer to the equations of Lotka-Volterra, also called "predator-prey models", that model the dynamics of interactions between prey and predators' biological systems.

2 The International Social Order Enables Predation

Veblen (1970) describes predation as a belligerent mindset, and a permanent rivalry between humans in the industrial era. In ordinary animal predation or within the social order of hunter-gatherers, the quest for food is the main driver and rents are collected from the natural environment. Veblen's predation goes beyond a simple quest for food; it is based on other rationalities and entails social costs[2] on the natural and human environments. The predator generates rents in a context of asymmetric power and domination, and so confiscates the rights of other parties involved in the transaction. Predation is therefore an exploitation of domination rents.

In North et al.'s view, predation thrives in an environment where institutions are simple and weak, and have not reached enough maturity to foster a Weberian monopoly of legitimate violence. Globalization has created an international social order in which actors are States, corporations, intergovernmental organizations, or non-governmental organizations. Since political and economic interactions are ruled through competition among actors without any global State, the international social order legitimizes predation in many areas.

2.1 Institutions of the International Order Lack Sophistication

In the international order, there is no global State endowed with the monopoly of legitimate force that might ensure stability and prosperity for all. It is not even certain that a global State would be the most suitable model of international cooperation, given the risk of totalitarianism. With the move from a bipolar towards a multipolar world, there is much evidence that all configurations (uni/bi or multipolar) can produce abuse. Each country abides to its own laws, although international law is still being developed. The sophistication of the international social order's institutional network always lags behind the continuing complexification of transactions between international players.

Moreover, all States are not party to all international agreements, and international law covers only a limited field of international relations and global commons. For example, the international community is still looking for an effective international mechanism against tax avoidance and against global warming, while these global phenomena have long been identified as predatory practices. International law often lacks effectiveness in its application because control mechanisms are slow by nature and might be too expensive to activate. The United Nations (UN) system

---

[2]Pigou (1932) introduced the concepts of social costs and private costs. Social costs are all costs borne by society (including private costs) due to the existence of the business, while private costs are all costs incurred or considered by the author of the activity.

emerged as a means to organize international cooperation and to reduce the risk of predation. However, the UN does not enjoy the sovereign power of a State, and this severely limits its ability to thwart violence.

The international social order has neither police nor an army. The UN "Blue Helmets" are only peacekeepers; they cannot compete with organizations such as NATO (North Atlantic Treaty Organization) that enjoy more power and proven autonomy. The intervention of the United States in 1999 in Kosovo without a UN mandate and its entry into the war in Iraq in 2003 without any resolution of the UN Security Council have shown that the UN lacks political and military power and must deal with parallel initiatives from powerful States. In addition, the International Criminal Court is only qualified to judge mass crimes and human rights violations, and based on its present operation, it is possible for powerful States to avoid their international responsibilities.[3]

The international social order has no government, to speak of. The UN Security Council consists of five permanent members who have the power of veto—USA, Russia, France, the United Kingdom, and China—and ten non-permanent members who sit a two-year term. It is possible for powerful States to instrument this international body for their strategic interests under the guise of defending the public interest or human rights.[4] Through various means, powerful States can direct the operation of the United Nations and its specialized agencies. For example, in 2012, the United States stood against the entry of the Palestinian State to UNESCO by removing its significant funding to the organization.

The international order has certainly found some stability with the advent of the UN, which so far has served as a space for dialogue, and has helped avoid further world wars and reduced transactions costs for States. However, with the prevailing lack of sophistication, it is possible for powerful States to dominate.

2.2 Powerful Actors Dominate the International Order

For North et al. (2009: 131), the domination by powerful States is the condition of their survival: *"To survive, open access orders must have the ability to succeed, not only in economic competition but also in violent competition. Without this ability, they risk succumbing to the ambitions of authoritarian states. (...) This risk remains today, as international terrorism and the events of 9/11 emphasize."*

Within the international social order, powerful States may manipulate rents and privileges through aid and multidimensional cooperation, or through the expansion

---

[3]For example, for various reasons including refusal to sign or ratify the Rome Statute, the United States and the United Kingdom have been able to evade their responsibilities in the war and chaos in Iraq since 2003.

[4]The UN Resolution 1973 in 2011 which enabled the international military intervention in Libya was diverted by leading powerful States, including France, and this led to the killing of Muammar Gaddafi and destabilization of the whole Sahel.

of their TNCs. As North et al. (2009: 132) explains in terms of the Cold War: "*US aid often depended on market reform; for example, the famous Marshall Plan after World War II required as a condition that the countries of Western Europe lower tariff barriers to one another, create a realistic plan for macroeconomic management, and join a new organization for economic cooperation called the Organization for Economic Co-operation and Development (OECD). Aid focused on market economies for providing prosperity in part as a means of making socialism a less attractive alternative.*" The array of sanctions against an uncooperative State range from the withdrawal of funding to banishment in terms of embargo, civil war or targeted killings. For example, in 2013, the United States issued reports showing how and why, in recent history, the US government inspired, supported, or sponsored various coups.[5] Powerful countries make use of secret services, armies, and diplomacy as weapons for their geostrategic interests, including their TNCs' expansion.

Until recently, the main TNCs were from the western world or Russia. Now they also come from emerging countries (see Nurdin and Djermoun 2015), like ArcelorMittal in India, Petronas in Brazil, MTN in South Africa, ONA in Morocco, Dangote in Nigeria, or Huawei in China. These companies are involved in the defense of their home State's economic and geostrategic interests. TNCs forge political alliances and shape institutions to maintain their competitiveness and ensure their domination over national and international competitors. Robert Reich (2011: 120) illustrates these alliances in the United States: "*In recent years, Wall Street has shown extraordinary generosity to the two major US political parties; it is even one of the greatest donors of the Democratic Party. Overall in 2009, the financial world has spent more than $300 M in lobbying to influence the representatives and senators. During the 2008 election, Wall Street donated more than $88 M to Democratic candidates and more than $67 M to Republican candidates, placing the world of finance at the forefront of generous donors.*"

Because of these interdependent relationships between TNCs and home States, it is common to see the image and reputation of a TNC associated with that of its home country and vice versa. It is also common for States to equate national economic interests to those of their TNCs in international competition. Heads of States and Governments mobilize to promote their corporations, for example, by bringing delegations of TNC representatives during official travels abroad. Globalization has increased the geostrategic role of TNCs by aligning their objectives to the interests of States, thereby strengthening TNCs' predatory potential.

---

[5]For example, in Guatemala in 1954 against Jacobo Arbenz (who had openly questioned the land interests of the US TNC United Fruit Company), or in Iran in 1953 against Mohammed Mossadegh (who had decided upon the nationalization of oil, then controlled by the British company Anglo-Iranian Oil Company, when oil was essential to the recovery of England after World War II) (Le Monde 2013; NSA 2013).

3 The Predatory Potential of a TNC

The predatory potential of an actor refers to its propensity to develop predatory behaviors. To move and settle in another social order, various motivations guide a TNC, including the existence of business opportunities, the ability to mobilize resources for this development, and incentives offered by the host social order. From an institutional perspective, a corporation based in only one country is mainly subject to national regulation. Once settled in an additional country, a TNC is subject to three regulatory systems: (i) its home social order (which is an open access order or a limited access order); (ii) the host social order (which is an open access order or a limited access order); and (iii) the international social order (which is an international order of predation as demonstrated above).

Concerning the international social order, a mix of national and international regulations governs the operations of TNCs (including between its subsidiaries and headquarters, or among its subsidiaries, or with other partners). These regulations stem from central banks, regional organizations like the European Union, or international organizations like the World Trade Organization (WTO). There is often a lack of consistency between various regulations, yet international transactions continue to increase in sophistication.

Let's analyze in this section the predatory potential of a TNC by observing its behavior when it moves from one social order to another. This will enable the identification of the determinants that will foster predatory tendencies of a TNC: some of these determinants are intrinsic while others are related to its home social order. This section will conclude with the presentation of some predatory behavior commonly observed in the activities of TNCs.

3.1 Behavioral Adjustment in Different Social Orders

Does a TNC behave in the same manner when it moves into another social order? To support their commitment to ethical behavior, TNCs usually claim that they implement the same rules in every location. However, they behave differently in different social orders, as *"the same institutions work differently in different circumstances, particularly in the absence or presence of open access."* (North et al. 2009: 256). So how do TNCs adapt their behavior to their institutional environment?

When a TNC settles in a new social order, it may keep the same behavior if the host social order is comparable to the home social order. If the social order differs, it may also experience a transition to become compatible with the host social order's institutions. Table 1 specifies four cases (a, b, c and d):

Table 1 TNCs' behavioral dynamics from one social order to another

		HOST Social Order	
		Open Access Order	**Limited Access Order**
HOME Social Order	**Open Access Order**	a. Actor of an Open Access Order	d. MUTATION Into an Actor of a Limited Access Order or of an Order of Predation
	Limited Access Order	b. MUTATION Into an Actor of an Open Access Order	c. Actor of a Limited Access Order or of an Order of Predation

Source Author

a. When a TNC moves from an open access order into another, it finds organizations and norms of the same level of sophistication. It also finds the same operating mode (free political and economic competition), though differences may still exist. The host social order will then compel the TNC to remain compliant to these open access institutions, as they easily detect predatory behaviors and apply dissuasive sanctions. Consequently, the TNC will keep behaving like an actor of an open access order.

b. When the TNC moves from a limited access order into an open access order, it finds organizations and institutions of a higher level of sophistication. The host social order will appear more demanding in the fight against predation because of high detectability and heavy sanctions. The TNC must transition into an actor of the open access order or experience risk of penalties or expulsion. The violent turmoil faced by Arcelor-Mittal in France in 2012–2013 due to the closing of a production site[6] showcases the level of vigilance that institutions and organizations (government, trade unions, media, etc.) in an open access order (France) can develop in order to force an actor of a limited access order (India), however it is economically powerful, to comply with open access host institutions.

c. When the TNC moves from a limited access order into a limited access order, it finds organizations and institutions of the same operating mode (manipulation of rents and privileges). Differences in rules and enforcement may be notable, especially between primary natural States and mature ones, but in any natural State, personalized interactions remain. Thus, the TNC will remain an actor of

---

[6]See L'Humanite.fr (2012) and the outcome with Lang-Roth (2013).

limited access orders. It may also develop predatory practices if its bargaining power is much higher than the host social order's. Thus, the risk of predation between a TNC from China (mature natural State) and an African country (fragile or primary natural States) is high because of the huge bargaining power of the Chinese TNC, especially when it is sponsored or owned by the government.

d. When the TNC moves from an open access order into a limited access order, it finds organizations and institutions of a lower level of sophistication. The host social order will appear alien to the TNC because of the local tendency to personalize relationships and manipulate rents and privileges. Used to impersonalized relationships and free political and economic competition, the TNC will need to adapt to local customs. The more it will need to interact with local organizations and population, the more it will be required to adapt to their manner of functioning. This adaptation consists of a moral transition that transforms the TNC into an actor of the limited access order. The TNC may also develop predatory practices if its bargaining power is much higher than the host social order's. This is the case of western TNCs, like the French Bolloré, Areva, or Total, or the American ExxonMobil when they settled in Africa.

Ultimately, a TNC is likely to sustainably develop predatory behaviors when it moves into a limited access order, be it from an open or a limited access order (cases c and d). The greater the TNC's predatory potential, the higher the probability it will develop predatory behaviors.

3.2 Characteristics of the TNC and Its Home Social Order

Now let's define some characteristics of the TNC's predatory potential. There are four: two intrinsic to the TNC (economic weight, and predatory nature of the products or services), one related to the unique relationship between the TNC and its home social order, and the last one related to the home social order itself. All four are specified below, but for simplicity, this work will focus on three.

3.2.1 The Predatory Nature of Products and Services of the TNC

Some products and services have predatory attributes, in that the production process or their use generates high social costs. One of the most obvious predatory attributes is pollution. Such products include oil and gas, uranium, phytosanitary products, etc. Among the most iconic illustrations of the predatory nature of a product or a production process, let's cite the case of the US TNC Union Carbide and Carbon Corporation (UCC) that caused the Bhopal disaster in India in 1984, which affected almost 600,000 people, including 20,000 killed (Amnesty International 2014).

Other predatory characteristics are less obvious as they affect lifestyles and institutions within a host social order. As Ozawa (2016: 6) states regarding TNCs: "*They are innovators, disseminators of commercial knowledge, and prompters of structural change in home and host countries alike. [...] TNCs are a puissant agent of structural change and growth across the global landscape.*" In their tendency to innovate, multinationals may prove predatory. This is the case, for example in developing countries, where some luxury goods that are not manufactured locally (champagne, luxury vehicles, jewelry, etc.) are highly consumed, thus generating an exsanguination of local purchasing power which would have better served to develop local economies. As another predatory attribute, one can evoke the propensity of some natural resources, such as wood, oil or minerals, to foster social tensions and even fuel civil wars.

The clear majority of TNCs handling these predatory products (oil, mining, pharmaceuticals, energy, chemicals, etc.) also display significant economic power. Therefore, to simplify this framework, let's assimilate them with companies that have significant economic power (see 3.2.2 below). This limits the characteristics defining a TNC's predatory potential to the following three.

3.2.2 The Economic Power of the TNC

When the economic power of a TNC is important, the TNC is likely to build strong impersonal and personalized relationships with its home social order. For example, given their economic weight in France, Total and Alstom groups are close to French public officials, and have built privileged relationships with MPs and government representatives. Similarly, ArcelorMittal maintains privileged relationships with Indian authorities.

The economic power of a TNC is appreciated here in absolute terms with respect to other actors in the international scene. It is also perceived in relative terms with respect to the home or host social orders. Economic power may refer to the sales of the company, its market capitalization, and its brand reputation. It may also refer to the TNC's ability to mobilize resources in financial markets, or from its home social order (including subsidies, exemptions, and public support for international development). For example, as Total Group is one of the most powerful corporations in the world, it is obvious that in Nigeria its economic power is also seen as significant in absolute terms. Moreover, in that country, Total represents approximately 15% of oil production, and is thus among the top four producers, so even its relative economic weight is significant. Therefore, in an analysis of Total in Nigeria, its economic power will be important. The French group *Boissons et Glacières Internationales (BGI)* has negligible absolute economic power, but it has important relative power in a limited access order like Cameroon, with its subsidiary *Brasseries du Cameroon*, which is a top five company; therefore, BGI will be important in Cameroon due to its relative economic power. A significant absolute economic power often implies a significant relative weight, but not vice versa.

Economic power is dynamic and changes dependent on the economic and financial situation of the company. An important economic power is based on the existence of substantial financial resources that enhance and sustain the bargaining power of the TNC, as well as its corruptive power. Because of its economic power, the TNC can build predatory alliances with local actors to secure its rents. It can also mobilize savvy and costly legal advice to protect these rents. For example, it is now established (see Le Floch-Prigent and Decouty 2001) that the defunct French company Elf forged predatory alliances with some African governments partly because it could generate almost limitless financial resources for African leaders, and thus fund their armies or militias. Such economic power also allowed Goldman Sachs in 2014 to spend up to 800,000 EUR in lobbying the European Commission and 3.4 M USD in the US to influence political decisions in its favor (David and Lefèvre 2015). TNCs that enjoy such economic power are able to develop their rents, to endorse high penalties when their predatory behaviors are sanctioned, and to render these behaviors less detectable.

3.2.3 The Strategic Importance of the TNC for the Home Social Order

Strategic importance refers to the importance of the company's business to the home social order: either the State is the owner of the company, or the business is important for the survival of the State, or the TNC's economic power is so important that the home social order considers it as one of its flagship businesses. For example, Areva Group is highly strategic to the French State because of its key role in the energy independence of the country. To some extent, Alstom, Air France, or Total groups are also strategic. Regarding US companies, and according to Gilpin (1987: 241), "*American corporate and political leaders have in general believed that the foreign expansion of American corporations serves important national interests in the United States. American policies have encouraged corporate expansion abroad and have tended to protect them.*"

Powerful States mobilize whenever they are requested by their TNCs within the country or abroad to support their expansion through economic diplomacy mechanisms. For Stopford and Strange (1991), whatever the internationalization of its operations, a TNC maintains an interdependent relationship with its home State, and the TNC psychologically and sociologically belongs to its home country. Even when the TNC's economic power is not important, should it prove strategic to its home country, the TNC is likely to develop predatory behaviors when operating abroad.

3.2.4 The Power of the Home Social Order

For Keohane and Nye (2012: 10), "*Power can be thought of as the ability of an actor to get others to do something they otherwise would not do—and accept at an acceptable cost to the actor. Power can be conceived in terms of control over outcomes*." Gilpin (1987) and Keohane (1984) consider the power of a social order in terms of the effective control it exerts on wealth creation, including raw materials, sources of capital and markets, or the manufacture of high added value products. Power relates to a proven ability derived from low vulnerability to internal and external shocks and from real influence through demonstrated military capabilities.

Strange (1988, 1996: 70) attributes the current hegemony of world powers to the mastering of four factors of power related to international political economy (security, finance, production, and knowledge). Strange (1988, 1996) highlights the importance of structural power that confers the capacity to dominate without that intention. To describe a country's power and influence, Knorr (1975: 6) distinguishes military power, economic power, and what he calls political penetrative power, which is a *"variety of overt or clandestine activities"* like *"propaganda, fomenting of political unrest and strikes, support of opposition parties or revolutionary groups, bribing of officials or political leaders."*

To summarize, the power of a social order refers to its actual ability to defend its national interests in the international scene by mobilizing required economic and political resources. Power depends on a social order's technological prowess and the effectiveness of its governance system.[7] This enables a social order to withstand internal and external shocks, generates multifaceted resources (financial, military, technological, diplomatic, etc.) and supports the expansion of TNCs. Therefore, a powerful social order is likely to enable predatory behaviors by its TNCs.

3.3 Analysis of the Predatory Potential of a TNC

Table 2 provides an assessment of the predatory potential of a TNC based on the three criteria specified above. It is an attempt to estimate a propensity, not a mathematical calculation, and is intended to be logical and empirically verifiable.

The predatory potential of a TNC is high when it has economic power; in fact, economic power turns out to be the most decisive criterion. However, when there is a combination of a strategic TNC and a powerful home social order, the TNC's economic weight is not important, as the home social order will expend effort to ensure the sustainability of the TNC in the host social order. For example, this is the case of TNCs within the military weapons industry: regardless of their economic weight, their promotion is de facto undertaken by the home social order.

---

[7]The characteristics of the social order will be specified when defining the prey potential (Sect. 3).

Table 2 The predatory potential of a TNC

Economic power	Yes	Yes	Yes	Yes	No	No	No	No
Strategic importance	Yes	Yes	No	No	Yes	Yes	No	No
Power of the home social order	Yes	No	Yes	No	Yes	No	Yes	No
Predatory potential	**High**	**High**	**High**	**High**	**High**	**Medium**	**Low**	**Low**

Yes = Important and No = Not important. For simplification, only these two possible answers have been used

Source Author

3.4 Example of Predatory Behaviors of TNCs

A TNC with a high predatory potential does not always act as a predator. However, if it does, it typically utilizes various dominating behaviors, especially within natural States. Some of these behaviors are detailed below:

- Corruption of government officials due to financial resources that sometimes exceed those of host natural States.
- Tax avoidance: the most sophisticated accounting practices allow TNCs to legally obtain revenues from host countries through tax havens or transfer prices manipulation (see OECD 2013).
- Intimidation or violence against local stakeholders (employees, unions, NGOs, etc.) opposed to the company's practices.
- Use of production techniques, processes, or raw materials prohibited in their home social orders, but tolerated or uncontrolled in the host social order, while the negative impact on health or environment is evidenced.
- Waste discharges without treatment, or natural environment destruction without repair.
- Development of transactions with co-contractors, subcontractors, suppliers, or customers who maintain predatory behaviors in their own value chains.
- Complicity in destabilizing institutions of host social orders, through fueling of militias or coups.
- Large philanthropic engagements while there are unaddressed negative impacts of business core activities on human and natural environments: in this case, philanthropic actions appear as a corruptive approach to divert attention.
- More broadly, the violation or complicity of violation of human rights in the company's sphere of influence.

This list is obviously not exhaustive. Predatory behaviors refer to all TNCs' activities that generate unaddressed social costs. While representing an opportunity for extra profits or savings for the company, these social costs are incurred by stakeholders without their knowledge, without their free and informed consent, or without fair compensation.

4 The Prey Potential of a Social Order

In this section, factors that dictate the prey behavior of social orders in the international social order are addressed. A social order is as exposed to predators as it is lacking in power. Coming back to the determinants of the power of a State (cf. 3.2.4) developed by Strange (1988), namely security, finance, production, and knowledge, let's group these into two major factors: Governance[8] and Innovation.

North et al. (2009: 133, 136, 270) define Governance in terms of the Hayek's adaptive efficiency. This concept describes the ability of a social order to constantly adjust its decision-making processes, and the effective implementation of these decisions. North et al. (2009) define Innovation in terms of the Schumpeterian dynamics of creative destruction conducive to economic development.

Governance encompasses the whole process of coordination of actors to achieve collectively bargained plans (Dubresson and Jaglin 2002), while Innovation is the process and outcome of creating something new of value. These two axes respectively evoke the political capacity and economic capacity, and are both embedded in a virtuous circle of development. The political capacity (Governance) enhances the ability of institutions and organizations to act with effectiveness, while the economic capacity (Innovation) enables financial, technological and military means that support the social order's ambitions. Some measurements will be provided in Sect. 3.2 when illustrating the prey potential of some African countries.

The power of governance and innovation systems reflects respectively the quality of political and economic factors; economic factors being capital, labor, technology, knowledge, and institutions. All military powers and all open access orders have built effective governance and innovation systems that support political responsiveness when they face any adversity. The quality of governance and innovation systems determines the social order's resilience against predators, but also its ability to behave as a predator.

4.1 Power and Resilience of the Host Social Order

Governance and Innovation represent the resilience of the social order. North et al. (2009: 42) portray a fragile natural State as an institutional environment where resilience is weak: *"the State can barely sustain itself in the face of internal and external violence. Contemporary examples include Haiti, Iraq, Afghanistan, Somalia, and several other places in sub-Saharan Africa. In a fragile natural State,*

---

[8]Governance should not be reduced to the 'good governance' doctrine constructed for developing countries in the 1980s by the Bretton Woods institutions and international development finance institutions for structural adjustment plans and democratic reforms. Such an approach of governance is exogenous. In contrast, governance is a mix of endogenous leadership and relevant decisions that are successfully implemented.

commitments within dominant coalition are fluid and unstable, often shifting rapidly, and dependent on the individual identity and personality of the coalition members. The coalition is fragile in the sense that small changes in the situation of the coalition members—changes in relative prices, any number of shocks from climate, neighboring peoples, disease, and so on—can upset the coalition. (…) Because of their fluidity, fragile natural States are also characterized by simple institutional structures." Therefore, powerlessness is a matter of weak governance and poor innovation systems.

As Diamond (1997) highlights, germs brought by Europeans killed most of the population of the Incan Empire (up to three-quarters in some cases) in the sixteenth century. However, it was only the European governance system and their innovation system (technological, military, and political superiority) that enabled them to reach the South American coast, thus surprising the Incas. The latter certainly could never have considered reaching Europe and invading Spain. Building on institutions that were more conducive to technological progress, Europeans resisted their predators and exerted predation over other social orders.

4.1.1 Governance Axis—Innovation Axis

The Governance or political axis refers to the ability to make the right decisions and organize and mobilize resources to address the challenges faced by the social order. A well-governed social order can avoid being predated by surprise, whether by natural disasters or foreign TNCs. Governance is not necessarily equivalent to what is commonly called democracy; here it relates to making the right decisions in a timely manner. Without being a democracy, the regime of General Park Chung-Hee transformed South Korea in the 1960s into an open social order, thus escaping its prey status. Contemporary China is not a democracy, but it provides an example in which the prey status has been avoided under the party leadership.

It is one thing is to be able to organize, and another to provide effective material means to achieve organization through innovation. Material means does not simply refer to the funds available, but to the endogenous capacity to generate these financial resources, which requires entrepreneurial, scientific, technical, and technological aptitudes of the social order to address adversity. This innovation axis reflects the ability to invent, learn, and renew methods of handling the changing natural and human environment. It refers to the accumulated stock of knowledge, the quality of human resources, and the capacity of institutions to develop knowledge. Overall, it determines the ability of a social order to conquer and dominate, or at least to withstand adversity.

If a social order is weak on these two axes, it is thus vulnerable and exposed to predators, displaying a high prey potential.

Table 3 Assessment of the prey potential of social orders

Prey potential		Governance	
		Low	High
Innovation	High	Medium	Low
	Low	High	Medium

Source Author

4.1.2 Summary Diagrams of the Prey Potential of a Social Order

Both the governance system and innovation system can be simplified as either high or low. Combining the two criteria, Table 3 presents the four possible situations regarding the prey potential of a social order.

With Governance along the x-axis and Innovation along the y-axis, the prey potential of a social order can be interpreted on the four dials of Fig. 1.

Dial I: Strong governance is coupled with a strong innovation system; the social order is likely to escape TNCs' predatory practices. This social order is strong and can sustain economic and geo-strategic ambitions, including through its own TNCs. The prey potential is low.

Dial II: There is a strong governance system but the innovation system is still weak. The social order can lead and implement reforms, but under an inefficient innovation system. In such conditions, predators may thrive; at least until the governance mechanisms enable the technical and technological capacity to resist. In the meantime, the social order is vulnerable to predation. The prey potential may be high or medium.

Dial III: There is a strong innovation system but governance is still weak. Sophisticated technical and technological capacities are overseen by poor management and leadership. Such a social order remains vulnerable to predation. The prey potential may be high or medium.

Dial IV: A weak governance capacity coupled with an inefficient innovation system inevitably exposes the social order to predators. There is an inability to lead, implement, fund, or support governance and innovation systems. Such a social order is not resilient to predators or natural disasters. The prey potential is high.

Now, let's illustrate this prey potential assessment framework by analyzing the prey potential of some African countries.

4.2 Assessment of the Prey Potential of Some African Countries

Data that are analyzed here on the level of governance in Africa come from the Mo Ibrahim Foundation, which defines governance as *"the provision of the political,*

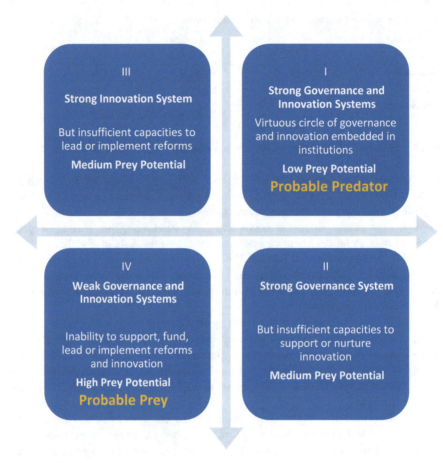

Fig. 1 Typology of the prey potential of social orders

social and economic goods that a citizen has the right to expect from his or her State, and that a State has the responsibility to deliver to its citizens".[9]

Regarding the innovation system, the INSEAD-WIPO-Cornell University Global Innovation Index (GII)[10] is used, which covers all continents.

---

[9]For more information on this organization and index construction, see http://mo.ibrahim.foundation/fr/iiag/.

[10]For more information on this index, see https://www.globalinnovationindex.org/.

4.2.1 Governance: The Ibrahim Index of African Governance (IIAG)

The Mo Ibrahim Index of African Governance (IIAG) has four categories, 14 subcategories, and over 90 indicators from 30 independent institutions, and stands as the most integrated measurement of governance in Africa. Since 2006, its ranking has earned a consistently high reputation and is now a reference for systematic and regular studies on governance in Africa. The edition published in 2015 ranked the 54 countries. The categories and subcategories are:

- Safety and Rule of Law
- Participation and Human Rights
- Sustainable Economic Opportunity
- Human Development.

4.2.2 Innovation: The Global Innovation Index (GII)

Originally launched in 2003 by INSEAD Business School (Fontainebleau, France), as of 2016 the GII is in its ninth edition, published in partnership with the World Intellectual Property Organization (WIPO) and the Johnson Cornell University. The six main components are:

- Input: Innovation Institutions
- Input: Human Capital and Research
- Input: Infrastructures
- Input: Market sophistication
- Output: Knowledge Products
- Output: Inventions.

Going beyond the usual measures of innovation that focus on the level of research and development, the GII develops a horizontal vision of innovation that is applicable to both developed and developing countries. In the 2016 edition, only 28 African countries were ranked. Table 4 and Fig. 2 are based on the 28 African countries where there are both IIAG and GII data.

4.2.3 The Governance-Innovation Relationship for Africa

Given that there are only African countries presented in Fig. 2, the four dials have been adjusted to the data of the continent in order to obtain an intelligible display.[11] It is obvious that the introduction of a European country would upset the positioning of African countries, as these countries would all (Mauritius and South

---
[11]This adjustment involves a shift (in equal proportion) to the right on the Governance axis and up on the Innovation axis.

Table 4 2015 IIAG on governance and 2016 GII on innovation in Africa

Country	Governance	Innovation
Mauritius	79.9	35.86
Botswana	74.2	28.96
South Africa	73.0	35.85
Namibia	70.4	28.24
Ghana	67.3	26.66
Tunisia	66.9	30.55
Senegal	62.4	26.14
Rwanda	60.7	29.96
Zambia	59.5	19.92
Kenya	58.8	30.36
Benin	58.8	22.25
Morocco	57.6	32.26
Malawi	56.7	27.26
Tanzania	56.7	26.35
Ouganda	54.6	27.14
Algeria	52.9	24.46
Mozambique	52.3	29.84
Burkina Faso	52.2	21.05
Egypt	51.3	25.96
Madagascar	49.1	24.79
Mali	48.7	24.77
Ethiopia	48.6	24.83
Niger	48.4	20.44
Togo	48.4	18.42
Côte d'Ivoire	48.3	25.80
Cameroon	45.9	22.82
Burundi	45.8	20.93
Nigeria	44.9	23.15

Source Author, according to 2015 IIAG and 2016 GII reports

Africa included) join the dial IV. However, it would not change the relative positioning of different African countries within the dial.

According to Fig. 2:

- Dial I: Three countries of the 28 (Mauritius, South Africa, Tunisia) represent a low prey potential. South Africa, which already possesses TNCs, is likely to develop predatory behavior.
- Dial II: Four countries (Botswana, Namibia, Ghana, Senegal) represent a medium or high prey potential, as their innovation system is still weak while their governance system is improving.

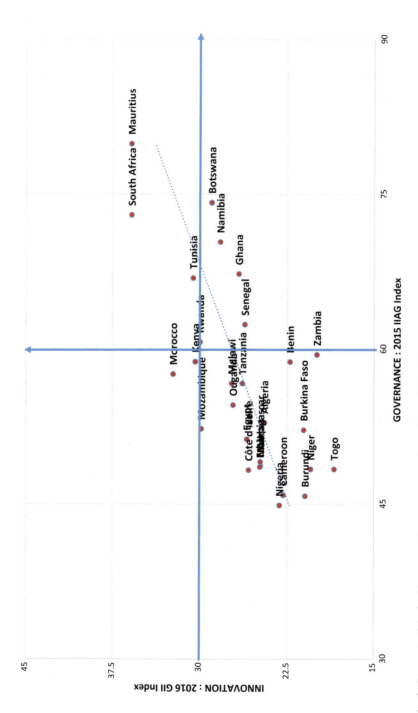

Fig. 2 Prey potential of African countries: governance—innovation relationship

- Dial III: Four countries (Morocco, Kenya, Mozambique and Rwanda) represent a medium or high prey potential, as their governance system is still weak while their innovation system is improving.
- Dal IV: The remaining 17 countries represent a high prey potential, as their weak governance and innovation systems expose them to predators.

The strong correlation between Governance and Innovation appears very clearly in Fig. 2 and highlights a progressive trend from dial IV to dial I (following the dashed line). Passage through dials II and III appears to be optional. Such a correlation is not surprising given the overlapping of political and economic capacity reflected in the content of both indices.

5 The Risk of Predation

The definition of the predatory potential of a TNC and the prey potential of a social order enables the overall assessment of the risk of predation. From the three values (high, medium, low) of both predatory and prey potentials, there are nine possibilities for the risk of predation, as presented in Table 5.

The risk of predation by a TNC is high when its predatory potential and the prey potential of the social order are high. It may also be high when the predatory potential is high while the prey potential is medium, and vice versa.

As the behavioral dynamics of TNCs according to institutional environments have now been specified, let's explore the conditions required to effectively regulate the activities of TNCs though sustainable development and corporate social responsibility standards.

6 Regulating TNCs Behavior Through SD and CSR

From a focus on the natural environment, the sustainable development (SD) and corporate social responsibility (CSR) movements have gradually extended their attention to all dimensions of human and social life. Today, they broadly address human rights violations and thus actually combat predation. Basically, SD and CSR

Table 5 The risk of predation by a TNC

		Prey potential of the social order		
		High	Medium	Low
Predatory potential of the TNC	**High**	High	High	Medium
	Medium	High	Medium	Low
	Low	Medium	Low	Low

Source Author

movements are aiming for the transformation of predatory practices into responsible behaviors.

I assume that a global code of conduct on TNCs would consist of mechanisms to combat predation based on SD/CSR standards, strategies, and tools. Some of the now existing SD/CSR standards, like the Global Compact, the Extractive Industry Transparency Initiative (EITI), or OECD Principles for TNCs, have paved the way towards more effective and operational tools. Effective regulations depend not only on their intrinsic quality but also on the institutional environments where they are applied and the parties involved. I draw upon the concept of crypto-morality to sketch the institutional conditions under which TNCs are likely to effectively implement SD/CSR standards against predation.

6.1 Crypto-Morality

The concept of crypto-morality developed by Greif and Tadelis (2010) is based on the work of Bisin and Verdier (2001) on socialization. Socialization is the process by which social norms are transmitted and internalized by individuals. The postulate is as follows: in institutional environments where the intrinsic morality of an individual is easily detectable and highly penalized, a moral transition to the new morality is observed; elsewhere, the individual operates a simple behavioral transition and maintains a hidden practice of his intrinsic morality, a crypto-morality.

Applied to TNCs, their predatory or responsible rent-seeking activities will depend on the cost-benefit analysis they undergo when interacting with society. In this analysis, the characteristics of the institutional environment are pivotal, especially due to stakeholders' propensity to detect and penalize TNCs' predatory practices. There are four potential scenarios, but before specifying them, let's explore the notions of detectability and penalties.

A TNC's predatory practices are detectable when stakeholders (especially the State) have the right, the opportunity, and the ability to observe them, and they can provide evidence and enforce penalties. As such, strong economic and political inequalities between a company (more powerful) and stakeholders may undermine detectability. Mitchell (2013) shows how oil production activity is anti-democratic in nature because of its short value chain, its high technological intensity, and its isolation at sea or in rural areas where stakeholders can be little informed.

Penalties are the stakeholders' response to a TNC's predatory practices. Penalties include sanctions (when suitable enforcing institutions exist and they are effectively implemented), and any negative impact that stakeholders' actions may cause on the TNC's image and reputation, and incidentally on its economic and financial performance. A penalty is typically sufficient for victims if it is at least equivalent to the social costs incurred, and it is sufficiently dissuasive for a TNC if it exceeds extra savings or profits the TNC has incurred due to the challenged predatory practices.

Table 6 TNCs' strategies vis-à-vis SD/CSR engagement

	High penalties	Low penalties
Detectable predation	1. Moral transition	2. Behavioral transition (crypto-morality)
Non-detectable predation	3. Behavioral transition (crypto-morality)	4. Behavioral transition (crypto-morality)

Source Author

6.2 TNCs' Cost-Benefit Analysis of Predation

Depending on the detectability of predation and the level of penalties, there are four scenarios corresponding to two behaviors: behavioral transition under crypto-morality, and moral transition (see Table 6).[12]

Scenario 4—Non-Detectable Predation and Low Penalties: it is almost impossible to detect the TNC's predatory behaviors, and any potential penalties are low. The company will be encouraged to continue predation as long as resulting savings or benefits outweigh penalties. The TNC's SD/CSR commitment will consist of a simple behavioral transition to assure a positive image and reputation.

Scenario 3—Non-Detectable Predation and High Penalties: the TNC would pay heavy penalties if its predatory behavior became detectable. Therefore, the TNC will strive to keep its predatory practices non-detectable. It may hide pollution, or bribe and intimidate the most threatening stakeholders to ensure their cooperation. The TNC's SD/CSR commitment will consist of a simple behavioral transition to assure a positive image and reputation.

Scenario 2—Detectable Predation and Low Penalties: it is possible for stakeholders to easily identify that the TNC practices predation, but penalties are low. The company will only endorse these residual penalties while reducing its exposure to stakeholders, and therefore, any SD/CSR commitment will consist of a simple behavioral transition.

Scenario 1—Detectable Predation and High Penalties: the TNC's SD/CSR commitment may consist of a moral transition to an actual fight against predation. This is the case in environments where institutions are strong and credible. Here, stakeholders are informed and able to enforce penalties against predators. The TNC does not stop innovating regarding methods of predation, but the institutional environment is so dynamic that stakeholders are also able to keep innovating to detect and penalize any new predatory practices.

In all three scenarios 4, 3 and 2, the TNC's SD/CSR engagement remains superficial. It is manipulated through various ethical codes and standards to cover predatory rent-seeking activities. Scenario 1 represents a situation where the TNC is forced to undertake a moral transition as its predatory attempts are regularly detected and punished. Such a moral transition does not immunize the company to

---

[12]This cost-benefit analysis has been introduced in Lado (2016).

predation. Crypto-morality is merely reduced and is likely to re-emerge once the company notices a slackening in detection practices and penalties. Thus, the TNCs' SD/CSR engagement against predation is dynamic: it evolves alongside the regulation and stakeholders' ability to maintain an active watch on predatory practices.

7 Conclusion

In the search of conditions for a successful development of a global code of conduct for TNCs, the ambition of this work was to analyze the behavioral dynamics of transnational corporations (TNCs) with respect to the institutional environments in which they operate. In fact, effective regulations for responsible behavior depend not only on their intrinsic quality but also on the institutional environment where they are applied and behavior of parties involved in their implementation. Building on North et al. (2009)'s conceptual framework on the categorization of social orders (limited access order or developing countries vs. open access order or developed countries), I have developed an analytical framework on the behavioral dynamics of TNCs when they move from one social order to another. The analysis of predator-prey dynamics between TNCs and States (in what I have defined as an international order of predation) reveals that TNCs are more likely to develop predatory practices in limited access orders where the prey potential is high. Greif and Tadelis (2010) concept of crypto-morality provides grounds for the demonstration that the sustainable development (SD) and corporate social responsibility (CSR) movements are likely to be effective in mandating responsible behavior in institutional environments where TNCs' predatory behaviors are highly detectable and heavily penalized.

To describe predatory and prey potentials, I have made use of the indicators 'important', 'high', 'low' or 'medium'. I'm aware that these terms only partially represent a reality that is complex by nature and varies from one TNC or social order to another. An attempt to move towards a more predictive analysis framework would require definition of discrete thresholds of these indicators; however, the elaboration of a predictive tool was not the purpose of this work. The aim was to provide a framework that depicts actors, institutional environments, and interactions that underlie predatory behaviors among TNCs and States. This should aid the design of a global code of conduct for TNCs; a promising approach is to focus on transparency and penalties mechanisms, and to foster capacity building in limited access orders for increased resilience and boldness.

In this analytic framework, the configuration in which a TNC is the prey and a social order the predator has not been considered. However, this case exists, especially in the situation where TNCs' investments or revenues are coveted by government officials. This is also the case when local populations perceive the TNC only as a provider of rents they can capture through violence. Furthermore, this work has demonstrated that limited access orders are most likely subject to predation, but this should not lead to the conclusion that predation does not exist in open access orders.

In fact, as open access orders' institutions and organizations are more sophisticated, predation is likewise sophisticated. When predatory practices thrive, they may be spectacular and their spillovers may impact the entire world, like the subprime crisis in 2007/2008 and the Volkswagen scandal in 2016. However, as limited access orders suffer most in terms of poverty, security, and other basic needs, predation is likely to cause more vital damages in terms of human rights.

This framework could be enriched with the analysis of predatory or prey potentials of other international actors such as intergovernmental organizations or non-governmental organizations. The influence of these international players in the international social order is significant, especially as in recent decades authority has moved from States to international organizations, as noted by Strange (1996). This framework would thus gain complexity with the consideration of the interplay between several international actors.

Finally, it should not be inferred from this work that TNCs concentrate all evils when operating in limited access orders. Their significant contribution to wealth creation and technology transfer has been well documented. However, even though host social orders must play a leading role in the protection of human rights, it is obvious that in their legitimate quest of rents, responsible TNCs must remain vigilant in their operations in institutionally weak social orders if they do not wish to foster predation. A global code of conduct for TNCs should consider transparency and dissuasive penalties as key drivers of responsible practices, and should target an improvement of the capacity of host countries in the fight against predation.

References

Amnesty International. (2014). *30 Après la catastrophe de Bophal, ils continuent à demander justice*.
Bisin, A., & Verdier, T. (2001). The economics of cultural transmission and the dynamics of preferences. *Journal of Economic Theory, 97*, 298–319 (2001).
David, E., & Lefèvre, G. (2015). *Juger les Multinationales. Droits Humains Bafoués, Ressources Naturelles Pillées, Impunité Organisée*. Editions Mardaga—GRIP.
Diamond, J. (1997). *Guns, germs, and steel. The fate of human societies*. New York: W. W. Norton & Company.
Dubresson, A., & Jaglin, S. (2002). La gouvernance urbaine en Afrique subsaharienne: pour une géographie de la régulation. In F. Bart, J. Bonvallot & Pourtier R. (Eds.), *Regards sur l'Afrique, Historiens et Géographes* (pp. 67–75). IRD. (Online) Available http://www.documentation.ird.fr/hor/fdi:010029294. 04 Jan 2017.
Gilpin, R. (1987). *The political economy of international relations*. Princeton: Princeton University Press.
Greif, A., & Tadelis, S. (2010). A theory of moral persistence: Crypto-morality and political legitimacy. *Journal of Comparative Economics, 38*(3), 229–244.
Keohane, R. (1984). *After hegemony: Cooperation and discord in the world political economy*. Princeton: Princeton University Press.
Keohane, R., & Nye, J. (2012). *Power and interdependence*, 4th Ed. Logman.
Knorr, K. (1975). *The power of nations. The political economy of international relations*. New York: Basic Books Inc. Publishers.

Lado, H. (2016). Les responsabilités sociétales obligatoires et volontaires des entreprises. *Revue Française de Gestion, 42*(260), 143–157.

Lang-Roth, C. (2013). ArcelorMittal: un accord social trouvé à Florange. *France Bleu (30 May 2013)*. (Online) Available https://www.francebleu.fr/arcelormittal-un-accord-social-trouve-florange-1369886400. 04 January 2017.

Le Floch-Prigent, L., & Decouty, E. (2001). *L'affaire Elf, affaire d'Etat. Entretiens avec Eric Decouty.* Paris: Ed. Le Cherche Midi.

Le Monde. (2013). La CIA reconnaît son rôle dans le coup d'Etat en Iran en 1953. (Online) Available http://www.lemonde.fr/ameriques/article/2013/08/19/la-cia-reconnait-avoir-renverse-le-premier-ministre-iranien-en-1953_3463576_3222.html. 04 January 2017.

L'Humanité. (2012). Florange sera "le cauchemar du gouvernement". (Online) Available http://www.humanite.fr/social-eco/florange-sera-le-cauchemar-du-gouvernement-491101. 04 January 2017.

Mitchell, T. (2013). *Carbon democracy. Le pouvoir politique à l'ère du pétrole.* Ed. La Découverte.

North, D., Wallis, J., & Weingast, B. (2009). *Violence and social orders. A conceptual framework for interpreting recorded human history.* Cambridge: Cambridge University Press.

North, D., Wallis, J., Webb, S., & Weingast, B. (2013). *In the shadow of violence: Politics, economics and the problem of violence.* Cambridge: Cambridge University Press.

NSA. (2013). *CIA confirms role in 1953 Iran Coup.* (Online) Available http://nsarchive.gwu.edu/NSAEBB/NSAEBB435/. 04 January 2017.

Nurdin, G., & Djermoun, S. (2015). *Les multinationales émergentes. Comment elles changent la donne mondiale.* L'Harmattan.

OECD. (2013). *Addressing base erosion and profit shifting.* Paris: OECD Publishing.

Ozawa, T. (2016). *The evolution of the world economy. The 'Flying-Geese' theory of multinational corporations and structural transformation.* Cheltenham: Edward Elgard Publishing.

Pigou, A. C. (1932). *The economics of welfare.* London: Macmillan and Co.

Reich, R. (2011). *Le Jour d'Après, Sans réduction des inégalités, Pas de sortie de crise.* Vuibert.

Stopford, J. M., & Strange, S. (1991). *Rival states, rival firms. Competition for world market shares.* Cambridge, NY: Cambridge University Press.

Strange, S. (1988). *States and markets.* Pinter Publishers.

Strange, S. (1996). *The retreat of the state. The diffusion of power in the world economy.* Cambridge: Cambridge University Press.

Veblen, T. (1970). *Théorie de la classe de loisir.* Trad. de Louis Evrard (édition originale en 1890). Gallimard.

Hervé Lado holds a Ph.D. in economics from the University Paris 1 Panthéon-Sorbonne and a Master in Finance and Strategy from Sciences Po Paris (Institute of Political Studies). His thesis was on the Corporate Social Responsibilities (CSR) of oil TNCs in Nigeria. Hervé served in the French economic diplomacy network in Africa for several years, advising corporations for their development in Africa. Recently, he was the Team Leader for social and environmental issues of a major hydroelectric dam project in Cameroon (420 MW, €1bn) sponsored by the Government of Cameroon, EDF and IFC. He is currently the Country Manager for Guinea of Natural Resource Governance Institute (NRGI), providing technical assistance and capacity building to the government and the civil society for a better governance of natural resources. Associate Researcher in the Programme Companies and Development (CODEV/IRENE) at ESSEC Business School in Paris, he has authored publications on the process of sustainable development in Africa, CSR and predation, including a book on political and economic dynamics in the history of Nigeria.

The UN Global Compact for Transnational Business and Peace: A Need for Orchestration?

Mariko Shoji

1 Introduction

IGO (Inter Governmental Organization) orchestration is more extensive in issue areas such as human rights and environment than in international security and finance," Abbott et al. (2015) claim. This chapter examines these less extensive issue areas of international security. In exploring the issue of security, Haufler (2015) describes the UN Security Council (UNSC) as an orchestrator. Here, Abbott et al.'s (2015) theoretical framework of IGO orchestration is used to analyze the field of the UN Global Compact (UNGC), "Business for Peace." As the author is involved in this issue,[1] this paper uses the viewpoint of an insider or intermediary.

Based on the experience of the author, we shall proceed as follows. First, several theoretical questions will be examined and an analytical framework is introduced. This is because "Business for Peace" of the UNGC differs in many aspects from typical IGO orchestration theory. Second, four specific cases are examined. Case 1: at the June 2010 Leaders' Summit of the UNGC, *the Guidance Document* entitled

---

[1] From 2011 to 2013, I served as a member of the expert meeting of "Business for Peace" of the UN Global Compact.

The original version of the book was inadvertently published with incorrect information. The correction to this chapter is available at https://doi.org/10.1007/978-3-030-10816-8_9

The author wishes to thank Dr. Mia Mahmudur Rahim for the opportunity to join this project. A draft version of this chapter was originally submitted as a paper at *the International Studies Association* (ISA) Annual Convention 2016, Atlanta, United States on 16 March 2016. The title was "Business for Peace: The Four Cases of Orchestration in the UN Global Compact." This has now been revised and I am particularly indebted to Neil Cowie and one anonymous peer reviewer in helping me do so.

M. Shoji (✉)
Department of International Studies, Keiai University, Chiba, Japan
e-mail: stmari@u-keiai.ac.jp

© Springer Nature Switzerland AG 2019
M. M. Rahim (ed.), *Code of Conduct on Transnational Corporations*, CSR, Sustainability, Ethics & Governance,
https://doi.org/10.1007/978-3-030-10816-8_5

Guidance on responsible business in conflict-affected and high-risk areas: a resource for companies and investors was adopted (United Nations Global Compact Office [UNGCO] 2010). The norm-creating (rule-making) process of *this Guidance Document* is analyzed. Case 2: on 25 June 2013, a "Business for Peacebuilding" Conference was held, co-hosted by the UN Peacebuilding Commission and the UNGC. It proved to be a very difficult event to jointly organize. Case 3: *The Business for Peace* (B4P) document was published by the UNGCO (UNGCO 2013a). This includes deliberation processes with multi-stakeholder initiatives. Case 4: The Oslo Business for Peace Award (B4P award) was initiated by the Business for Peace Foundation in 2007,[2] which was very helpful for the operation of the UNGC. Using this last case, observations based on the theory of IGO Orchestration are put forward.

2 What is an IGO and What is the Theory of IGO Orchestration?

Abbott et al. (2015) examine many case studies of orchestration by IGOs. What are IGOs? Many scholars defined them differently in the research literature. According to Claude (1971, p. 4), "International Organization is a process; international organizations are representative aspects of the phase of that process which has been reached at a given time." Haas (1990, p. 14) states that "International Organizations are part of everybody's experience because they are mediators of policies. They are a part of the international repertory of fora that talk about and authorize innovation." Therefore IGOs include the aspect of process and inherent societal experience. In order to expand on the theory of orchestration, it is important to analyze the operation of IGOs. Bennett and Oliver (1995, pp. 2–3) provides a more distinct explanation with the following five aspects: "(1) a permanent organization to carry on a continuing set of functions; (2) voluntary membership of eligible parties; (3) a basic instrument stating goals, structure, and methods of operation; (4) a broadly representative consultative conference organ; and (5) a permanent secretariat to carry on continuous administrative, research, and information functions. IGOs are, additionally, established by treaty... in order to safeguard state sovereignty." Furthermore, from the viewpoint of international law, IGOs are legally independent subjects of international law (Shearer 1994, p. 543; Shaw 2008, pp. 259–260; Yokota 2015, p. 23). IGOs can be not only forums but also independent actors.

The explanation by Abbott et al. (2015, pp. 3–4)," IGOs have ambitious governance goals but moderate governance capacity". And IGO orchestration means *"an IGO enlists and supports intermediary actors to address target actors in pursuit of IGO governance goals.* The key to orchestration is that the IGO brings third parties into the governance arrangement to act as intermediaries between itself

---

[2]http://businessforpeace.no/award/about-the-award/ (visited 8 March 2016).

and the targets, rather than trying to govern the targets directly". In IGO orchestration, an Orchestrator (O), Intermediaries (I) and Targets (T), these three actors perform interactively, and it is referred as the O-I-T model.

In this paper, the following organizations are analyzed: the UNGC, the United Nations Peace Building Commission (PBC), the United Nations Peace Building Support Office (PBSO), the UNSC, and the United Nations Economic and Social Council (ECOSOC). These bodies are included within the UN as a whole but in this paper only the interactions of parts of these IGOs are analyzed. The whole UN can be divided into two categories: the secretariat body and conference machinery. Conference machinery constitutes forums, such as the UNGC, the PBC, the UNSC and the ECOSOC. The secretariat body can be seen as an independent global actor[3] and includes the UNGCO and the PBSO.

3 The Role of an Intermediary

Abbott et al. (2015, pp. 12–13) explain that NGOs and other civil society organizations, trans-governmental networks, business organizations, transnational partnerships, and IGOs can be intermediaries. In this paper, these actors and also legal documents, state actors and individuals are considered as intermediaries.

What is the role of an intermediary? "The key to orchestration is that the IGO brings third parties into the governance arrangement to act as intermediaries between itself and the targets, rather than trying to govern the targets directly" and "an orchestrator works through intermediaries; orchestration is an ***indirect*** mode of governance. In addition, because an orchestrator has no hard control over the activities of intermediaries, but must mobilize and facilitate their voluntary cooperation in a joint governance effort, orchestration is a ***soft*** mode of governance" (Abbott et al. 2015, p. 4). Intermediaries must have the voluntary intention to enlist with an orchestrator. An intermediary can play several roles, ranging from a passive link between an orchestrator and its targets, to acting as a catalyst, or playing an active role as a bridge-builder, an organizer and a conductor.

One special feature of the theory of IGO orchestration is the acknowledgment of intermediaries. In this article four cases are studied. In case 1, an individual character, Sir Mark Moody-Stuart, plays the most important role as an intermediary. In cases 2 and 3, UN documents are important intermediaries. And as another important intermediary is the Principle of Responsible Investment (PRI).[4] In case 4, the Business for Peace Foundation, is the intermediary (Table 1).

---

[3]The Japan Association for United Nations Studies (2002), *The United Nations secretariat as a global actor*, Kokusai Shoin.

[4]https://www.unpri.org/ (visited 20 May 2018).

Table 1 O-I-T chart of business for peace (*Source* complied by author)

	O (Orchestrators)	I (Intermediaries)	T (Targets)
Case 1: *Guidance Document*	UNGCO	Sir Mark Moody-Stuart, PRI, Institute for Economics & Peace, etc.	Business (Investors & Companies)
Case 2: GC&PBC Conference	UNGCO, PBC, PBSO	*PBC/1/OC/12 Document* Japanese Mission	Business, UNSC, ECOSOC & Member States of the PBC
Case 3: *Business for Peace*	UNGCO PRI	*Guidance Document*	Business (Investors & Companies),etc.
Case 4: Business for Peace Prize	UNGCO (Business for Peace Foundation)	Business for Peace Foundation (UNGCO)	Business (Investors & Companies

4 Who Are the Targets?

Abbott et al. (2015, p. 6) explain that "the targets of IGO orchestration may be either states or private entities." They distinguish two general forms of IGO orchestration based on the identity of targets: "managing states" and "bypassing states." In the four cases presented in this chapter, the main targets are businesses such as investors and companies. In case 3, the targets are not only businesses but also the UNSC, the ECOSOC, and Member States of the PBC. In this case, IGOs can be a target of orchestration. In all four cases, the main focus is not on "managing states" or "bypassing states", but instead "managing businesses."

5 What Kind of Rules?: Hard Law to Super Soft Law

Mattli and Seddon (2015, p. 316) divide orchestration partners into "whether orchestrators or intermediaries… assume one of two complementary roles: rule-making and rule-supporting." The rule-making role can be explained as a process of creating international treaties or positive international laws, and the activities of intermediaries enlisted with IGOs can be illustrated as types of IGO orchestration. In this chapter, the four cases analyze rule-like documents stipulating processes among businesses. It is well-known that the ten principles of the UNGC act as soft laws for business. As Table 2 shows, positive international law has a high profile and states need rigid procedures to conclude or join positive international law. On the other hand, the ten principles of the UNGC have a lower profile than positive international law. In this chapter, the four cases analyze rule-like documents under the ten principles of the UNGC. These are subordinate documents of soft law. Table 2 illustrates that these rule-like documents have low profiles. Given that IGO orchestration is a soft mode of governance for states, the four cases in this article illustrate what could be called a super soft mode of governance for businesses.

6 What Are the Tools for Targets?

Even if O-I-Ts were classified, one important aspect is the way in which they are orchestrated together. According to IGO orchestration, "convening," "agenda setting," "assistance," "endorsement," and "coordination" are important techniques of orchestration (Abbott et al. 2015, pp. 14–16). These activities have also been used as important methods in negotiating international treaties (Shaw 2008, pp. 911–913).

Table 2 Hard law to super soft law (*Source* complied by author)

High Profile	Law	Rule	Hard to Join
	Semi Law	Principle	
	Soft Law	Guidance Principle	
Low Profile	Super Soft Law	Guidance Point	Easy to Join

Additionally, it is important to figure out what methods are successful from the perspective of awakening the targets' consciousness. In this chapter, the following techniques are seen as useful for IGO orchestration: raising awareness of common goals, acknowledging the importance of goals, and ensuring the motivation of targets.

In the context of Business for Peace, there are five levels of motivations by businesses (see Table 3). It is most important for business actors to *do no harm* to a society. Businesses have the ability to contribute to peace but it can be dangerous if they do not have the motivation to support peace and security. Businesses can be a cause of conflict if it is possible for them to profit from war and unrest. To prevent this dangerous situation, it is necessary to develop the network of Business for Peace. The next level is procurement from IGOs and government actors. If there are enough procurement opportunities for companies to invest and develop their business, they can much more easily enter the field and contribute to peace on site. The third level is profit-led motivation. In a post-conflict case of a former battlefield, there may be few business opportunities without an armament industry. In the disarmament case, post-conflict states have to abandon their armament industry and focus demand on more constructive industries. On the other hand, some businesses are reluctant to become involved in a post-conflict society. However, there are various opportunities for business development. Post-conflict society can constitute a new market with comparably little competition. The fourth level is contribution. Companies that have a high level of awareness, such as through Corporate Social Responsibility of the UNGC, and an interest in the maintenance of international peace and security, can actively contribute to peace and security. The fifth level is the Oslo Business for Peace Award, including Best Practice, which is an excellent way to raise the motivation of targets. It is also very important to keep lines of communication open with multi-stakeholders across these five cases. Whether by webinar meetings or through conferences and so on, it is indispensable to continue undisrupted communication with multi-stakeholders (Shoji 2012a) (Table 3).

Table 3 Level of Motivations (*Source* complied by author)

Do No Harm	Low Motivation
Procurement	
Profit Led	
Contribution	
Best Practice	High Motivation

6.1 Case 1: Creating a Process of Guidance on Responsible Business in Conflict-Affected and High-Risk Areas: A Resource for Companies and Investors *(UNGCO 2010)*

Before 2010, there were no transnational rules for business and peace. After the ten principles of the UNGC were established, from 2001, the role of conflict prevention by businesses began to be considered. *Guidance on responsible business in conflict-affected and high-risk areas: a resource for companies and investors* (UNGCO 2010) was finally adopted at the tenth anniversary of the UNGC Leaders' Summit, held in June 2010 in New York. It had taken ten years for the UNGC to create *this Guidance Document*.

There were three phases in the construction of *the Guidance Document*. The first phase was from March 2001 to May 2004, wherein the first activity on this theme of business and peace started; that is, the Policy Dialogue Series on the Role of the Private Sector in Zones of Conflict. The second phase was from October to December 2004, when a series of expert workshops were held, entitled "Identifying public policy options to promote conflict-sensitive business practices." The third phase was from January 2007 until 2010, when the Expert Group on Responsible Investment was organized to discuss creating *the Guidance Document* (Shoji 2012b).

During the first phase of the genesis of the business and peace issue, there were seven meetings, mainly organized by the UNGCO. These meetings were held in New York, at the headquarters of the UNGCO, in Switzerland, and also in many conflict sensitive places such as South Africa, Kazakhstan, Columbia and the Sudan. The participants in these meetings were multi-stakeholders and the main topic discussed was suitable policy for businesses to follow in order to prevent conflict. In this first phase, the orchestrator was the UNGCO enlisted with local networks of the UNGC. Meetings were open to multi-stakeholders who were interested in this issue and the targets were the private sector, mainly businesses, and NGOs. One important intermediary was the fact sheet entitled "Voluntary principles on security and human rights",[5] which had been cooperatively created by the governments of the United States, the United Kingdom, the Netherlands, and Norway, companies in the extractive and energy sectors, and by NGOs (Bureau of Democracy, Human Rights, and Labor, U.S. Department of State 2000). These voluntary principles had been already created by a multi-stakeholder process and were a firm basis for policy dialogues through the UNGC. During these policy dialogues, working groups were established to discuss various topics including: (a) Multi-Stakeholder Initiatives; (b) Revenue-Sharing Regimes; (c) Impact Assessment and Risk Management; and (d) Transparency.

In the second phase, the above-mentioned working groups were developed as expert workshops. One interesting feature is that the government actor of Germany

---

[5]http://www.voluntaryprinciples.org/ (visited 20 May 2018).

played an intermediary role. In addition, until 2004, many documents outside of the UNGC were created. These include the Kimberly Process Certification Scheme (KPCS) in 2002; the DAC Guidelines "Helping prevent violent conflict" (Michel 2001), and the Extractive Industries Transparency Initiative (EITI) principles in 2002.[6] These documents played a role as intermediaries, although the KPCS specializes in only the diamond industries and the EITI is only for extractive industries. The DAC Guidelines were proposed by the OECD Development Assistance Committee. All of these documents were very useful in helping to create the UNGC *Guidance Document*. In this second phase, the main orchestrator was the UNGCO and the main targets were businesses. NGOs became consultative participants in a multi-stakeholder process.

In the third phase, the UNGCO and the PRI cooperatively led the initiative as orchestrators. The goal of this initiative was to make *the Guidance Document*. After the PRI began to cooperate with the UNGCO as an orchestrator, many investors began to participate in the meetings and became the main targets of this initiative alongside companies. There were also many intermediaries such as the Comptroller of the City of New York,[7] the Strategic Foresight Group (SFG),[8] the Academic Group of India,[9] the AlBadayel Advanced Training Center, the Sudanese Businessmen and Employers Federation, the Ahfad University for Women (UNGCO 2008), the UN Alliance of Civilization (Wallace Aramian 2008), Sir Mark Moody-Stuart, and the Academic Group of Japan.[10] It can be seen that academics in many countries played a crucial role in organizing meetings for this initiative. In addition, a powerful tool for change was the Global Peace Index created by the Institute of Economics and Peace that served as a very useful measure concerning business and peace.[11]

---

[6]https://eiti.org/eiti/principles (visited 9 March 2016).

[7]First Consultation on Responsible Investment in Weak States, New York January 17, 2007.
http://www.unglobalcompact.org/Issues/conflict_prevention/meetings_and workshops (visited 9 August 2007).

[8]The Strategic Foresight Group (SFG) is a think tank engaged in crafting new policy concepts that enable decision makers to prepare for a future in uncertain times. http://www.strategicforesight.com/about-us.php#.VuKC_-KLTrc (visited 9 March 2016).

[9]Mr. Kumar Ketkar, Chairman, Conference Organizing Group; Dr. Arun Sawant, Pro-Vice Chancellor, University of Mumbai; Mr. B. P. Bam, Director, Purushottam Academy; Mr. Sunil Karve, Vice Chairman, Mumbai Education Trust; Mr. Sundeep Waslekar, President, Strategic Foresight Group; and Ms. Ilmas Futehally, Vice President, Strategic Foresight Group cooperatively organized the meeting in Mumbai in 2008 (Chandra 2008).

[10]Dr. Tatsuro Kunugi, Visiting Professor, UN University-Institute of Advanced Studies and former UN Assistant Secretary General, Mr. Yasunobu Sato, a professor of the University of Tokyo; and, Ms. Mariko Shoji, professor of Keiai University cooperatively organized the meeting in Tokyo in 2010 (Keiai University 2010).

[11]http://economicsandpeace.org (visited 9 March 2016).

From this study of the process of the creation of *the Guidance Document*, the following seven points can be made. First, orchestration occurred during the rule-making process of *the Guidance Document*. In parallel to this rule-making activity, the UNGCO convened conferences, set agendas, and coordinated among many intermediaries and targets. These were also awareness raising activities. Second, throughout this process, the targets were narrowed down from the private sector in general to companies and investors. Third, NGOs and academia became intermediaries. Fourth, the role of academia as an intermediary was conspicuous. As Haas (1992, p. 4) mentions, "academia; an epistemic community, is a network of professionals with recognized expertise and competences in a particular domain and an authoritative claim to policy-relevant knowledge within that domain or issue-area." Academics have the "power of ideas" to propose, organize and coordinate in the process of orchestration.[12] During the process of creating *the Guidance Document*, many academics played an important role in inviting the UNGC to their country and organizing workshops or conferences. Fifth, the role of NGOs and academia was reconsidered. Although not clearly outlined, in the process of making *the Guidance Document*, there may have been some misunderstanding of civil society, NGOs and academia. The UNGCO reported that "the views of civil society and academics were also sought, especially in the context of ongoing divestment campaigns" (2007, p. 1). However, in reality, most NGOs and academics did not want to divest businesses but to transform harmful businesses into useful ones that could contribute to peace (Shoji 2012b). Sixth, Sir Mark Moody-Stuart was very active in creating *the Guidance Document*, especially at the final stage of rule-making. He was Chairman of the Foundation for the Global Compact and an ex-chairman of Royal Dutch Shell.[13] His leading role in creating *the Guidance Document* was remarkable. He created the draft of the document and revised the document again and again in meetings of the third phase. He is a powerful intermediary and was almost like a conductor of the orchestration. However, there are pros and cons concerning Moody-Stuart's role in the process of rulemaking. On the one hand, without his strong leadership, *the Guidance Document* could not have been finalized. On the other hand, although he and the UNGCO tried to achieve a consensus and include as many opinions as possible, it was a totally derailed rule-making process compared with the international treaty-making process. Seventh, the normative character of *the Guidance Document* is a very soft mode and has weak enforcement ability. Until November 2009, the contents of this document were called "guidance principles", but because companies were worried about being bound by this new framework, in addition to the ten principles of the UNGC, it was decided to change the contents to "guidance points." The word "points" is used as "a point of reference." It is regrettable that by changing the word

---

[12]"Epistemic community" and "power of ideas" can have enormous networking and norm creating power. See Thakur et al. (2000), Emmerij et al. (2001), Goldstein and Keohane (1993).

[13]It is well known that tensions arose between the native Ogoni people of the Niger Delta and Shell in the 1990s. See http://www.essentialaction.org/shell/issues.html (visited 10 March 2016).

from "principle" to "point," the normative character of the document becomes weaker (Shoji 2012b, pp. 154–155). However, as mentioned above, if a rule has a low profile character, it is expected that many targets would join *the Guidance Document*.

6.2 Case 2: 25 June 2013 "Business for Peacebuilding" Conference

After the creation of *the Guidance Document*, there was a need to create a partnership between the UNGC and the main bodies of the UN in the field of peace and security. Regarding the theory of Global Governance, the following three factors are indispensable: (1) Global Norm: the sum of laws, norms, policies, and institutions; (2) Transnational Relations: mediation of trans-border relations; and (3) Multilateral Actors: states, citizens, intergovernmental and nongovernmental organizations, and the market (Weiss and Thakur 2010, pp. 31–32). *The Guidance Document* is super soft, but we can say that it is the Global Norm. The UNGC itself has the nature of a transnational network (Transnational Relations). As seen in case 1, the norm-creating process of *the Guidance Document* involves a multi-stakeholder process that includes multilateral actors such as citizens, intergovernmental and nongovernmental organizations, and the market, who all participate in the process of peacemaking and peacebuilding.[14] In 2004, not only the UNGC but also the UNSC discussed this issue, expanding it to include civil society in the process of peacebuilding (UNSC 2004, 2005). At the meeting of the Security Council, one of the representatives from the NGOs mentioned that "Engagement with civil society is not an end in itself, nor is it a panacea, but it is vital to our efforts to turn the promise of peace agreements into the reality of peaceful societies and viable States. The partnership between the United Nations and civil society is therefore not an option; it is a necessity" (UNSC 2004, p. 4). Furthermore, in this UNSC meeting the importance of businesses in the process of peacebuilding was discussed. Businesses can, with their local partners, mobilize the will of broad economic and social sectors. Businesses can offer financial support for productive quick-impact projects, for example through employment initiatives for former combatants (ibid., p. 19). The UN, the UNSC and the PBC perceived that an important role for the UN was to convene, facilitate, and lead partnerships not only of governments, but also of all stakeholders including civil society and businesses so that multi-stakeholder processes (MSPs) could become key elements in the field of peace and security. Brozska et al. (2011, p. 259) state that "MSPs are not only a

---

[14]The "Arria-formula" was introduced to the UNSC in 2006, wherein the "Security Council may invite on an informal basis any Member State, relevant organization or individual to participate in 'Arria-formula' informal meetings" (UNSC 2006, para. 54).

promising but also already an effective instrument for improving human security and development."

Even if the importance of partnerships between the inter-governmental bodies of the UN (such as the UNSC or the PBC) and non-state actors was understood, few partnerships between the UNGC and the PBC have actually been created. In 2007, the Permanent Mission of Japan to the UN sought to establish a partnership with civil society. As Uhlin (2010, p. 16) note, it was a very important issue to include non-state actors and MSPs in UN governmental meetings. Even if non-state actors were included in peacebuilding activities on the ground in post-conflict countries, it was not satisfactory for the whole peacebuilding process to be carried out without including such non-state actors in the PBC at the headquarters of the UN in New York. As a result, the Japanese Mission proposed a document entitled "Provisional guidelines for the participation of civil society in meetings of the Peacebuilding Commission" (UN Peacebuilding Commission 2007). The document suggested that civil society and the private sector could be invited to informal and formal meetings, which signified great progress in the field of peace and security. The UNSC can only include non-state actors in "Arria-formula" informal meetings, whereas the PBC can invite non-state actors to both formal and informal meetings.

Although a procedure for including the private sector was established, bridge building between the PBC and business was still required. In February 2008, the first meeting between the UNGCO and Japanese Mission staff in charge of peacebuilding took place.[15] They discussed how to build partnerships and linkages between the UNGC and the PBC. It was relatively easy for government representatives to the UN and UN officials in New York to contact each other, but there were some obstacles regarding contact between the UNGC and the PBC. This is one difference between the UNGCO and the UNGC and is also a difference between the PBSO and the PBC. UN officials tried to make a linkage between the UN and business, but it took five years to organize a joint conference. The PBC is a conference body among government representatives. From the viewpoint of business, the PBC looks like a collective of government actors. Within the UNGC network, businesses have transnational ownerships and do not always obey government orders, so the UNGCO could not compel businesses to meet with the PBC.

The first joint meeting between the PBC and the UNGC was held on 25 June 2013.[16] At this meeting, there were 42 representatives of the private sector of the UNGC (28 companies, five business associations, nine NGOs, and a number of academics), 31 member states of the PBC, nine staff members from the UNGCO and the PBSO, and eight staff members from other IGOs. The aim of this meeting was to "bring together business and political leaders to explore venues for enhanced business engagement in post-conflict countries and identify concrete entry points

---

[15]The author could contribute to bring Ms.Melissa Powell of the UNGCO and Minister Toshiya Hoshino from the Japanese Mission together on 28 February 2008.
[16]"Business for Peacebuilding" Conference, 25 June 2013, United Nations, New York, Co-hosted by the UN Peacebuilding Commission and the UN Global Compact.

and opportunities for partnerships and collaboration at ground level."[17] At this multi-stakeholder meeting, participants agreed that the primary responsibility for peace, security and development rested with governments, but that the private sector can make a meaningful contribution to stability and security in countries emerging from conflicts. Although not noted as an objective on the official agenda, one purpose of the meeting was to inform the main bodies of the UN of the importance of the role of businesses. To this end, the presidents of the UNSC and ECOSOC were invited to a joint meeting. Although some participants suggested that this joint meeting should be repeated annually or biannually, it ended after just one lavish ceremony.

The orchestrators of the joint meeting of "Business for Peace" between the PBC and the UNGC were the UNGCO and the PBSO. Their contribution was invaluable as it was so difficult to realize a meeting between business and government representatives. The most important intermediary was *the PBC/1/OC/12 Document* (UN Peacebuilding Commission 2007), which encouraged the private sector to participate in a formal meeting of the PBC. In addition, bridge building activities by the UNGCO officials and the Japanese Mission were also essential. In this case, the main targets of orchestration were businesses and member states of the PBC, whilst other important targets were the UNSC and ECOSOC. In the end the event was purely ceremonial because of the gap between business and government. Concerning goal divergence, it would be difficult to continue the project if there was a significant gap between O-I-Ts; it might be a better choice for O-I-T governance to maintain a fundamental goal. All parties are for the proposal in principle but against specific details. This has to be overcome by sheer perseverance and gradually goal divergence can be diminished, ultimately allowing convergence to be achieved.

6.3 Case 3: **Business for Peace Document *(UNGCO 2013a)***

It was very difficult to create *the Guidance Document*, but it has proven even more difficult to implement it. After *the Guidance Document* was established, the UNGCO enlisted with the PRI to set up a "Pilot Project" which aimed to promote the Guidance's content and encourage its implementation by companies and investors operating in challenging environments (UNGCO 2010).

There were two main challenges in this case. One was to promote the existence of the document and to develop understanding of it within the UNGC. The second was to ensure the implementation of the document. The UNGCO announced that "This voluntary guidance is designed to stimulate learning and dialogue and to promote collective action and innovative partnerships through Global Compact

---

[17]Ibid.

Local Networks and other initiatives."[18] However, in reality, it was very hard to promote and implement a voluntary and super soft law to businesses.

For MSPs, the UNGCO held webinar meetings, which was easier for many participants to join compared to a face-to-face meeting. The first webinar was held on 20 November 2010 and was open to multi-stakeholders of the UNGC. Pre-registration, a password and ID were required for participants to enter the webinar conference. There were 108 seats for participants from all over the world. All the participants could see the presenter by screens but they could not see other participants' faces and only one person at a time could speak. If a participant wanted to give their opinion, they had to signal this by pushing a button on the screen. Six webinar meetings were held until September 2013.[19]

A webinar conference is a distinctive method for MSPs as they can easily meet wherever they are in the world. Webinar meetings do have some pros and cons. Of course, participants do not have to travel to a meeting place and are able to join in from their office or home, but the time difference cannot be easily overcome. The locations of the orchestrator, such as the UNGCO in New York or London, are the focal points of a webinar meeting. For the participants from different time zones, it is difficult to adjust the meeting time to that of the focal point. Whether New York or London was a focal point, it was always difficult for people from South Asian countries, such as India, because the webinar conferences took place in the middle of the night in those countries. Sometimes, greeting words required attention; for example, "Good morning from London" is not appropriate for a global webinar meeting.

Brozska et al. (2011, p. 7) note that membership of MSPs can be highly flexible and sometimes ad hoc, which means that in contrast to formal organizational bodies, a MSPs group of participating actors must quickly adapt to cope with a changing environment. At the UNGC webinar meetings, the persons in charge from businesses were constantly changing. With newcomers at each meeting, the UNGCO had to consistently explain the initiative from a basic level. It might be useful for MSPs networks to prepare a document explaining this initiative in a basic way, as one aim of these meetings was to promote and develop an understanding of this issue. On the other hand, some participants became super experts, which became an obstacle. Super experts began to use technical jargon, which was typically hard to understand for MSPs newcomers. If O-I-T orchestration wishes to maintain MSPs, it is indispensable to devise a suitable introductory document or

---

[18]UNGCO, "New phase of business and peace initiative launched," New York, 11 November 2010, https://www.ideaspaz.org/tools/download/50924 (visited on 6 March 2012).

[19](1) 11 November 2010 Webinar: New phase of business and peace initiative launched. (2) 5 April 2011: Webinar for local network on responsible business in conflict-affected and high-risk areas: agenda and technical instructions. (3) 20 September 2012, PRI/UNGC webinar: Responsible business in Iraq: how to build constructive relations with the government. (4) 26 June 2013 (8 am EST): for GC Local Networks only. (5) 25 July 2013 (8 am EST): all GC participants. New "Business 4 Peace" initiative under development: The UN Global Compact Office. (6) 22 August 2013, final webinar consultation: Business for Peace.

beginner's webinar session prior to the main webinar conference. MSPs form a new mode of governance and could be a useful tool for O-I-T orchestration. Brozska et al. (ibid.) observe that it has become clear that "governance" by government is only one form of addressing policy issues. Modern governance often combines international, national, and sub-national elements.

In the discussion of MSPs, the UNGCO noted three important issues. First, to simplify *the Guidance Document* and make it accessible; second, to create measures for implementation of the document; and third, to collect successful concrete examples on the ground from local UNGC networks. In order to achieve these three goals, it was necessary not only to have a series of webinar meetings but also to hold face-to-face meetings with experts. The Expert Group on Responsible Business and Investment in High-risk Areas was organized by the UNGCO and the PRI. Members of the expert meeting included company representatives, investors, civil society leaders, UN representatives, and others from all regions of the world. As of September 2013, six expert meetings had been held in Copenhagen, New York, Colombia, Rio de Janeiro, London, and Beijing.[20] It was important for the UNGCO to visit many places around the world and to explain what the document was with face-to-face talks on the ground. For the UNGCO, it was also necessary to acquire information about concrete examples of local networks.

As a result of these intensive discussions and deliberations, the *"Business for Peace" (B4P) Document* was endorsed at the event for a new leadership platform of the UNGC on 20 September 2013 (UNGCO 2013a). *The B4P Document* is just a simple four-page pamphlet. It can be used as an entry point for new participants because it explains the importance of participation, ways to participate in this initiative, a list of MSPs who can participate in this platform, and a statement of support. It is simple to understand and includes three important pieces of information: *The Guidance Document*, a guide for Communication on Progress (COP),[21] and *the Local Network Document* (UNGCO 2013b). This was created by the UNGCO after extensive deliberations with local networks and by collecting information from many stakeholders and local networks. The guide to the COP is an explanation for companies who are expected to reference progress made in implementing *the Guidance Document* in the context of the annual COP.[22]

---

[20](1) 17 May 2011, "Responsible business and investment in high-risk areas," Copenhagen. (2) 8 November 2011, "Responsible business and investment in high-risk areas," New York, UNHQ. (3) 29 May 2012, "Advancing responsible business in Colombia: engaging with local communities and addressing grievances." (4) 17 June 2012, "Business, peace and sustainable development", at Rio+20, Rio de Janeiro. (5) 27 Nov. 2012 "Responsible business and investment in high-risk areas," London. (6) 16 April 2013, "Business executives conference: sustainable business and investment in the global context; rights, risk and responsibilities," Beijing, China.

[21]COP is a key component of stakeholders' commitment to the UN Global Compact. Every stakeholder has to submit a report on what it has implemented each year. Reporting to stakeholders in a transparent and public manner is fundamental for companies committed to sustainability.

[22]UNGC & PRI, *Note on the Pilot Project on Responsible Business in High-Risk Areas*, UNGCO, March 2011.

Referring to the theory of O-I-T orchestration, the UNGCO enlisted with the PRI were orchestrators. The powerful intermediary was *the Guidance Document*. *The Guidance Document* is soft and weak by nature, but it could be used as a solid foundation for the next step, which was to create *the B4P Document*. Furthermore, it could also be used as a step for creating *the Local Network Document*. In this regard, local UNGC networks were also effectual intermediaries in creating *the Local Network Document*. The main targets were companies and investors and, additionally, governments, especially in high-risk areas, civil society, academia, and other UN main bodies and agencies. In this process, three remarkable points are indicated for orchestration by the UNGCO: making rules simple to understand, showing concrete examples, and giving recommendations that refer to activities which should be mentioned in the COP reports.

6.4 Case 4: The Oslo Business for Peace Award

O-I-T orchestration by the UNGCO is a very soft mode of governance. *The Guidance Document* is simply a subordinate rule within the ten principles of the UNGC. The ten principles do not have any legal binding force against targets but are a self-restraint norm for corporations. *The Guidance Document* is a super soft law that does not have any compulsory power, but urges voluntary and self-regulating activities by businesses. B4P required a degree of positive stimulus to raise the motivation of businesses. One resulting project was the "Business for Peace Award" (B4P Award). This award was separately established from the B4P initiative of the UNGC. It was introduced in 2007 by the Business for Peace Foundation "in the belief that socially responsible and ethical initiatives should not be merely window dressing, but must stand the test as a business case, and gradually, as the moral culture of corporations matures, will constitute an integrated part of modern business."[23]

It is an award for individuals who exemplify the Foundation's concept of being business worthy by ethically creating economic value that also creates value for society.[24] Honorees were selected by an independent committee of Nobel Prize winners in peace and economics in closed-door meetings.

In this case, from the viewpoint of the B4P Foundation, the B4P Foundation is an orchestrator and the UNGCO is an intermediary. For the B4P Foundation, the UNGCO is a reliable partner because it is very knowledgeable and can present many examples of good practice for the B4P initiative. However, from the viewpoint of the UNGCO, the UNGCO is an orchestrator and the B4P Foundation is an intermediary. This is interchangeable. The B4P Foundation has a measure of

---

[23] http://businessforpeace.no/about-us/mission-and-vision/ (visited 7 March, 2016).

[24] http://businessforpeace.org/award/about-the-award/ (visited 7 March, 2016).

authority to lead the award project. The B4P Foundation and the UNGCO worked cooperatively to encourage businesses to contribute to a peaceful society. Their targets were business and related individuals.

It is very hard for the UNGCO, as a very soft mode of governance, to implement its goals. However, different kinds of events to raise the motivation of targets are good triggers to activate B4P initiatives. Competitive methods such as best practice surveys can make orchestration more active.[25]

7 Concluding Note

In this concluding note, the author classifies the four cases as per the typology of the theory of O-I-T orchestration. In Table 4, the four cases are analyzed using several important techniques of orchestration. It can be seen that one very important role for the orchestrator is to convene conferences and meetings. For the intermediaries, agenda setting is critical. *The Guidance Document* and *B4P Document* are super soft laws for which it is vital to be endorsed by targets. In many cases, the orchestrators coordinated the process. In IGO orchestration, the orchestrators, intermediaries, and targets all have specific roles. For example, orchestrators tend to convene meetings or conferences, set agendas and coordinate the different parties. Intermediaries tend to set agendas and assist in coordination. In many cases, the role of targets is that of endorsement. This chapter has analyzed just one case of B4P and the UNGC; further case studies need to be examined to make further generalizations.

Table 5 examines whether the six hypotheses of IGO orchestration are applicable or not. Abbott et al. (2015, pp. 20–30) define six hypotheses as analytical tools of IGO orchestration. (1) Orchestrator capabilities hypothesis: Governance actors are more likely to orchestrate when they lack certain capabilities needed to achieve their goals through other governance modes. (2) Intermediary availability hypothesis: Governance actors are more likely to orchestrate when intermediaries with correlated goals and complementary capabilities are available. (3) Orchestrator focality hypothesis: Governance actors are more likely to orchestrate when they are focal within the relevant issue area. (4) Orchestrator entrepreneurship hypothesis: Governance actors are more likely to engage in orchestration when their organizational structure and culture encourage policy entrepreneurship. (5) Goal divergence hypothesis: IGOs are more likely to orchestrate when there is a divergence of goals among their member states and/or between member states and IGO orchestration. (6) State oversight hypothesis: IGOs are more likely to engage in

---

[25]There are examples of the UN using best practice methods. See "UN expert launches survey to identify best practices to protect human rights defenders," *UN News Centre*, 4 November 2015. Also, *UNSC resolutions 1373* (2001) and *1624* (2004) promote best practice of states. They were prepared pursuant to several resolutions of the UNSC referring to best practices, codes, and standards as tools that can assist states in their implementation of the resolution.

Table 4 Several important techniques of orchestration (*Source* complied by author)

		Convening	Agenda Setting	Assistance	Endorsement	Coordination	Other
Case 1	O	O	O			O	
	I	O	O	O			
	T				O		
Case 2	O	O					
	I		O	O		O	
	T				O		
Case 3	O	O				O	
	I		O		O		
	T				O		
Case 4	O				O	O	
	I	O	O	O	O		
	T						O

orchestration when their member states have weak institutional control mechanisms. In this chapter, the main targets are not states but businesses. Exceptionally, in case 2, states can be added as targets.

Using the data from Table 5, whether or not the six hypotheses are applicable to these four cases in this chapter will now be examined. The six hypotheses are as follows.

(1) Orchestrator capabilities hypothesis: Case 1: The UNGCO did not have any clear guidelines for the enforcement of Business and Peace. The creation of a guidance document was mainly orchestrated by the UNGCO with the assistance of many business actors, including Sir Mark Moody-Stuart. Case 2: The governmental body of the PBC and the UN required a partnership with business communities at the post-conflict stage. Although it was only a first step for the PBC and the UNGC to hold a joint meeting, it was a precious example of potential future cooperation between the UN and business communities. Case 3: Although *the Guidance Document* that was produced in 2010 is an excellent example of guidelines for Business and Peace, it is too large and may be difficult for business people to understand or access. The UNGCO needed a simple flyer to overcome these issues. The PRI and the expert meeting were very helpful in creating a simplified version of *the Guidance Document*.

Table 5 Six hypotheses of IGO orchestration (*Source* complied by author)

	Case 1	Case 2	Case 3	Case 4
Orchestrator capabilities hypothesis	GCO did not have any forcible enforcement power.	GCO & PBC jointly.	GCO held webinar meetings and on site meetings with intermediaries.	GCO does not have such a resource like the B4P Foundation.
Intermediary capability hypothesis	Strong leadership and high motivation	*PBC document* enables business to join PBC meetings.	*Guidance Document* provides many indicators.	B4P Foundation has strong leadership.
Orchestrator focality hypothesis	There is no other existing entity that has a rule-making ability without GCO.	GCO and PBSO are both UN secretariat offices.	GCO played a secretariat role for these meetings.	GCO has greater network among targets than B4P Foundation.
Orchestrator entrepreneurship hypothesis	GCO tried to be a norm entrepreneur.	Entrepreneurships are comparably weak.	GCO would like to make *the Guidance Document* much more understandable and simple.	It was led by strong entrepreneurship of intermediary.
Goal divergence hypothesis	Investors and companies have different goals	There are differences between intention of member states and that of businesses.	Goals are different from target to target.	GCO and B4P Foundation have a common goal to raise the motivation of targets.
State (Targets) oversight hypothesis	Businesses may not be able to manage conflict.	Stance of the PBC and businesses are totally different.	Many oversights are found in this discussion.	Businesses may not have high motivation to participate in B4P.

Case 4: It was difficult for the UNGCO to enforce B4P within business communities. The Oslo B4P Award helped to motivate these communities to practice B4P. From these observations, the orchestrator capability hypothesis is applicable to all four cases. The UNGCO was the orchestrator in these four cases and was assisted by various intermediaries.

(2) Intermediary Capability hypothesis: Case 1: As an intermediary, Sir Mark Moody-Stuart (a former chairman of Royal Dutch Shell) was highly motivated to settle the conflict between oil companies and oil producing countries, especially in Africa. He played an active role in drafting and adopting *the Guidance Document*. Case 2: *The PBC/1/OC/12 Document* (UN Peacebuilding Commission 2007) had a strong impact as an intermediary on the joint meeting between the PBC and the UNGC. *The PBC/1/OC/12 Document* encouraged the private sector to participate in a formal meeting with the PBC. Case 3: *The Guidance Document* was a powerful intermediary in creating *the B4P Document*. Without the existence of *the Guidance Document*, the UNGCO would not have endeavored to create *the B4P Document*. Case 4: The support

of the B4P Foundation was very influential. The B4P Foundation is not a part of the UN but an independent organization based in Oslo. It acted as a driving force, helping the UNGCO to increase the motivation of companies to contribute to B4P. Each of these cases has different intermediaries. In case 1, it was Sir Mark Moody-Stuart; in case 2, it was the *PBC/1/OC/12 Document*; in case 3, it was *the Guidance Document*; and, in case 4, it was the B4P Foundation. Through the work of these intermediaries, the UNGCO was able to pursue the goal of B4P.

(3) Orchestrator focality hypothesis: Case 1: There is no other existing entity that has a rule-making ability except the UNGCO. In 2010, the UNGC created a worldwide network among business communities. The UNGCO has been a focal point in the promotion of the ten principles of the UNGC and it might be easier for the UNGCO to create a network in the field of B4P compared with the other organs of the UN. Case 2: The UNGCO and the PBSO are both UN secretariat offices which might make it easier for them to communicate with each other in order to set up joint meetings between the PBC and the UNGC. Case 3: The UNGCO played a secretariat role in meetings to create *the B4P Document*. Case 4: Whilst the UNGCO does not have any power to increase the motivation of business communities, it has a greater network among targets than the B4P Foundation. In these cases, the UNGCO as the orchestrator displayed a focality, especially in cases 1 and 3 where the UNGCO was a main actor. In case 2, the PBSO had a focality to cooperate with the UNGCO, and in case 4, the B4P Foundation had a powerful focality for supporting the goal of the UNGCO.

(4) Orchestrator entrepreneurship hypothesis: Case 1: In this case, the UNGCO attempted to act as a norm entrepreneur and contributed to the creation of *the Guidance Document* in 2010. Case 2: The UNGCO and the PBSO tried to create a partnership between the PBC, a governmental body, and the UNGC; but it was too early to create a strong tie between them. Case 3: The UNGCO wanted to make *the Guidance Document* more accessible and understandable, which successfully resulted in *the B4P Document*. Case 4: The Oslo B4P Award was pursued by the strong leadership of the B4P Foundation. In all cases, the UNGCO, as orchestrator, needed to cultivate and construct the organizational structure and culture of B4P. Of course, within the network of the UNGC (which has a corporate social responsibility framework), it might have been easier for the UNGCO to initiate B4P compared with outside the network. There were few B4P policies before *the Guidance Document* was created.

(5) Goal Divergence hypothesis: Case 1: Investors and companies have different opinions but in the process of creating *the Guidance Document*, opinions and understanding regarding business and peace converged. Case 2: There were differences between the intentions of member states and that of businesses. Although it was very hard to close the gap between them, it was useful to hold a joint meeting between the PBC and the UNGC. Case 3: The ultimate goal of members of B4P is the same, but there might be a variety of possible goals for the targets of members or possible members of B4P. Case 4: In this case, the UNGCO and B4P Foundation had a common goal to raise the motivation of

targets. There were a variety of opinions between investors and companies in case 1; between member states and businesses in case 2; and between expert members and businesses in case 3. Often, there were too many opinions, which was an obstacle in attaining a common goal. In case 4, the UNGCO and the B4P Foundation had almost the same goal, which worked well to raise the motivation of businesses for B4P.

(6) State (Targets) oversight hypothesis: Case 1: Business communities may not be able to manage conflict and may require assistance not only from government but also from the UN. Case 2: The stance of the PBC, member states, and businesses are totally different. Sometimes the PBC does not have sufficient resources and sometimes businesses need assistance from the UN in the post-conflict stage of a country. Case 3: Many oversights were identified during the discussion that led to the creation of *the B4P Document*. For example, *the Guidance Document* 2010 is too large and inaccessible for business communities. Case 4: Businesses may not be motivated to carry out B4P. The Oslo B4P Award helped to raise such motivation. In this IGO orchestration study, the main targets are not member states but businesses. Businesses in general do not have any capability to govern B4P issues, but the situation might be different for individual businesses. In many situations, businesses did not implement B4P perfectly. This was not because of their weak institutional control mechanisms but because of their lack of motivation. The UNGCO needs to further raise business awareness regarding B4P.

Table 5 indicates that the six hypotheses as analytical tools of IGO orchestration are almost, but not perfectly, applicable to these four cases. It can be observed that orchestration occurred in the four cases. As mentioned above, *the Guidance Document* and *B4P Document* are super soft laws. It is much easier to enforce a hard law than a soft one. In contrast, for many targets, a soft law is much easier to join (and more attractive) than a hard law.

It is very difficult for an orchestrator to enforce a super soft law. To enforce such a law, the orchestrator must exert considerable effort, for example, to persuade, explain, enlist, ask for contributions, endorse the targets' COP, and to motivate targets. Communication through a transnational network is an important pathway for effective orchestration. Motivating targets through an initiative such as the B4P Foundation is a useful and effective means of establishing best practice.

From these observations, we can conclude that the theory of orchestration is useful for analyzing the functions relating the B4P project with the UNGC. This is because the project is not underpinned by hard laws but by super soft laws such as *the Guidance Document, the B4P Document*, and the B4P award. It is very difficult to explain the effectiveness of the UNGC soft mode of governance, where everything must be managed through the self-restraint regulations of business. However, using the theory of orchestration, this chapter precisely explains the soft mode of governance process of the B4P.

Further questions remain to be answered, including how best to operate the orchestration and soft mode of governance, whether transnational networks should be more active and fluent, and the utility of nets of transnational global networks. Additional tools are required to make even more effective use of the theory of orchestration.

References

Abbott, K., Genschel, P., Snidal, D., & Zangl, B. (Eds.). (2015). *International organizations as orchestrators*. Cambridge: Cambridge University Press.

Bennett, A., & Oliver, J. (1995). *International organizations: Principles and issues* (6th ed.). Englewood Cliffs, NJ: Prentice Hall.

Brozska, M., Ehrhart, H.-G., & Narten, J. (Eds.). (2011). *Multi-stakeholder security partnerships: A critical assessment with case studies from Afghanistan, DR Congo and Kosovo*. Baden-Baden, Germany: Nomos Verlagsgesellschaft.

Bureau of Democracy, Human Rights, and Labor, U.S. Department of State. (2000). *Voluntary principles on security and human rights,* Bureau of Democracy, Human Rights, and Labor, U.S. Department of State, Washington.

Chandra, K. (2008). *Responsibility to the future: Business, peace, sustainability,* Conference Report, Strategic Foresight Group, 26–28 June, Mumbai, India.

Claude, I. (1971). *Swords into plowshares* (4th ed.). London: University of London Press.

Emmerij, L., Jolly, R., & Weiss, T. (2001). *Ahead of the curve?: UN ideas and global challenges*. Bloomington, IN: Indiana University Press.

Goldstein, J., & Keohane, R. (1993). *Ideas and foreign policy: Beliefs, institutions, and political change*. Ithaca, NY: Cornell University Press.

Haas, E. (1990). *When knowledge is power: Three models of change in international organizations*. Berkeley: University of California Press.

Haas, P. (1992). Introduction: Epistemic communities and international policy coordination. *International Organization, 46*(1), 1–35.

Haufler, V. (2015). Orchestrating peace? Civil war, conflict minerals and the United Nations Security Council. In K. Abbott, et al. (Eds.), *International organizations as orchestrators* (pp. 214–236). Cambridge: Cambridge University Press.

Keiai University. (2010). *United Nations global compact business and peace workshop: How business can contribute to peace and development through multi-stakeholder collaboration,* United Nations Global Compact Business and Peace Workshop, 25–26 April, 2010, Organized by Global Compact Network Japan, University of Tokyo and Keiai University. Available: http://www.unglobalcompact.kr/wp/wp-content/uploads/2014/03/20100331_BP_Programme.pdf (visited 27 February 2017).

Mattli, W., & Seddon, J. (2015). Orchestration along the Pareto frontier: Winners and losers. In K. Abbott, et al. (Eds.), *International organizations as orchestrators* (pp. 314–348). Cambridge: Cambridge University Press.

Michel, J. (2001). *DAC guidelines: Helping prevent violent conflict, organization of economic cooperation and development*. Paris: OECD Publications.

Shaw, M. (2008). *International Law* (6th ed.). Cambridge: Cambridge University Press.

Shearer, I. (1994). *Starke's international law* (11th ed.). London: Butterworths.

Shoji, M. (2012a). 'Research note; business and peace project of Columbia University,' Peace activities and the United Nations: Focusing on the interrelationship among conflict, movement of people, and governance, 『科研費報告書』 *KAKEN Report,* 21200047, University of Tokyo, Tokyo.

Shoji, M. (2012b). The United Nations global compact and peace: Guidance on responsible business in conflict-affected and high-risk areas: A resource for companies and investors. *The Keiai Journal of International Studies, 25,* 135–159.

Thakur, R., Cooper, A., & English, J. (Eds.). (2000). *International commissions and the power of ideas*. Tokyo: United Nations University Press.

The Japan Association for United Nations Studies. (2002). 『グローバルアクターとしての国連事務局』 *The United Nations secretariat as a global actor*. Tokyo: Kokusai Shoin.

Uhlin, A. (2010). Democratic legitimacy of transnational actors: Mapping out the conceptual terrain. In E. Emran & A. Uhlin (Eds.), *Legitimacy beyond the state?: Re-examining the democratic credentials of transnational actors*. Basingstoke, UK: Palgrave Macmillan.

United Nations Global Compact Office. (2007). *Report of the informal consultation with the institutional investor and business communities: Responsible investment in weak or conflict-prone states*. New York: United Nations Global Compact Office.

United Nations Global Compact Office. (2008). *Launch of global compact network Sudan, meeting report*, United Nations Global Compact Office, New York.

United Nations Global Compact Office. (2010). *Guidance on responsible business in conflict-affected and high-risk areas: a resource for companies and investors*. New York: United Nations Global Compact Office.

United Nations Global Compact Office. (2013a). *Business for peace*. New York: United Nations Global Compact Office.

United Nations Global Compact Office. (2013b). *Responsible peace advancing peace examples from companies, investors & global compact local networks*. New York: United Nations Global Compact Office.

United Nations Peacebuilding Commission. (2007). *Provisional guidelines for the participation of civil society in meetings of the Peacebuilding Commission, PBC/1/OC/12*. New York: United Nations Peacebuilding Commission.

United Nations Security Council. (2004). *Role of civil society in post-conflict peace building, S/PV.4993*, United Nations Security Council, New York.

United Nations Security Council. (2005). *The role of civil society in conflict prevention and the pacific settlement of dispute, S/PV.5264*, United Nations Security Council, New York.

United Nations Security Council. (2006). *S/2006/507*. New York: United Nations Security Council.

Wallace Aramian, C. (2008). *Doing business in a multi-cultural world: Challenges and opportunities*. New York: United Nations Alliance of Civilization & United Nations Global Compact Office, United Nations.

Weiss, T., & Thakur, R. (2010). *Global governance and the UN*. Bloomington, IN: Indiana University Press.

Yokota, Y. (2015).「国際機構の歴史的発展と現況」 International organizations: Historical development and present condition. In S. Watanabe & Y. Mochizuki (Eds.), 『国際機構論[総合編]』 *International organizations: A comprehensive study* (pp. 13–40). Kokusai Shoin, Tokyo.

Mariko Shoji is a professor in the Department of International Studies at Keiai University, where she specialises in international organisations, law and politics. She is the Committee member for Academic Exchange and Cooperation of the Japan Association for United Nations Studies (JAUNS), and an executive board member of the Japan Association of Global Governance since 2011. She also serves in the executive board of the JAUNS. She was a chief editor of the JAUNS from 2009 to 2010. She is a member of International Exchange Committee of the Japanese Association of International Relations (JAIR) and a representative of JAIR to the World International Studies Committee (WISC). She presided the United Nations Global Compact Business and Peace Workshop: Business' contribution to Peace and Development through Multi-stakeholder Collaboration with the United Nations Global Compact Office in 2010. Since 2011, she has been serving as a member of the expert meeting of "Business of Peace" of the UN Global Compact.

Transnational Corporations' Social License to Operate—The Third Facet of Corporate Governance

Indrajit Dube

1 Introduction

The decline of colonialism and post-war growth accelerated transnational investments. Many states integrated their economy with the international order to achieve sustainable growth in the national economy. Countries realigned and redefined their trade policies to participate and attract the foreign/overseas investments. Different international and regional economy groups were created to facilitate and strengthen this process. The initial objectives of these international and regional groups were to secure foreign investment in host countries and to receive equal treatment with domestic players. These groups helped host countries to develop economic and business policies, business infrastructure, regulatory institutions, and legal frameworks to facilitate foreign investment. Evidence suggests that foreign investment contributed strongly to the inclusive development of many host countries. To that end, the Trans-National Corporations (TNCs) were a preferred vehicle for foreign investment. The initial attraction of these companies was to source cheap raw material and competitive labour to maximise profit. While TNCs operations were mostly within transnational business operations at the primary stage of globalisation, they became the vital actors in global policy framing. The global economy provides an opportunity for TNCs to leverage their strength.

I. Dube (✉)
Rajiv Gandhi School of Intellectual Property Law,
Indian Institute of Technology, Kharagpur 721302, India
e-mail: indrajit@rgsoipl.iitkgp.ac.in

© Springer Nature Switzerland AG 2019
M. M. Rahim (ed.), *Code of Conduct on Transnational Corporations*,
CSR, Sustainability, Ethics & Governance,
https://doi.org/10.1007/978-3-030-10816-8_6

2 Guidelines for TNCs

The post-World War II economy witnessed an increased movement of FDI through the investments of TNCs, which served as the drivers of economic growth. TNCs established their headquarters and operations in multiple countries. Sauvant (2015, p. 64) notes that 'the number of TNCs headquartered in developed countries had risen from at least 7000 in the late 1960s, to at least 24,000 as of 1990, to over 70,000 at the end of 2010... over 100,000. TNCs controlled over 1 million foreign affiliates at the end of 2010' (see generally, 'World Investment Report 2011: Non-Equity Modes of International Production and Development', 2011). They were not only involved in the trade but also established production facilities that influenced the social fabric of their host countries and increasingly contributed to the development of host countries. This also led to a potential increase in conflict with host countries and produced several negative impacts (see Coonrod 1977, p. 278), which triggered regulatory concerns. The key question was whether TNCs would be regulated by their country of origin or their host countries.

The 1970s and 1980s saw a serious attempt to negotiate the interests of transnational corporations within different economic blocks. By this time there were three distinct economic blocks,[1] i.e. developed economy, socialist economy, and developing economy (see Sauvant 2015, p. 20). Each block demonstrated different characteristics relating to the operation of inbound and outbound TNCs. Developed economies had multifaceted concerns regarding outbound investment through their TNCs (see generally, Coonrod 1977, p. 285). These included the protection of investment; fair and equitable treatment of investors and investment; effective, adequate compensation upon expropriation; and the right to repatriate profit (Sauvant 2015, p. 22). The often weak and not necessarily impartial judiciaries or dispute settlement bodies in developing economies (countries) and reluctance towards applications of international investment rules added to the complexity of the problem for developed economies (countries). Socialist economies were rigid regarding inbound foreign investment in the domestic market, and they had very few TNCs invested in other countries. Most of these TNCs were under the direct control of the Government. The operation of TNCs did not significantly impact these economies, but they were interested in contributing to the international politics surrounding the issue (Sauvant 2015, p. 21). Developing economies comprised mostly decolonised economies struggling to strengthen and consolidate their domestic economy. Their ambition for growth was fuelled by Transnational Investment/Foreign Direct Investment (FDI) on mineral acquisitions, manufacturing, and low-end labour-intensive jobs. During this period, developing economies were overwhelmed by FDI flow from developed economies, leading to competition

---

[1] These economic blocks indicate groups of countries with similar national economy conditions.

amongst developing economies to secure regulatory concessions to strengthen the flow of FDI. Typically, the national government was too weak or disparate to attract FDI or too dependent on corporate contribution: 'the complexity of many firms' global operations has made it increasingly difficult for national governments to monitor and address a wide range of problems, from tax evasion to anti-competitive practices' (Anderson 2006, p. 7). Developing economies lobbied for more flexible national policy regarding FDI flow and transnationally binding guidelines to protect against the negative effects of FDI. Developing economies had extremely limited outbound TNCs during this period (see Sauvant 2015, p. 21).

2.1 Approaches at the Domestic Level

Developed economies (countries) attempted to frame domestic laws to regulate the affairs of their TNCs in host countries. The primary concern was not related to the negative impact of TNCs in the host country, but rather the effects of the economy of developed countries.[2] However, the corporate community[3] viewed these regulations as an infringement on their freedom of profit from different sources. Broad and Cavanagh (1999, p.24) note, '... on four occasions over the past decade, the U.S. Congress has passed legislation linking trade and investment privileges to respect for worker rights. First, in 1984, the U.S. Generalized System of Preferences, whereby many goods from the Third World entered the United States without paying tariffs, was amended so that if a country was found to be violating internationally-recognised worker rights, it could be denied the duty-free benefits. Similar amendments were attached to the Overseas Private Investment Corporation, the Caribbean Basin Initiative, and the Trade Act of 1988.' Choice of host countries by TNCs was based on several factors (see generally, Ghemawat n.d.) such as economic advantage, arbitration among alternate regulations, economic requirements, availability of natural resources for manufacturing inputs, low environmental compliance, and cost-effective labour force. Developing host economies typically had weak and inefficient governance systems, and TNCs were typically more powerful than the Government in power in these countries. This made it difficult for developing economies to manage the activities of TNCs (Scherer et al. 2006, p. 508) and their influence on social, economic, and political spheres (see generally, Coonrod 1977, p. 278).

---

[2]Issues like transfer pricing, taxation, etc.
[3]TNCs.

2.2 Major Approaches at the International Level

2.2.1 UN Code for Transnational Corporations

The failure of domestic regulation of TNCs led to a unified call for a United Nations Code of Conduct for TNCs from different economic blocks. Sauvant noted, "TNCs were seen as having a substantial impact on individual national economies and international economic relations, and there were widespread suspicions that—given the global profit maximising strategies of TNCs' versus national development objectives of governments—this impact was negative in terms of distribution of benefits and the ability of indigenous firms to grow and prosper.' In 1975 the United Nations formed a Commission on Transnational Corporations (UNCTC) and entrusted with the mandate to negotiating a 'UN Code of Conduct on Transnational Corporations' (Broad and Cavanagh 1999, p. 18). The UNCTC became operational on 1st November 1975 by a resolution of the United Nations Economy and Social Council (adopted through resolution 1908 (LVII) on August 2, 1974) (Sauvant 2015, p. 13). The objectives of the United Nations Code include social and political issues (respect for national sovereignty and observance of domestic laws, regulations and administrative practices; hearings of economy goals and development objectives, policies and priorities, adherence to social-cultural objectives and values; respect for human rights and fundamental freedoms); economic and financial issues (ownership and control; balance of payment and taxation; transfer pricing; technology transfer; competition and restrictive business practices) and disclosure of information (general treatment of TNCs by the countries in which they operate; nationalisation and compensation; jurisdiction; international institutional machinery) (see also, Broad and Cavanagh 1999, p. 18; Sauvant 2015, p. 41; see generally, 'UN Intellectual History Project' 2009, p. 1).

The negotiation within the intergovernmental working group on the code of conduct began in January 1977, with a total of 17 sessions. The working group submitted a draft Code of Conduct for TNCs with brackets indicating unsolved issues and alternative text (Sauvant 2015, p. 38). The negotiation attempted to deal with a large number of complex issues and to involve a range of countries, with mixed success. To quote Sten Niklasson, the Chair of the working group: 'as it played out in reality, most things happened more or less simultaneously and in great haste. Many countries came to meetings of the Commission and Working Group having but the faintest idea of the practical issues to be tackled'. In the initial part of the negotiation, the legal nature of the code and implementation mechanisms was not the primary focus. However, during the progress of negotiation, it became clear that the code should provide a balanced mechanism to control the behaviour of TNCs and government treatment of TNCs. Sauvant (2015, p. 43) records that developing countries could achieve '…[a]dherence to economic goals and development objectives, policies and priorities; adherence to socio-cultural objectives and values; respect for human rights and fundamental freedoms; non-collaboration by transnational corporations with racist minority regimes in South Africa; ownership and control; competition and restrictive business practices; consumer protection; and disclosure of information. In case of other topics, certain aspects were agreed upon (e.g. some issues relating to balance of payments and financing; transfer of technology) or depended on resolution of provisions elsewhere in the instrument (e.g. renegotiation of contracts).'

Developed countries were not in principle against the code negotiated, but they rejected any change in the customary international (investment) law (Sauvant 2015, p. 45). There was an undercurrent during this process about the legal nature of the code, as there was no clarity regarding the implementation of the code. During the negotiation, several other issues were raised relating to international law/obligations, fair and equitable treatment, nationalisation and compensation, jurisdictional settlement of disputes, and respect for national sovereignty. It was particularly difficult for developing countries to protect their interests against developed countries. Subsequently, from 1983 to 1990 there was a special session of the Commission on Transnational Corporations open to participation from all states to resolve these issues. However, no further progress was made during this time. In 1991 the United State Government sent messages to the embassies of countries abroad to lobby for the termination of the negotiated code, 'we believe that the Code is a relic of another era when the foreign direct investment was looked upon with considerable concern. The code does not reflect the current investment policies of many developing countries.... In light of the above, Washington agencies have decided to seek the support of host government officials responsible for foreign investment and quietly build a consensus against further negotiation.... We stress that the Demarche should be given to officials responsible for investment not/not those responsible for UN affairs' (Sauvant 2015, p. 54).

Due to lobbying by the United States and the United Kingdom in addition to nonparticipation of eastern countries, the negotiation failed to conclude on the remaining points. The President of the UN General Assembly reported in September 1992 that, 'it was the view of the delegation that no consensus was possible on the draft code at present. The delegation felt that the changed economic environment and the importance attached to encourage foreign investment required that a fresh approach should be examined...' (Sauvant p. 55). At the nineteenth session of the Commission of Transnational Corporations, it was recommended that the United Nations Economy and Social Council (ECOSOC) adopt a resolution to take note of the result of the draft negotiation. This formally ended the commission's work to create an International Code on Transnational Corporations. Although an implementable code could not be negotiated, the entire exercise brought an immense understanding of the complexities of TNCs regarding their ownership structure and business models. It was also clear that the core objectives of TNCs were business risk management through territorial expansion and maximising profit, which facilitated rapid movement of funds within TNC networks, further exacerbating impacts on the economies of host countries.[4] The author believes that negotiation failed to capture the finer micro level regulatory and political issues.

2.2.2 OECD Guidelines on Transnational Corporations

Regional groups like the Organisation for Economic Cooperation and Development (OECD) created the accepted norms to facilitate capital movement. The 1961 Code of Liberalisation of Capital Movements facilitated capital movement within developed countries. To build further efficiency in capital movement and transnational investment, in 1976 the OECD developed the Guideline for Multinational Enterprises.[5] In 1975 the OECD Governing body, the Council of Ministers, established a committee on International Investment and Multinational Enterprises (IME Committee) with the mandate to prepare a proposal for voluntary guidelines for an enterprise to engage in transnational investment. This includes the development of uniform standards of behaviour applicable to Transnational Corporations (see generally, Rojot 1985). In 1976, the Council of Ministers adopted the proposals prepared by the IME Committee, issuing the 'Declaration Principles', which had two basic objectives. The first objective was 'to encourage the positive contribution multinational enterprises can make to economic and social progress and to minimise and resolve the difficulties to which their various operation may give rise' and the second objective was to prevent differential treatment between multinational and domestic enterprises (Hägg 1984, p. 72).

The OECD is widely viewed as a club of developed countries, and these 'Declaration Principles' mainly evolved to protect the common interests of this economy block. It attempted to guide TNCs to align their activities with the economic goals of the host country and to encourage accommodating treatment by the host country. Interestingly, the guidelines were not intended to address complex tasks such as defining 'multinational enterprises'; however, TNCs were entrusted with the responsibilities of their subsidiaries and the group companies (Hägg 1984, p. 72). Furthermore, the guidelines stipulated that TNCs should not be given any responsibility than their counterparts (i.e. domestic companies) did not have in the host country. Guidelines on the disclosure of information were a significant milestone in the development of guidelines on TNCs. The guidelines proposed that a regular financial statement and pertinent information relating to the principal activities of TNCs (including their affiliates, subsidiaries, and group companies) should be published at least once a year (Rojot 1985, p. 73). Intra-group transfer

---

[4]When TNCs move funds (read as Capital) from one country to another country, the exit country stands to lose local liquidity, employment, and revenue (taxes), etc. On the other hand, during the TNCs' period of operation the exit country maximizes profit through consumption of local recourses and benefits.

[5]Read as Transnational Corporations.

pricing should also be disclosed as a part of the financial statement.[6] Guidelines on competition specified that TNCs should refrain from practices/actions that would adversely affect competition in the relevant market.[7] The financing guidelines emphasise that TNCs should manage their assets and liability according to the established objectives of the host country. The guidelines also attempted to deal with the complexity of 'transfer pricing' and taxation issues. TNCs practised 'transfer pricing' to gain a competitive advantage in the market. On the issue of standards of employment, the guidelines proposed that TNCs should conduct a similar kind of treatment to that of another employer in the host country: "it is said that enterprises should not in bona fide negotiations with representatives of employees 'threaten to utilise a capacity to transport the whole or part of an operation unit from country concerned in order to influence unfairly those negotiations'" (Hägg 1984). Guidelines on science and technology emphasised that TNCs should take serious steps to distribute research and development activities within the countries of their operation (Hägg 1984, p. 75).

The guidelines were purely voluntary. Over time, the guidelines became more dynamic and flexible to adapt to changing domestic and international investment needs. The guidelines were subjected to several revisions in the years 1979, 1984, 1991, and 2000 (Melgar et al. 2011, p. 10). Several emergent issues were incorporated, including key concepts and principles, human rights, combatting bribery, bribe solicitations and extortion, and consumer interest. Some guidelines were dropped due to a lack of clarity. Procedural revisions included the possibility for non-governmental organisations and the public to formally bring concerns about a company regarding compliance of the guidelines to 'National Contact Points' (NCP). However, this procedural revision failed to live up to the expectations of stakeholders (Melgar et al. 2011, p. 11).

2.2.3 ILO Guidelines on Transnational Corporations

Another United Nation agency, the International Labour Organisation (ILO), began a similar exercise to protect the rights of the workforce within TNCs. Traditionally in a single enterprise model, a company developed social policies (read as workforce welfare) for application within the organisation. With the emergence of the global economy, transnational corporations began to operate through subsidiaries, supply contractor licenses, strategic alliances, and joint ventures. TNCs have inherent limitations preventing the implementation of social policies as a single enterprise (Diller 2000). To address this gap, ILO pioneered international public regulations related to multinational corporations concerning the workforce and labour. ILO relied on the effectiveness of a consensus building approach amongst

---

[6]This is a contentious problem regarding TNC operation and is further examined in the chapter discussing competition and taxation.
[7]This includes abusing a dominant position of market power.

the tripartite members, namely, government, workers, and employers. In contrast to other multilateral systems, the legal text of ILO, including constitutional amendments, conventions, recommendations, and declarations, are adopted in votes in which government voting power is matched by combined votes of workers and employers (Diller 2000; see, Sauvant 2015, p. 30).

ILO adopted the 'Declaration on Principles Concerning Multinational Enterprise and Social Policy' in 1977[8] based on general principles to 'obey national laws and regulations, give due consideration to local practices, and respect relevant international standards.' The principles relied on the promotion of employment, security of employment, equality of opportunity and treatment, training, conditions of work and life, and industrial relations. It also covered matters relating to joint ventures, contractual relationships with suppliers or licensees, and private policies of local operations. However, transparency in the decision-making process was not evident. Accountability was equally elusive in the context of social commitment and improvement (see generally, Diller 2000).

2.3 Responsibility of Business to Uphold the Human Rights—UN Initiative

But the hind side of this economic integration though TNCs surfaced with the reports of instances of human rights violations (see generally, *Summary Report on Geneva Consultations, Geneva, Switzerland, December 4–5, 2007, Corporate Responsibility to Respect Human Rights* n.d.).

The challenges of regulating TNCs are multi-faceted and dynamic due to the evolving business models of TNCs.[9] In addition to human rights violation cases, these challenges include corruption in the bureaucratic system of many host countries, ineffective enforcement mechanisms and lack of competent dispute resolution systems for individual grievances, and exploiting resources[10] in the name of protectionism. Among all other sectors oil, gas, and mining dominate the accounts of human rights abuses. The office of the UN High Commission for Human Rights conducted a study in support of The Special Representative of the UN Secretary-General on Business and Human Rights (SRSG) to analyse more than 300 corporate human right abuses from all sectors. The initial findings identified that companies are accused of negative impacts on a full range of human rights (*Summary Report on Geneva Consultations, Geneva, Switzerland, December 4–5, 2007, Corporate Responsibility to Respect Human Rights* n.d., p. 2).

Extensive consultations by the SRSG revealed different facets of business human rights. A number of participants in the consultation suggested that the companies

---

[8]Since adoption, addendums were added in 1987 and 1995.
[9]Conducting business through associates, alliances, joint ventures, and supply chains.
[10]Natural and human resources.

(read TNCs) might exercise greater control of extended business associates and supply chains when they enter a contractual relationship. Companies should acknowledge human rights violations committed by their associates and document measure undertaken to prevent such violations. The consultation argued in favour of the incorporation of a human right clause in the business contract. (*Summary Report on Geneva Consultations, Geneva, Switzerland, December 4–5, 2007, Corporate Responsibility to Respect Human Rights* n.d., p. 8).

The "Protect, Respect, and Remedy" framework of the SRSG rests on three pillars. The first is the state duty to protect against human right abuses by third parties, including business enterprise through appropriate policies, regulations, and adjudication. Secondly, companies have a responsibility to respect human rights, which means business enterprises should act with due diligence to avoid infringement on the rights of others and to address adverse impacts in which they are involved. The third is greater access by victims to effective remedy, both judicial and non-judicial (Human Rights Council, United Nations 2011). These guiding principles were not intended to stipulate a new international order but to elaborate on existing standards and practices for states and businesses and integrate them into a logical and comprehensive template.

The operation of TNCs has impacted nearly the entire spectrum of internationally recognised human rights. Some human rights may be at greater risk, particularly in industrial operations. The responsibility of TNCs to respect human rights stand separate from the issues of legal liability, which is defined mostly by national law in the relevant jurisdictions. TNCs need to consider high standards within their operations, while circumstances demand, to uphold and respect individual's human rights (Human Rights Council, United Nations 2011, p. 14).

TNCs have a responsibility to respect human right in the conduct of all business wherever they operate. Their responsibility stands irrespective of a state's ability or willingness to discharge human rights obligations. This responsibility exists over and above the compliance of national law relating to the protection of human rights. TNCs may need to consider additional standards relating to human rights for specific groups in addition to protecting the rights of woman, children, persons with disabilities, indigenous people, ethnic groups, religious and linguistic minorities, and migrant workers and their families (Human Rights Council, United Nations 2011, p. 14). TNCs should publicly announce their responsibility expectations and commitment to uphold human rights (Human Rights Council, United Nations 2011, p. 15).

3 TNCs Towards Social Sustainability

Social sustainability aims to identify and manage business impacts on the people either positively or negatively. Company engagement with stakeholders is a critical aspect of socially sustainable business practices. It is important for TNCs to manage their business impact proactively, including employees, workers in the supply chain, customers, and local communities. TNCs' social license to operate largely depends on their efforts towards social sustainability.

The United Nations Global Compact Principles is an initiative of the UN Secretary 'to give a human face to globalisation'. The Compact address the environment, human rights, and worker rights, uniting global principles with local networks to create fluid networks. The Compact is a global multi-stakeholder, multi-issue network with more than 40 regional and national-sub networks. As a voluntary initiative, the Global Compact includes all key social actors: companies, labour, civil society organisations and Government (Leipziger 2015; see United Nations Global Compact, The UN Global Compact Ten Principles and Sustainable Development Goals: Connecting, Crucially).[11] The principles cover social sustainability specific to labour, women empowerment and gender equality, children, indigenous people, people with disabilities, and employ a people-centric approach to eradicating property. The primary responsibility to protect human rights lies with the government, but business (read as TNCs) should undertake proper care to avoid harming human rights. Also, businesses should take adequate steps to improve the lives of stakeholders by creating jobs, goods, and services that meet their basic needs and initiate social investment that supports social sustainability.

The 2003 Equator Principles introduced a different dimension to TNC operation by offering investment guidelines for financial institutions.[12] The principles advocate that creditors must conduct a social and environmental assessment before lending money for projects to a particular company. The principles state: 'we will not provide loans to projects where the borrower will not or is unable to comply with our respective social and environmental policies and procedures that implement the Equator principles' (Leipziger 2015, p. 426). The principles additionally contain measures for addressing grievances. The principles provide illustrative lists of potential social and environmental issues, including consideration of visible environment and socially preferable alternatives; observed host country laws and regulations; protection of human rights and community health, safety, and security; protection of cultural property and heritage; socio-economic impacts of business; and pollution prevention and waste minimisation.

On a similar understanding, the 2005 Principles for Responsible Investment [PRI] was developed by an international group of institutional investors and overseen by the United Nations Secretary-General. The initial focus of the PRI was on 'innovation, collaboration, and learning by doing.' It provided guidelines for investors regarding how to incorporate Environmental and Social Governance in investment decision-making. The six principles of PRI are based on environmental, social, and corporate governance issues that impact the performance portfolio across companies, sectors, regions, and asset class. It is an excellent example of

---

[11]https://www.unglobalcompact.org/docs/about_the_gc/White_Paper_Principles_SDGs.pdf (last visited Jan 13, 2017).

[12]The principles were revised in 2006 based on experience of its operation and stakeholder inputs (see www.equator-principles.com).

how principles can provide clarity and momentum and implement systematic change in the process of corporate function. PRI requires commitment from top leadership within the investment bodies, which is critical for effecting change within the organisation and other companies. There are three categories of signatories in PRI, namely asset owners, investment managers, and professional service partners (see generally, Leipziger 2015, p. 437). The PRI also works synergistically with a range of other initiatives, including the UN Global Compact and the UN Environment Programme. The strength of the PRI lies in transparent reporting which includes data on how the signatories are implementing the principles. Like the Equator Principles, PRI also underwent rapid modification as business practices evolved. This significant initiative further created a 'clearinghouse', an online platform for collaboration between the signatories.

3.1 Social Sustainability Through Mutually Accepted Trust-Based Guidelines

The core of the above international attempts was to ensure that TNCs adopt socially responsible and sustainable business operations. The relentless search for efficiency was the biggest allegation against TNCs, wherein they hollowed out industries in different countries by moving capital and technology to places where the labour is cheaper (Zinkin 2004). The guiding principles developed by different international and regional groups relied upon the concept of responsible corporate citizenship. From 1990, the term 'corporate citizen' was increasingly used in management texts to replace "business ethics" and "corporate social responsibility". The principles focus on the rights and responsibilities of all stakeholders, which are mutually interlinked and dependent on each other (Matten et al. 2003). The principles heralded an important transition in TNC governance from the development of mutually accepted guidelines to a trust-based approach to secure recognition or licence from the society in which it operates. The push for this transition was the role of TNCs in the process of designing global rules[13] and implementing citizenship rights. Matten et al. (2003) argue that if terms "such as a 'Corporate Citizenship' make any sense in the proper meaning of the term, Corporation and Citizenship in modern society come together at exactly the point where the state ceases to be the only guarantor of citizenship any longer. Seen in another light, it could be hypothesised that Corporations are compensating or correcting for Government failure." This transition enlarged the role of TNCs beyond the sole responsibility of the state (see generally Scherer et al. 2006, p. 515). TNCs should be proactive to enable, protect, and implement citizen's rights particularly in situations in which the state withdraws or has withdrawn these rights; the state has not yet implemented basic citizen rights; or the state is principally unable to do so (see

---

[13]Developed guidelines for all subsidiaries and associates of TNCs.

generally, Matten et al. 2003; Scherer et al. 2006, p. 515). In installing this trust, TNCs with different origins adopted various approaches. Western TNCs positioned themselves as socially responsible entities aiming for high-efficiency and world-class performance. Eastern TNCs expressed their goal to build world-class organisations without sacrificing relevant social dimensions (see, Zinkin 2004).

Understanding the social dimensions of TNCs in the context of Social License to Operate (SLO) has expanded over recent years. Non-state actors and citizen representatives became the key negotiators in this process. Negotiations include issues related to environmental compliance (see generally, Dube 2010); corporate conduct not in conformity with ethical production; activity against cultural integrity; descriptive marketing (including baby food formula to abandon breastfeeding); protection of women's rights; the abolition of child labour; recognising the ancient right of the local people; and enforcement of business human rights. Various states brought changes in the philosophy of domestic laws to provide relevant support to the process of negotiation and strengthened the position of non-state actors in this regard. The philosophical shift in domestic laws was implemented through different approaches. Firstly, the positive responsibility of the Board of Directors was specified. Secondly, the responsibility of shareholders was extended (see Afsharipour, Benefit Corporation). Mickels (2009) notes that 'socially responsible business and social enterprises in the US are catalysing a wave towards a new type of "hybrid" organization.... Businesses today are dedicating more resources than ever to providing social and environmental benefits. Similarly, government and social-sector organizations are beginning to emulate for-profit business by adopting earning-income governance models as a way to acquire the necessary capital to sustain their social mission'. Thirdly, newer development in the domain of Corporate Social Responsibility in China, Indonesia, and India has also facilitated this shift (see generally, Dube 2016).

3.2 Social Sustainability Through 'Social Licence to Operate'

The 'Social Licence to Operate' (SLO) emerged as a business concept in the 1990s to mitigate conflicts between local communities and businesses in the mining industry (Prno and Slocombe 2014). These conflicts included demands from the local population for a greater share of benefits, more involvement of local representatives in the decision-making process, and enhanced protection of health and the environment. Increased stress on 'Sustainable Development' where non-state actors are perceived to have an important role in governance decision-making contributed to the adoption of SLO. Recently, SLO has gained popularity within different business segments beyond mining, including agriculture, energy, manufacturing, pharmaceutical, telecommunication, and transport. The core of SLO is Polanyi's concept of social recognition of business.

In 1939 Karl Polanyi, a European—US Economist, emphasised the need to change the relationship between the economy and society. He viewed the economic process as consisting of social relations, shared rules, and beliefs (Maucourant and Plociniczak 2013, p. 514). Businesses developed as part of the economic process as an embodiment of social purpose. Therefore, a business must receive social recognition to establish legitimacy. Polanyi was not comfortable with the capitalist movement and the demand for business self-regulation. He interpreted laws on public health, factory conditions, labour unions, social insurance, public utilities, municipal services, and trade union rights as countervailing measures to check business dominance over the society (Maucourant and Plociniczak 2013, p. 516). Polanyi believed that social actors spontaneously respond through social movement against alleged self-regulation of business, leading to the development of a counter-movement in the form of social resistance. This tension arises due to organising principles of modern society, i.e. economic liberalism and social embeddedness (Maucourant and Plociniczak 2013, p. 519). As a result, Polanyi views the economy (i.e. business) as a natural social process (Maucourant and Plociniczak 2013, p. 522). The prime objective of a business is to satisfy human needs within the society.

Social dimensions in governance received increase focus to strick a balance between local expectations and cost to business through SLO. In fact, some countries including developing countries like India, have included these principles in corporation legislation. Directors' have the duty to protect the interests of the larger community is also incorporated into the Companies/Corporation Act and affirmed by various jurisdictions. Prominent examples of this approach are the United Kingdom, Australia, and India. Some states incorporate details of the responsibility of directors that were traditionally enforced under common-law and fiduciary duties. Other states provide guidelines about directors' duties. However, common factors regarding a director's positive responses to employees and customers are consistent across all states.

SLO principles complement the values of 'Enlightened Shareholder'. Enlightened Shareholder Value promotes the director's responsibility to regard the interests of employees, business relationships with suppliers, customers, and the impact of the corporate operation on the community and the environment. The director must uphold a high standard of business conduct. Although the director needs to promote the interests of shareholders, the interests of other groups upon whose activities the business of the company is dependent also be respected and protected. The director's actions should conform to the spectrum of stakeholder interests in conformity with the license to operate in a community (Dube 2011, p. 426).

Benefit Corporations Model in the United States are the result of a new generation of value-driven consumers and shareholders demanding that corporations deliver benefit to their communities (see generally, Hiller 2013). It is an another example of SLO. This approach attempted to develop alternative legal paradigms to meet the needs of social ventures. It conceived as a new class of organisation based on the philosophy of social purpose that seeks to be economically self-sustaining while also being social, ethically, and environmentally responsible. There are ten essential characteristics of a benefit corporation. These are a core commitment to a social purpose which is embedded in organisational philosophy and structure; freedom to engage in any legitimate business activity in pursuit of social goals; equitable distribution of ownership rights and distribution rights across all stakeholders; equitable compensation of employees, investors, and other stakeholder in proportion to their contribution and risk, subject to reasonable limitations that protect the ability of the organisation to achieve its mission; commitment of having a net positive social and environmental impact; commitment to accurate assessments and reporting of social, environmental, and financial performance; limited liability structure such that the directors of the organisation will not be held personally responsible for the action of the organisation (as long as the directors conduct any business activity that is consistent with its social purpose and stakeholder obligations); ability to accept debt and equity investment as well as tax deduction donations; and exemption on certain business taxes and lock on assets that prevent them from being privatised upon terminal event (Mickels 2009, p. 281). Benefit corporations are the classic example of seeking benefits not only for shareholders but also for all stakeholders.

The Corporate Social Responsibility movement reinforces the concept of social recognition of a business or license to operate. Several countries in South Asia have redefined the mandate of CSR for companies operating within their territory. Since 2004, CSR has been the focus of discussion at different policy forums in China. Chinese Company Law 2006, article 5 states that "[i]n the course of doing business, a company must comply with laws and administrative regulations, conform to social morality and business ethics, act in good faith, subject itself to the government and the public supervision, and undertake social responsibility" (Lin 2010). This requires companies to undertake social responsibility in the course of their business. Article 14 of the Corporation Law requires companies to comply with the law, conform to business ethics, and strengthen the construction of socialist civilisation. It also stipulates that companies should conduct their business under the supervision of the public and government. Public supervision may be understood as supervision by consumers, communities, and other stakeholders (see Lin 2010).

In 2007, the Indonesian Corporate Law No. 40 and Indonesian Investment Law provided a framework for CSR regulation in Indonesia. Article 15 of the 2007 Investment Law advocates that every corporation should implement corporate social and environmental responsibility: 'responsibly mounted in every investment company to keep creating relationship which is in harmony, in balance and sustainable to the local community's neighbourhood, values, norms and culture' (Waagstein 2011). The Article 75 of the '2007 Limited Liability Corporation Law' requires companies to create obligatory reserve funding to be spent on implementation of CSR, which can be considered as a corporate cost. The article proposed sanctions for failure to comply with such obligations. Article 74 creates provisions for mandatory CSR: '(i) companies doing business in the field of and/or in relation to natural resources must put into practice Environmental and Social Responsibility; (ii) the environmental and social responsibility contemplated in paragraph (i) constitute an obligation of the company which shall be budgeted for and calculating as a cost of the company performance of which shall be with due attention to decency and fairness; (iii) companies who do not put their obligation to practice as contemplated in paragraph (i) shall be liable to sanctions in accordance with legislative regulations; (iv) further provisions regarding environmental and social responsibility shall be stipulated by Government Regulations' (Waagstein 2011, p. 460). This mandatory nature of CSR supported by legal obligations is in contrast to the traditional voluntary statement of goodwill, the implementation of which is dependent on a corporation's strategy.

The Indian Companies Act 2013[14] incorporates a provision relating to a company's Corporate Social Responsibility in Section 135 such that: "(1) Every company having net worth of rupees five hundred crore or more, or turnover of rupees one thousand crore or more or a net profit of rupees five crore or more during any financial year shall constitute a Corporate Social Responsibility Committee of the Board consisting of three or more directors, out of which at least one director shall be an independent director; (2) The Board's report under sub-section (3) of Section 134 shall disclose the composition of the Corporate Social Responsibility Committee; (3) The Corporate Social Responsibility Committee shall (a) formulate and recommend to the Board, a Corporate Social Responsibility Policy which shall indicate the activities to be undertaken by the company as specified in Schedule VII; (b) recommend the amount of expenditure to be incurred on the activities referred to in clause (a); and (c) monitor the Corporate Social Responsibility Policy of the company from time to time; (4) The Board of every company referred to in sub-section (1) shall (a) after taking into account the recommendations made by the Corporate Social Responsibility Committee, approve the Corporate Social Responsibility Policy for the company and disclose contents of such Policy in its report and also place it on the company's website, if any, in such manner as may be prescribed; and (b) ensure that the activities as are included in Corporate Social Responsibility Policy of the company are undertaken by the company; (5) The Board of every company referred to in sub-section (1), shall ensure that the company spends, in every financial year, at least two per cent of the average net profits of the company made during the three immediately preceding financial years, in pursuance of its Corporate Social Responsibility Policy, provided that the company shall give preference to the local area and areas around it where it operates, for spending the amount earmarked for Corporate Social Responsibility activities, provided further that if the company fails to spend such amount, the Board shall, in its report made under clause (o) of sub-section (3) of section 134, specify the reasons for not spending the amount. For the purposes of this section 'average net profit' shall be calculated in accordance with the provisions of section 198" ('Companies Act 2013', n.d.). Further, Schedule VII stipulates that activities which may be included by companies in their Corporate Social Responsibility Policies Activities relate to: "(i) eradicating hunger, poverty and malnutrition, promoting

---

[14]This act replaced the Indian Companies Act 1956.

preventive health care and sanitation [including contribution to the Swach Bharat Kosh set-up by the Central Government for the promotion of sanitation] and making available safe drinking water; (ii) promoting education, including special education and employment enhancing vocation skills especially among children, women, elderly, and the differently abled and livelihood enhancement projects; (iii) promoting gender equality, empowering women, setting up homes and hostels for women and orphans; setting up old age homes, day care centres and such other facilities for senior citizens and measures for reducing inequalities faced by socially and economically backward groups; (iv) ensuring environmental sustainability, ecological balance, protection of flora and fauna, animal welfare, agroforestry, conservation of natural resources and maintaining quality of soil, air and water [including contribution to the Clean Ganga Fund set-up by the Central Government for rejuvenation of river Ganga]; (v) protection of national heritage, art and culture including restoration of buildings and sites of historical importance and works of art; setting up public libraries; promotion and development of traditional arts and handicrafts; (vi) measures for the benefit of armed forces veterans, war widows and their dependents; (vii) training to promote rural sports, nationally recognised sports, para-Olympic sports and Olympic sports; (viii) contribution to the Prime Minister's National Relief Fund or any other fund set up by the Central Government for socio-economic development and relief and welfare of the Scheduled Castes, the Scheduled Tribes, other backward classes, minorities and women; (ix) contributions or funds provided to technology incubators located within academic institutions which are approved by the Central Government; (x) rural development projects; (xi) slum area development (Notification No. 1/15/2013-CL.V 2.). This was substituted by Notification No. 1/15/2013-CL-V w.e.f. 1st April, 2014 regarding the following: "(i) eradicating extreme hunger and poverty; (ii) promotion of education; (iii) promoting gender equality and empowering women; (iv) reducing child mortality and improving maternal health; (v) combating human immunodeficiency virus, acquired immune deficiency syndrome, malaria and other diseases; (vi) ensuring environmental sustainability; (vii) employment enhancing vocational skills; (viii) social business projects; (ix) contribution to the Prime Minister's National Relief Fund or any other fund set up by the Central Government or the State Governments for socio-economic development and relief and funds for the welfare of the Scheduled Castes, the Scheduled Tribes, other backward classes, minorities and women; and (x) such other matters as may be prescribed" (Substituted by Notification From File No. 1/18/2013-CL-V Dated 06.08.2014 w.e.f. 01.04.2014.
4. Inserted vide Notification From File No. 1/18/2013-CL-V dated 24.10.2014. 'Companies Act 2013', n.d.). Section 135 provides the substantive law on CSR while Schedule VII explains the situations in which companies can undertake CSR activities. The act institutionalises CSR within companies by constituting a mandatory board committee which will be comprised of three or more directors, of which one director shall be an independent director (Sub-Section 1, Section 135 'Companies Act 2013', n.d.). Statutory CSR is only restricted to those companies having a net worth of rupees five hundred crores or more or turnover of rupees one thousand crores or more or a net profit of rupees five crores or more during any

financial year ('Companies Act 2013', n.d.). The committee responsible for formulating policies shall indicate the activities the company will undertake, expenditure for implementation of the activities, and propose the mechanism for monitoring the activities (Sub-Section 3, Section 135 'Companies Act 2013', n.d.). The Board must ensure that the company spends, 'in every financial year, at least two percent of the average net profits of the company made during the three immediately preceding financial years, in pursuance of its Corporate Social Responsibility Policy' (Sub-Section 5, Section 135 'Companies Act 2013', n.d.). The Board must also disclose the composition of the CSR committee and activities in the Board's report. Both the Section and the Schedule has undergone amendment under the New Government, with recent modification in 2014.

4 Conclusion

"Social" dimensions in governance have received increased focus[15] in order to strike a balance between local expectations and cost to business through SLO. Recently, the local community has typically emerged as a key arbitrator in this process because of their proximity to the project/business and their ability to affect the project outcome. The word 'license' in SLO has notional understanding instead of any legal significance. SLO, as perceived over the years, is not confined to a single definition but expands to fit different business segments, eras, societies, and legal regimes. Therefore, SLO continues as a concept associated with a spectrum of understanding. It may involve a business gaining the confidence and trust of society through their transparent, accountable, legitimate and socially acceptable method of business operation. There may be an unwritten agreement between the business and society for approval of their business operation. Often SLO is a project or is location specific, and the local communities are the 'key negotiator' to the activity of companies and their associated effects. The relationship between the parties of the agreement relies on trust, consistency, quality of information being provided, and flexibility received from all parties. SLO is difficult to earn and easily lost. In many societies/legal regimes, SLO is an integral part of Corporate Social Responsibility. Today, SLO is significant regarding the achievement of sustainable goals for societies across the world.

Social confidence in business has been shaken time and again due to the role of large corporations (Transnational Corporations) and their influence on the global financial system. This concern has been echoed in a social resistance movement protesting the disproportionate benefit to a group of people (who are in the minority) due to the concentration of wealth and economic/financial power of corporations (companies). The slogan coined in protest against this disproportionate benefit is 'we are 99%'. While many observed the slogan as indicative of a radical

---

[15]As Karl Polanyi advocated.

movement, this resistance movement actively draws attention to the need for greater ethics, accountability, and transparency from the business community in this increasingly connected global business environment. There is a need for greater transparency as business operations increasingly migrate from local to global platforms, with correspondingly higher expectations from global consumers. Non-state actors such as NGOs or financial institutions are likewise aligning their activity towards sustainable goals. This means that SLO is no longer an option but a requirement for business.

It is arguable that the seed of SLO slowly germinated in the post-war economy with the migration from a national to a global economy. The transnational economy became the norm.[16] The carrier of the transnational economy was Transnational Corporations (TNC). This economic transition created tension between business wealth creation and societal expectations. Several attempts have been made in different forums to mitigate this tension. Understanding of the issues and the mitigation processes move through several phases of argument, namely counter-argument, agreement—disagreement, and definition of acceptable procedures of accepted norms by involved parties. In all these attempts the core was Polanyi's argument of social recognition of the business. These attempts were reflected in UN agencies and regional groups conclaves, conferences, and incorporation of specialised agencies to frame Guidelines for Transnational Corporation (TNCs) with the underlying notion of aligning TNCs operation with national policies and societal expectations. Over time, new frontiers of tensions were recognised, and a new standard was developed through a bilateral agreement between countries in continuation with the transnational guideline developed and updated by different agencies. The guidelines advocate for the positive responsibility of TNCs to society; however, the response by TNCs typically fell short of social expectation. Today, societal expectations are enforced through SLO either by negotiation or legal sanctions.

The seamless integration of national economies within the global order has increased the transnational movement of TNCs from all economic blocks. To date, it is widely accepted that no economy can prosper in isolation. Therefore, the regulatory focus has shifted towards SLO. The majority of countries, utilizing either soft or hard laws, ensure that the community's preferences are considered in corporate policy—and decision-making. To achieve this, some countries impose positive responsibility on company directors, and others mandate spending of a percentage of corporate profit on the development of social infrastructure. This mandatory spending may be imposed on classes of corporations with specific net worth or financial turnover. Thus, the Social License to Operate (SLO) has developed as the third facet of governance for TNCs by means of this formal arrangement. This governance arrangement empowers society to determine the extent, and types of social benefit TNCs need to extend to the community.

---

[16]Though there was initial resistance from different quarters.

References

Anderson, S. (2006, December). International Regulation of Transnational Corporations. Retrieved 1 August 2016, from: http://www.policyinnovations.org/ideas/policy_library/data/01311/_res/id=sa_File1/

Broad, R., & Cavanagh, J. (1999). Corporate accountability movement: Lessons & opportunities. *The Fletcher Forum of World Affairs, 23,* 151.

Companies Act 2013. (n.d.). Retrieved 14 January 2016, from http://www.mca.gov.in/Ministry/pdf/CompaniesAct2013.pdf

Coonrod, S. (1977). United Nations code of conduct for transnational corporations. *Harvard International Law Journal, 18,* 273.

Diller, J. M. (2000). Social conduct in transnational enterprise operations: the role of the International Labour Organization. *Multinational enterprises and the social challenges of the XXIst century, Roger Blanpain, Ed., Kluwer Law International.*

Dube, I. (2010). Environmental governance–Future directions. *Chartered Secretary, Special Edition,* 1381–1384.

Dube, I. (2011). Is corporate governance the answer to corporate structural failure. *US-China Law Review, 8,* 413.

Dube, I. (2016). Statutory corporate social responsibility—A philosophical shift in decolonized company law. *Chartered Secretary, 46*(12), 28–32.

Ghemawat, Pa. (n.d.). The forgotten strategy. *Harvard Business Review, 81*(November), 76–84.

Hägg, C. (1984). The OECD guidelines for multinational enterprises. *Journal of Business Ethics, 3*(1), 71–76.

Hiller, J. S. (2013). The benefit corporation and corporate social responsibility. *Journal of Business Ethics, 118*(2), 287–301. https://doi.org/10.1007/s10551-012-1580-3.

Human Rights Council, United Nations. (2011). *Report of the Special Representative of Secretary-General on the issue of human rights and transnational corporations and other business enterprises, John Ruggie* (No. 17th Session, Agenda item 3) (p. 1 to 27). Retrieved from http://www.ohchr.org/documents/issues/business/A.HRC.17.31.pdf

Leipziger, D. (2015). *The corporate responsibility code book.* Viva Books Publishing.

Lin, L.-W. (2010). Corporate social responsibility in China: Window dressing or structural change? *Berkeley Journal of International Law, 28*(1), 64–100.

Matten, D., Crane, A., & Chapple, W. (2003). Behind the mask: Revealing the true face of corporate citizenship. *Journal of Business Ethics, 45*(1), 109–120. https://doi.org/10.1023/A:1024128730308.

Maucourant, J., & Plociniczak, S. (2013). The institution, the economy and the market: Karl Polanyi's institutional thought for economists. *Review of Political Economy, 25*(3), 512–531.

Melgar, B. H., Nowror, K., & Yung, W. (2011). *The 2011 update of the OECD guidelines for multinational enterprises: Balanced outcome or an opportunity missed?* Institute of Economic Law Transnational Economic Law research Centre, School of Law, Martin Luther University Halle Wittenberg. Retrieved from http://telc.jura.uni-halle.de/sites/default/files/BeitraegeTWR/Heft112_0.pdf

Mickels, A. (2009). Beyond corporate social responsibility: Reconciling the ideals of a for-benefit corporation with director fiduciary duties in the US and Europe. *Hastings International & Comparative Law Review, 32,* 271.

Prno, J., & Slocombe, D. S. (2014). A systems-based conceptual framework for assessing the determinants of a social license to operate in the mining industry. *Environmental Management, 53*(3), 672–689. https://doi.org/10.1007/s00267-013-0221-7.

Rojot, J. (1985). The 1984 revision of the OECD guidelines for multinational enterprises. *British Journal of Industrial Relations, 23*(3), 379–397.

Sauvant, K. P. (2015). The negotiations of the United Nations code of conduct on transnational corporations: Experience and lessons learned. *The Journal of World Investment & Trade, 16*(1), 11–87.

Scherer, A. G., Palazzo, G., & Baumann, D. (2006). Global rules and private actors: Toward a new role of the transnational corporation in global governance. *Business Ethics Quarterly, 16*(04), 505–532. https://doi.org/10.5840/beq200616446.

Social Licence to Operate. (n.d.). Retrieved 14 September 2016, from https://www.sbc.org.nz/__data/assets/pdf_file/0005/99437/Social-Licence-to-Operate-Paper.pdf

Summary Report on Geneva Consultations, Geneva, Switzerland, December 4–5, 2007, Corporate Responsibility to Respect Human Rights. (n.d.). Retrieved from https://business-humanrights.org/sites/default/files/reports-and-materials/Ruggie-Geneva-4-5-Dec-2007.pdf

UN Intellectual History Project. (2009, July). Retrieved 18 December 2016, from http://www.unhistory.org/briefing/17TNCs.pdf

United Nations Global Compact. (n.d.). The UN Global Compact Ten Principles and Sustainable Development Goals: Connecting, Crucially. Retrieved from https://www.unglobalcompact.org/docs/about_the_gc/White_Paper_Principles_SDGs.pdf

Waagstein, P. R. (2011). The mandatory corporate social responsibility in Indonesia: Problems and implications. *Journal of Business Ethics, 98*(3), 455–466. https://doi.org/10.1007/s10551-010-0587-x.

World Investment Report 2011: Non-Equity Modes of International Production and Development. (2011). Retrieved 17 December 2016, from http://unctad.org/en/PublicationsLibrary/wir2011_en.pdf

Zinkin, J. (2004). Maximising the'licence to operate': CSR from an Asian perspective. *The Journal of Corporate Citizenship, 14,* 67.

Professor Indrajit Dube works at Rajiv Gandhi School of Intellectual Property Law of the Indian Institute of Technology Kharagpur, India. His areas of specialisation include corporate laws and governance. He published numerous papers in high ranked journals and led many research projects funded by both national and international agencies. He has also been invited as Visiting Faculty at the University of Western Ontario and the University of British Columbia. He has the distinction of being invited to deliver the Kirby Lecture Series at the School of Law, University of New England, Australia. He has been invited to participate in multi-stakeholder expert consultation at Osgood Hall Law School of the York University organised in support of the mandate of the Special Representative, Prof. John G. Ruggie, at the United Nations on Business and Human Rights. He is awarded the School of Taxation and Business Law 2018 Fellowship.

Enforcement of a Global Code of Conduct on TNC's Operations

Vicki Waye

1 Introduction

As a result of their economic power, making transnational corporations accountable for human rights abuse has been problematic (Frynas and Pegg 2003). Escalating globalisation of trade and commerce over the past 25 years has led to rapid growth in the size, number and power of transnational corporations to the extent that in some cases their economic strength overshadows that of the States in which they operate (Whelan et al. 2009; de Jonge 2011). Powerful transnational corporations can bargain down human rights protections or else ignore them with impunity because States may be reluctant to enforce breach and alienate desperately needed foreign investment. Alternatively, to secure favourable operating concessions, transnational corporations may collaborate with corrupt governments intent on aggrandising themselves at the expense of the disenfranchised (Tsakaridis 2016; Aaronson and Higham 2013, pp. 334–335). Otherwise, States may lack the legal infrastructure to support effective redress, such as a strong and independent judiciary, accessible legal advice and representation, or processes for aggregating and efficiently dealing with common claims. Attempts to bring transnational corporations to account in home jurisdictions, which may be better endowed with legal resources and relatively free of institutional corruption are often thwarted by formalistic rules governing jurisdiction (Prihandono 2011).

While accountability for human rights abuse has been weak, by contrast, the ability of transnational corporations (hereafter TNCs) to operate and expand globally with the assurance that their proprietary and economic interests will be safeguarded has been reinforced through a series of multilateral, regional and bilateral trade agreements (Ruggie 2013, p. 165). This disparity has led to calls to

V. Waye (✉)
School of Law, University of South Australia,
GPO Box 2471, Adelaide, SA 5001, Australia
e-mail: vicki.waye@unisa.edu.au

© Springer Nature Switzerland AG 2019
M. M. Rahim (ed.), *Code of Conduct on Transnational Corporations*,
CSR, Sustainability, Ethics & Governance,
https://doi.org/10.1007/978-3-030-10816-8_7

rebalance the scales with greater TNC accountability for human rights violations, culminating most recently with the United Nation's (hereafter UN) formation of an open-ended intergovernmental working group (OEIWG) mandated to "elaborate an international legally binding instrument to regulate, in international human rights law, the activities of transnational corporations and other business enterprises" (United Nations Human Rights Council 2014).

However, the creation of a new international legally binding instrument that ensures TNCs respect human rights remains controversial. The Human Rights Council Resolution that proposed the establishment of the OEIWG was passed 20 votes to 14 with 13 abstentions, hardly a consensus. Subsequently, a number of contentious issues that require resolution have been identified including the extent of the rights which the proposed treaty might protect, the type of legal liability that might be imposed, the relevant definition of a TNC, the extent of TNCs' responsibilities for the acts of subsidiaries or entities within their supply chains, the means of compliance monitoring, and how the proposed instrument might interact with the Guiding Principles. Significantly, early meetings of the OEIWG have also indicated that the proposed treaty must develop and codify legal and non-legal measures for access to an effective remedy for human rights breaches against both States and business enterprises. The need for an international court or other international dispute resolution processes has also been raised (United Nations Human Rights Council 2016).

Arguably, it is the creation of the means to access and enforce human rights obligations beyond national boundaries that lies at the heart of the rationale for a legally binding instrument (Cassidy 2008) and which constitutes the focus of this chapter. The chapter will begin by examining the current international law framework governing business violation of human rights. As the chapter outlines, the framework imposes responsibility on States for ensuring that human rights breaches committed by transnational corporations operating within their jurisdictions are redressed. However, outside of specific supra-national and regional treaties, institutional enforcement mechanisms for ensuring States abide by these obligations are weak. Using illustrative case studies, the article outlines why relying on non-binding guidelines to ensure adequate redress can be problematic. The article goes on to consider how a legally binding instrument might address these problems, before examining the fora and forms of dispute resolution that might be used to sanction human rights breaches committed by TNCs. A multi-pronged approach distinguishing between egregious human rights violations likely to attract universal jurisdiction versus breaches of more contested social and economic rights will be considered. The chapter will also examine the range of remedies that might be imposed, including the balance between public and private law remedies. Intertwined with these questions, the chapter will touch upon issues such as standing to bring claims and the responsibility of the State to ensure that those who have been harmed have access to sufficient support to bring claims or to have claims brought on their behalf.

1.1 International Developments: Business and Human Rights

A. State obligations and remedies

Whatever future recommendations the OEIWG makes with respect to the international dimension of business and human rights, there is little doubt that currently every State is subject to an obligation to protect human rights, and that this extends to an affirmative duty on the State to provide a remedy to those harmed by breach (Ramcharan 2011, p. 35), including where the harm is committed by non-State actors (Clapham 2014, p. 535). However, except for certain international crimes such as genocide, slavery or child sexual exploitation (Cassell and Ramasastry 2016, p. 16), enforcement of this obligation at the international level is largely restricted to monitoring of compliance and to fostering adherence through dialogue, censure and exhortation (Donoho 2006). While quasi-judicial mechanisms for identifying and redressing human rights breach by States may be instigated by other States, by individuals, or by the Human Rights Council, use of these means to pursue human rights abuse has been limited. Insofar as State complaints are concerned, for example, it is notable that for diplomatic reasons these mechanisms are rarely used (Shelton 2013, p. 674). The limitations are even more acute where the breach is perpetrated by a TNC (McConnell 2017, 3.1.1; Nowak and Januszewski 2015). The mandate of international human rights monitoring bodies rests on the consent of those States party to the relevant treaty. Their jurisdiction *ratione personae* does not apply to TNCs (Karavias 2015, p. 105).

For 'consistent patterns of gross and reliably attested violations of all human rights and all fundamental freedoms occurring in any part of the world', it is possible for individuals or groups to make a confidential complaint to the Human Rights Council (United Nations Human Rights Council 2007). Additionally, the Human Rights Council may instigate 'special procedures' where it commissions rapporteurs or working groups to investigate and report on special country situations or thematic issues about human rights.

Individuals affected by breach may also be able to initiate complaints (known as communications) to treaty monitoring bodies. However, as outlined earlier, these individual complaints procedures are subject to major limitations. Not all States have adopted the procedures. Significantly, for example, China, the United States of America, India and the United Kingdom have not acceded to the First Optional Protocol to the International Covenant on Civil and Political Rights. Generally, complaints must be instigated by individuals. Although they may represent disempowered individuals, NGOs, which are likely to be much better resourced than individuals, have no standing (UR v Uruguay 1983; JHA v Spain 2008). Complaints take a long time to be heard, and even before complaints are heard, complainants must first establish that all avenues of redress within their own jurisdictions have been exhausted. Any subsequent findings of breach are not legally binding. Rather reports condemning the breach are forwarded to the relevant State and reported to the General Assembly.

Some States have acceded to enforcement of human rights obligations at the regional level and have created regional institutions for this purpose. Examples of these institutions include the European Court of Human Rights, the African Court of Human and Peoples' Rights, and the Inter-American Court of Human Rights. As with the international instruments and bodies outlined above, these institutions and the instruments underpinning them focus upon the acts and omissions of the State. Consequently, the application of international human rights obligations to business is almost entirely dependent upon the domestic institutions of the State (Hillebrecht 2012, pp. 964–965). As the law currently stands, neither the European Court of Human Rights or the Inter-American Court of Human Rights can hear claims made directly against TNCs nor does their jurisdiction extend to TNC activity occurring outside of the respective contracting States' territories. While the African Court of Human and Peoples' Rights has extended its jurisdiction to include corporate criminal responsibility for human rights violations (African Union 2014), at the time of writing the minimum number of relevant State parties had not ratified the amended protocol and so it has not yet entered force.

B. TNC related obligations

Although a series of aspirational norms governing TNCs can be traced as far back as 1977 when the International Labour Organization (hereafter ILO) adopted the *Tripartite Declaration of Principles covering Multinational Enterprises*, followed by the UN *Global Compact* (2000), and then the Organisation for Economic Cooperation and Development's (hereafter OECD) *Guidelines for Multinational Enterprises* (2000), designed as guidance for States and TNCs, none of these set out repercussions for breach or explained how those that suffered as a result of breach might obtain redress. The UN *Global Compact*, for example, was a voluntary initiative that aimed to encourage global business leaders to promote an array of human rights principles, as well as principles related to sustainable development and good government within their business domains. While the UN *Norms on the Responsibilities of TNCs and other Business Enterprises* (2003) comprised a comprehensive statement of human rights and other business related obligations that purported to bind States and TNCs, the *Norms* were never fully endorsed by the UN Commission on Human Rights, which in 2004 declared that although they contained useful ideas they had no legal standing (Feeney 2009, p. 165).

The making of the UN *Guiding Principles on Business and Human Rights 2011* (hereafter UNGPs) constituted a step forward in relation to breaches of human rights by explicitly linking States' obligations under international law with a duty to ensure that businesses within their jurisdictions were also compliant (Aaronson and Higham 2013, p. 336). However, rather than creating a new top down rights based hierarchy of legal obligations, the UNGPs set about demonstrating how existing domestic governance could be better aligned with respect to business and its adherence to human rights norms (Ruggie 2014).

There has been significant progress in implementing the UNGPs (European Commission 2015), including the formulation of a series of National Action Plans (Office of the High Commissioner, United Nations Human Rights 2016a) and the issue of elaborated guidance on State obligations (Office of the High Commissioner, United Nations Human Rights 2016b). Business and private stakeholder organisations such as the Thun Group of banks and the International Organisation for Standardisation are also aligning their activities with the UNGPs (Addo 2014). Nonetheless, a view that TNC accountability for human rights breach requires strengthening remains, especially with respect to redress for breach as those who whose rights have been violated rarely have the opportunity to have their grievances heard, let alone obtain redress. Many of the National Action Plans that have been produced to date almost completely overlook the role of legal access to remedies (Baughen 2015, p. 242). Even where redress is available it regularly fails to provide effective and prompt reparation (Office of the High Commissioner, United Nations Human Rights 2016b, p. 3). In some instances, the emphasis in the UNGPs on non-legal grievance mechanisms has created opportunities for offending businesses to extract a swathe of disclaimers, waivers and confidentiality obligations that disaffirm many claims, and there is no guarantee that the redress mechanisms will be administered by independent third parties (Baughen 2015, pp. 243–244; Knuckey and Jenkin 2015, pp. 807, 811). Moreover, while noting that a number of States already extend legal responsibility to instances of extraterritorial breach, the UNGPs fall short of requiring businesses domiciled within their territory to respect human rights abroad. Despite the UNGPs, existing domestic law remedies for alleged business related human rights breaches have thus been described as 'patchy, unpredictable, often ineffective and fragile' (Office of the High Commissioner, United Nations Human Rights 2016b, p. 3). Consequently, many regard the UNGPs as a step in the evolution of aspirational non-binding soft law into more durable and binding hard law obligations (Blitt 2012).

2 Current Domestic Law Enforcement

Within their jurisdictions and to differing degrees, all States have laws in place that impose labour rights, prohibit discrimination, promote indigenous and cultural rights, protect the environment, restrict incursion upon civil liberties, and address work and product safety. Many, including Great Britain, France, Australia, Indonesia, South Korea, Canada, Spain, and India, have also established human rights enforcement systems comprised of a human rights commission or ombudsman which may investigate complaints, and tribunals and courts which may hear claims and determine whether a breach has occurred. As a result, businesses that breach human rights articulated in these laws may attract criminal or civil liability or may be subject to administrative sanction.

Yet in spite of the apparent commitment to the protection of human rights through accession to human rights instruments as well as the translation of international obligations into domestic regulation, empirical findings demonstrate a significant compliance shortfall. The compliance shortfall varies according to the type of right under consideration, economic development, population size, state of democracy and war (Dai 2013; Hafner-Burton and Ron 2009) as well as the efficacy and rigour of States' compliance and enforcement measures (Cole 2012, 2015). To illustrate, the World Justice Project, Rule of Law Index 2016 reveals wide ranging performance for the protection of fundamental rights as between developed versus developing nations (World Justice Project 2016, p. 29). Particularly in less developed States, domestic policies and domestic institutions have at times proven to be ill equipped to address human rights abuse perpetrated by TNCs working hand in hand with corrupt governments (Tsakaridis 2016, p. 260). It is this compliance shortfall that underpins the OEIWG's mandate for strengthening State responsibility for TNC violations and for extending legal responsibility for reparation directly to TNCs. Without encapsulating the obligation to remediate human rights violations into a legally binding instrument it is feared that TNCs will be able to operate in a governance vacuum independent of the regulatory control of any one State (Grear and Weston 2015).

There are many examples that explain the governance vacuum which have been cited to the Office of the UN High Commissioner for Human Rights (hereafter OHCHR) (Zerk 2014) or which have been collated by NGOs with the assistance of human rights scholars (Skinner et al. 2013). Three will be discussed here: (1) Anvil Mining Ltd and allegations of complicity with the Democratic Republic of Congo armed forces in egregious human rights violations including summary execution, rape and torture; (2) Cisco systems and allegations of complicity in the supply of surveillance hardware used to identify and arrest members of the Falun Gong religious minority; and (3) Broadspectrum Ltd and allegations of complicity in Australia's off-shore detention policy for asylum seekers. These case studies were chosen to illustrate the diversity of limitations (both practical and legal) affecting access to domestic enforcement mechanisms for alleged human rights abuse perpetrated by business. They demonstrate that difficulties may be encountered by those seeking redress in both democratic and non-democratic States and that access to redress is limited whether the alleged violations by business involve direct or indirect participation in the breach.

2.1 Case Study One—Anvil Mining Ltd

In October 2004 Anvil Mining Ltd provided transportation (planes and vehicles) and other logistical support (food and money) to the armed forces of the Democratic Republic of Congo (hereafter DCR) while they were fighting an armed insurgency in the Congolese town of Kilwa. During the fighting the armed forces committed serious human rights breaches against the local civilian population including summary execution, rape and torture (Australian Broadcasting Corporation 2005). Later, a number of army and Anvil personnel were prosecuted in the DCR. Despite credible eye-witness testimony and other corroborative evidence supporting liability, the Lubumbashi Military High Court acquitted these personnel in 2007 finding that there had been no summary executions and that the civilian deaths had occurred as a result of fierce fighting between the army and the rebels (United Kingdom, Border Agency 2009, p. 38). Appeals followed, but amid allegations of political interference, the appellate court declined to review the earlier acquittals (McBeth 2014).

As Anvil Mining is an Australian company, in 2008 a class action was commenced in Australia on behalf of the victims in Kilwa (Pierre v Anvil Mining Management NL 2008). However, that action was discontinued because the DRC government had prevented NGOs and the class law firm from going to Kilwa to gather evidence, and because the lead plaintiffs had been subject to death threats and a campaign of harassment which caused them to withdraw from the proceedings. Subsequently, in 2010, a class action was lodged against Anvil Mining Ltd in the Superior Court of Quebec. At first instance, the Court determined there was sufficient jurisdiction to hear the case. However, on appeal this was reversed (Anvil Mining Ltd. c. Association canadienne contre l'impunité 2012) and the Supreme Court of Canada declined to overturn that decision (Association canadienne contre l'impunité c. Anvil Mining Limited 2012). The Quebec Court of Appeal found no real and substantial connection between the cause of action and Quebec's jurisdiction. Anvil Mining Ltd was an Australian company; its activities in Quebec were confined to maintaining relationships with investors and shareholders; and the events affecting the victims all occurred in the DCR.

2.2 Case Study Two—Cisco Systems and China

Cisco Systems, Inc., the world's largest supplier of internet networking equipment, tendered for and won a contract to design and supply a surveillance and security network for the Chinese government known as the Golden Shield. The Golden Shield system became operational in every Chinese province by June 2003. A number of NGOs allege that Cisco designed, customised and integrated the Golden Shield for the dual purpose of (1) gathering criminal and national security intelligence and (2) to suppress dissidents, especially members of Falun Gong. Since 1999, Falun Gong has been subject to widespread persecution in China comprised of threats, banning of activities, detention, beatings, torture, disappearances, and extrajudicial killings.

Falun Gong is heavily dependent on the internet for the dissemination of its views and for communication between adherents. The Golden Shield helped Chinese security officials monitor Falun Gong communication, and provided information to assist them apprehend, interrogate, forcibly convert and torture Falun Gong members.

In 2011, a class action was commenced in California on behalf of Falun Gong followers alleging that Cisco had assisted in the facilitation of human rights abuses against them in China by the Chinese government. The class action was dismissed on several grounds (Doe I v Cisco Systems, Inc. 2014). First, relying on the US Supreme Court decision in *Kiobel* (Kiobel v Royal Dutch Petroleum Co. 2013), the Court found that there was an insufficient nexus between Cisco's actions in designing and supplying the Golden Shield network and the alleged human rights abuses perpetrated against Falun Gong members in China. According to the Court it was not established that Cisco had participated in planning, directing or committing any human rights abuse in the United States or directed against the United States. Second, the Court found that liability for aiding and abetting human rights abuse could not be established. The Court determined that it was not shown that Cisco's conduct had a substantial effect on the alleged violations nor was it shown that Cisco was aware that its products would be used to facilitate human rights abuse. In that respect the Court found that Cisco did not obtain any benefit from the persecution of Falun Gong; did not have any influence or leverage over the Chinese government so as to dictate its policies; and did not take any action that might bear upon US policy towards China's treatment of Falun Gong. Lastly the Court found that Cisco was exempt from liability under the Electronic Communication Privacy Act. At the time of writing, an appeal to the United States Court of Appeals is pending.

2.3 Case Study Three—Broadspectrum Ltd and Asylum Seekers

In October 2012 Broadspectrum Ltd, formerly known as Transfield Services, was awarded the contract to manage Australia's immigration detention centres on Nauru and Manus Island, Papua New Guinea. The detention centres house persons who attempt to enter Australia irregularly by sea. Contrary to Australia's refugee and international human rights obligations, such persons are intercepted and forcibly detained by Australian law authorities, and then transferred to Nauru or Manus Island where their claims for refugee status are processed. Many are detained for very long periods. Reports from bodies like Amnesty International (Amnesty International 2016) and media outlets (SBS 2014) claim that the conditions in the detention centres are inhuman and degrading. A report prepared by NGO, No Business in Abuse, explicitly accuses Broadspectrum Ltd of being complicit in 'gross human rights abuses on a massive scale, violating 47 international laws…… with severe mental and physical harm inflicted upon detainees' (No Business in Abuse 2015). However, it is very difficult to substantiate the claims as the detention centres are not easily accessible and service providers and others working in the detention centres face criminal prosecution and civil penalties if they disclose any information about detainees' living conditions (Australian Border Force Act 2015 (Cth), Pt 6). Nonetheless, the UN Committee on the Rights of the Child has indicated that it is deeply concerned by the conditions facing asylum seeking children on Nauru (United Nations, Committee on the Rights of the Child 2016).

A challenge to the detention centre on Nauru launched in the Australian High Court failed (M68/2015 v Mins for Immigration and Border Protection 2016). The Court found that Australia's actions in detaining and transferring detainees to Nauru and entering into an arrangement with Nauru to process detainees' refugee claims were lawful and constitutional. As Australia adopts a dualist approach to the reception of international law, the Court was not called upon to consider whether the arrangements breached Australia's international human rights obligations. By contrast with the decision of the Australian High Court, the Papua New Guinea Supreme Court determined that the detention centre on Manus Island was unconstitutional (Namah v Pato 2016). Consequently the Manus Island detention facility has been forced to close.

2.4 Discussion

Although the volume of human rights litigation against TNCs is increasing, a number of common threads throughout the case studies outlined above and those cited in reports compiled by NGOs and UN bodies demonstrate the limitations of existing domestic legal systems insofar as TNC human rights violations are concerned. These include problems associated with bringing claims in the host countries where the courts in the host countries lack the power to consider whether a business has violated human rights (Broadspectrum) or where the courts are subject to political pressure or interference (Anvil Mining) or are otherwise not in a position to act in a manner contrary to governmental policy (Cisco). Attempts to bring cases in home countries are often inhibited by a lack of territorial connection to the violations (Cisco, Anvil Mining), or through doctrines such as the common law doctrine of *forum non conveniens*, which is frequently applied by courts outside of Europe to decline jurisdiction (Anvil Mining). The cases indicate that short of direct involvement (Anvil Mining, Broadspectrum) it will be very difficult to establish liability merely because the relevant enterprise is doing business with the host State where human rights violations have occurred (Cisco). As a result of the doctrine of the separate legal personality of corporations, even where direct involvement is shown, the relevant acts committed by a poorly capitalised subsidiary based in the host State may be difficult to attribute to the wealthier parent company in its home State. Although domestic courts may be persuaded in some instances to find a duty of care owed by the parent company to victims of breaches committed by subsidiary companies, they have largely eschewed imposing liability upon parent companies on the basis of 'enterprise theory' (Zerk 2014, p. 46). Obtaining an effective remedy against a business in the host State may therefore be futile if the majority of that business's income and assets have been remitted to a parent business in another State. Meanwhile, despite strong arguments in favour of liability (Rott and Ulfbeck 2015), legal responsibility for actions of independent firms within a TNC's global supply chains is almost non-existent (Sarfaty 2015).

Intimidation of victims (Anvil Mining) can also make it difficult to prove human rights violations. The cost of initiating human rights litigation is very high and in most cases victims are either impoverished or oppressed, and therefore heavily reliant on NGO or pro bono law firm assistance (Anvil Mining, Cisco, Broadspectrum). Apart from this kind of noblese obligé assistance, there is little victim support available for bringing claims and obtaining redress.

In light of these deficiencies, the UN OHCHR has issued a report (Office of the High Commissioner, United Nations Human Rights 2016b) and guidance (Office of the High Commissioner, United Nations Human Rights 2016c) to improve corporate accountability and victims' access to remedies for business-related human rights abuse. The report and guidance focus upon improving domestic State-based judicial mechanisms on the ground that these lie at the 'core of ensuring access to remedy.' In terms of enforcement, the report and guidance recommend that State agencies responsible for investigating and enforcing business-related human rights abuse be given a clear mandate to act independently of political interference, and that they are appropriately resourced and staffed by persons with suitable levels of training and expertise. It is recommended that any enforcement discretion reposed in these bodies be exercised in a clear and transparent manner and in accordance with a comprehensive enforcement policy. Where a decision is made not to investigate or prosecute for breach, it is also recommended that complainants be appropriately advised of their rights and of the procedures that may apply for those rights to be exercised. Enforcement agencies are urged to protect complainants from intimidation and reprisals, and to ensure that when dealing with complainants that proper account is taken of individuals' vulnerabilities.

States are encouraged to take steps to improve cross-border cooperation between State agencies and judicial bodies and where appropriate to carry out cross-border investigations through joint investigation teams, to share information support and training, and to provide mutual legal assistance. States are also pressed to strengthen their domestic legal responses to cross-border human rights abuses. This extends to ensuring that domestic private law regimes are sufficiently robust to ensure proper deterrence and an effective remedy for proven abuses, including abuses perpetrated by third parties, where the relevant business entity has aided and abetted or fostered breach. Importantly, the OHCHR recommends that victims have access to diversified sources of litigation funding and that States should prioritise the provision of funding for victims who are able to show financial hardship or increased risk of vulnerability. Systems of collective redress should also be made available to allow claims to be advanced cost-effectively. Where possible court procedures should include readily identifiable and affordable opportunities for mediation and settlement.

At the time of writing, the OEIWG was still in the early stages of its work and had not yet produced a draft legally binding instrument for substantive negotiation. It therefore remains to be seen whether its draft will incorporate the details set out in the OHCHR guidance outlined above or whether it will proceed as a framework

Enforcement of a Global Code of Conduct on TNC's Operations

convention with optional protocols that subsequently define obligations with respect to enforcement in more detail. At this stage, it appears that diplomatic consensus around TNC accountability will take considerable time to construct.

If a framework approach is adopted, at the very least the International Commission of Jurists (hereafter ICJ) has proposed that the treaty should incorporate (International Commission of Jurists 2016, p. 8):

1. An affirmation of the basic human rights obligations of States and business enterprises
2. An international framework to facilitate national level prevention and legal accountability of TNCs and other business enterprises
3. A national system of remedies for victims of human rights abuse perpetrated by business enterprises; and
4. An international framework for international cooperation including mutual legal assistance to address business-related human rights abuse

In respect of remedies for business related human rights abuses the ICJ recommends that judicial remedies must always be available in respect of serious crime and other public law offences. Insofar as private civil cases are concerned the ICJ recommends that jurisdiction be established over business enterprises domiciled in the relevant jurisdiction extending to the acts of subsidiaries wherever they are based, and that domestic courts are able to exercise universal jurisdiction if there is no other effective forum. Thus, like the OHCHR, the ICJ also favours strengthening domestic legal systems so that enforcement occurs within local judicial forums supervised and monitored by an international committee of experts rather than the creation of an international human rights court or arbitral tribunal.

Key global business organisations adopt a similar approach and insist that the OEIWG should maintain the UNGPs' strict division between, on the one hand, the State's duty to protect human rights, and on the other, companies' responsibility to respect human rights (International Organisation of Employers; International Chamber of Commerce, Business and Industry Advisory Committee and World Business Council for Sustainable Development 2016). They regard a focus upon the development of transnational accountability mechanisms as misplaced, and consistent with the UNGPs, favour the strengthening of existing national accountability processes. As a result of the high cost of pursuing breach in foreign courts, these organisations contend that attempts to establish universal jurisdiction will not substantially improve access to justice or advance the rule of law very far. They therefore maintain that any proposed instrument should make the preparation and implementation of National Action Plans binding and explicitly require States to report on their implementation of the UNGPs to a treaty monitoring body. A similar position has been adopted by the Committee of Ministers of the Council of Europe (2016) and has been referenced in OEWIG panel discussions.

Given the strong positioning in favour of the strengthening of national mechanisms from key protagonists like the OHCHR, the ICJ and global business and the lack of any consensus in favour of formal international dispute resolution fora from

OEIWG panellists, it therefore seems unlikely that proposals for an international arbitration or an international court put forward by some academics and NGOs will be successful. However to fully complete the discussion and in light of the international community's lukewarm response to these suggestions, the various advantages and disadvantages of these organs will be considered below.

3 International Mediation and Arbitration

As of 2016 it is estimated that there are over 3000 international investment treaties worldwide and the number is growing. As a result, the number of investor-state arbitrations arising from the treaties is also increasing. Investors have initiated over 700 known arbitrations challenging State regulation straddling areas such as taxation, energy and public health (Cotula 2016). While there have been a small number of investors seeking redress for breach of human rights, generally speaking human rights arguments are raised by host States in response to investor party claims as justification for the implementation of State policy on matters such as health, energy and the environment. Currently, investment treaties do not provide a basis for initiating claims against TNCs for breach of human rights, and so their impact on victims' access to justice for human rights violations by TNCs is negligible.

Nor is there currently any international body accessible to victims for either mediation or binding arbitration in relation to human rights violations. However, as a result of the retreat from extraterritorial exercises of jurisdiction by national courts, a number of scholars have suggested that an international arbitral tribunal may provide victims with recourse and encourage TNCs to respect human rights (Zambrana-Tevar 2015; Cronstedt and Thompson 2016). Their proposals recommend the establishment of an international arbitral tribunal that would administer mediation followed by binding arbitration if a settlement cannot be reached.

Identified advantages of an international arbitration tribunal include: deployment of mediation before the dispute escalates and party positions become entrenched; avoidance of arid jurisdictional arguments once party consent is established; speedier and less costly proceedings; party choice as to the seat of the arbitration and the composition of the arbitral tribunal; customization of procedures and processes to suit the parties' needs; party specification of the substantive and procedural law governing the arbitration; less use of adversarial court trappings; confidentiality of proceedings; and global enforcement under the New York Convention 1958 (Zambrana-Tevar 2015; Cronstedt and Thompson 2016).

Litigation funding, contingency fees and collective redress are already well established in international commercial arbitration (Strong 2013) as well as international investment arbitration (Abaclat v Argentina 2011), and provide a model for the proposed international arbitral tribunal that is likely to improve access to justice for victims of human rights violations where host States are unwilling to provide finance to instigate claims before domestic courts. Moreover, there are already a number of precedents for arbitrating and processing mass claims in international law including the Iran-United States Claims Tribunal, the Eritrea-Ethiopia Claims Commission and the Claims Resolution Tribunal for Dormant Accounts in Switzerland (Rosenfeld 2013) that should reassure victims that their claims will be dealt with fairly and appropriately. By transferring human rights redress to an international neutral forum like the proposed tribunal, home States would thereby be discharged from having to adjudicate upon the domestic policies of host States apropos their relationship with powerful TNCs (Pak and Nussbaumer 2009, p. 36). Provided the tribunal is composed of a well-balanced selection of eminent jurists and experts from a variety of legal traditions, cultural and socio-economic backgrounds, proponents argue that these advantages will attract both business and victims to this forum.

Those opposed to the idea of an international arbitral tribunal question whether TNCs would voluntarily submit to its jurisdiction (Childress III 2015, pp. 44–45). To make the proposed tribunal feasible, a large number of TNCs must be willing to expose their business practices to international scrutiny. Given that it is unclear whether consent to arbitration would prevent proceedings being instigated in domestic courts, those opposed to the proposal believe that TNCs have little to gain by giving a wide berth to favourable domestic laws and procedures, which the case studies demonstrate insulate them from both scrutiny and accountability.

The proponents of the tribunal claim that businesses will accept the tribunal's jurisdiction for two reasons. First, the tribunal would provide a fair, efficient and confidential disposition of human rights claims. Second, it is claimed that businesses would participate to obtain reputational benefit. Proponents also argue that in the latter regard, businesses can be encouraged to submit to jurisdiction by inserting pre-dispute arbitration clauses into instruments such as bilateral investment treaties, economic development agreements, free trade agreements, conditions attached to national and international financial assistance, and various codes of conduct. Certainly, the new generation of model economic development and bilateral investment treaty templates could be updated to incorporate such provisions if the proposed arbitral tribunal gained support in the OEIWG. Alternately home States may be willing to grant TNC operating licenses on the condition that the TNC is willing to submit to arbitration in favour of claimants from countries where the TNC does business (Zambrana-Tevar 2015, p. 20).

Given the track record of international commercial arbitration, detractors of the arbitral tribunal proposal also argue that the efficiencies of arbitration are often over-stated and that arbitration can be as resource intensive and protracted as litigation (Cassell and Ramasastry 2016, p. 35; Childress III 2015, p. 46). Furthermore, arbitration is generally a confidential process with limited capacity for NGO oversight or involvement. From a normative perspective, some question whether privacy is consistent with the need to deter TNC human rights breach and with victims' needs for recognition of their plight. Coupled with the lack of transparency, there are few means to guard against disparate outcomes between arbitral tribunals which are composed ad hoc and not subject to appeal.

Clearly, the proposed arbitral tribunal would be limited to hearing only civil claims. As essentially private processes founded on party consent, mediation and arbitration are wholly unsuited to dealing with criminal breaches of human rights obligations, which should be dealt with by domestic courts or bodies such as the International Criminal Court armed with powers of arrest and punishment. Consideration will need to be given to the procedural rules and processes the proposed tribunal may adopt. Existing commercial arbitration rules administered by institutions such as the International Chamber of Commerce or the International Centre for Settlement of Investment Disputes may not be suitable for addressing human rights violations where the parties seek remediation or reparation (Zambrana-Tevar 2015, p. 27). The inquisitorial procedures and evidential techniques adopted by the international mass claims tribunals (Rosenfeld 2013) with their focus on providing reparation and practical justice (Giroud and Moss 2015) are more likely to produce fair and efficient disposition of claims.

4 The Creation of an International Court

While the idea of a World Court on Business and Human Rights has been raised during OEIWG deliberations, it has not been the subject of detailed discussion in that forum. There are many questions that would need to be addressed if such a proposal were to be entertained, including whether the court would have both criminal and civil jurisdiction, the body of law it would apply, where it might be located, and how it might be resourced. Furthermore, while it might be feasible for a Human Rights Committee to formulate non-binding expert guidance in relation to particular State practice, it would be an entirely other matter for a court to deliver binding adjudication on domestically contentious matters such as development, health, privacy and rights to access resources in respect of States with diverse legal and political frameworks, demography and cultures (Alston 2014, p. 202).

It may be argued that the European Court of Human Rights (hereafter ECHR) model depends on cultural and social affinities across the European Union (hereafter EU) and upon social, political and economic linkages between the Court and other EU member organs of state that provide substantial incentives for compliance with the Court's decisions that are not replicated on a global scale (Donoho 2006, p. 45). The recent enactment of a law in Russia allowing its Constitutional Court to review rulings of bodies like the ECHR and pronounce them 'non-executable' if they are deemed to contradict the Russian constitution (Russian Federation 2015) and intimations that in the wake of BREXIT the United Kingdom will cut ties with the ECHR (Giannoulopoulos 2016) illustrate how much the Court's authority can be diminished when these linkages are severed. The notion that matters of development, health, privacy and access to resources lend themselves to a single universal resolution from a World Court across States with very divergent cultures and stages of socio-economic development is difficult to sustain.

The recently announced withdrawal from the International Criminal Court (hereafter referred to as the ICC) by Burundi, Gambia and South Africa and the failure of dominant States like the United States of America, Russia and China to accede to or ratify the Rome Statute further suggests that obtaining backing for a new international human rights court is going to be difficult. That view is reinforced by the failure of ASEAN and Arab nations to implement any regional human rights enforcement mechanism (Alston 2014, p. 201). Strong opposition to the OEIWG's formation by the United States, the United Kingdom, and the European Union also indicate that even if such a court could be established, that not many States would agree to submit to its jurisdiction.

Nevertheless, there is historical precedent for a court with authority to deal with gross human rights violations that could entertain complaints against States and TNCs. Moreover, recent amendments to the Protocol on the Statute of the African Court of Justice and Human Rights provide a model that could be considered as part of an additional future protocol to any framework treaty that might be drafted by the OEIWG. Gallegos and Uribe cite the establishment of international courts against the slave trade during the early 1800 s as one of the first examples of international bodies set up to adjudicate upon human rights violations (Gallegos and Uribe 2016) noting that during the lifespan of a network of treaties between Great Britain, the Netherlands, Portugal and Spain, over 600 cases were heard and 80,000 slaves recaptured and freed. Martinez forcefully argues that the conceptualization of the slave trade as a crime against humanity and of slave traders as *hostes humani generis* during this period helped to lay the conception of modern day international human rights law (Martinez 2012). Indeed, it was on the basis of *hostes humani generis* that directors of German companies that manufactured and sold gas used in the Nazi death camps or collaborated in other ways with the Nazi regime throughout World War II were convicted of war crimes. During the Nuremberg proceedings, corporate assets were seized and corporate status terminated for businesses directly involved in genocide and other crimes against humanity (Cassell and Ramasastry 2016, pp. 35–36).

One issue that might be considered is whether a separate World Court of Human Rights is necessary given that the ICC is already established. For example, the ICC's jurisdiction could be expanded by adding the words 'and legal' to Article 25.1 of the Rome Statute, which currently provides: "The Court shall have jurisdiction over natural persons pursuant to this Statute" (Cassell and Ramasastry 2016, p. 36). Although incorporation of corporate criminal liability within its jurisdiction was rejected at the ICC's foundation (Gallegos and Uribe 2016, p. 8) and notwithstanding that the ICC appears to have fallen out of favour among some nations, expanding the existing ICC to enable it to rule on all gross human rights violations committed by TNCs as well as individuals has a number of advantages. First, the ICC constitutes the first permanent, general oriented court tasked with enforcing international criminal law not imposed by powerful States, but founded upon the voluntary participation of 124 State parties. It has been in operation since 2002 and has built up a highly distinctive approach and set of procedures focusing upon reparation for mass atrocities. As such it contributes to reconciliation, strengthens accountability for human rights violations, and contributes to promoting world peace (Mariniello 2015, p. 4). Expanding its jurisdiction to include egregious corporate criminal conduct, would be consistent with the ICC's overall mandate, the requirement that in applying the law the Court adhere to international human rights standards, and with the Court's focus upon reparation for harm.

Second, the ICC's jurisdiction does not apply to violations of the whole range of civil, political, social and economic rights but rather to a very small sub-set of crimes including torture, summary execution, genocide and crimes against humanity. Although international law regarding crimes against humanity was not fully developed until the early 20th century, the prosecution of individuals for war crimes can be traced back to the ancient Greeks (Schabas 2011, pp. 1–2). The prosecution of war crimes is thus more firmly embedded within human culture than the enforcement of modern human rights such as economic and social rights, which mostly rely upon voluntary compliance. A focus on egregious rights violations related to *jus cogens* and universal jurisdiction is more likely to attract international consensus than an array of contested human rights that many States are likely to baulk at applying (Trechsel 2004; Donoho 2006, p. 8). According to Donoho, restricting jurisdiction to crimes against humanity increases institutional legitimacy, alleviates fears about usurpation of State sovereignty and improves the prospects for effective enforcement (Donoho 2006, p. 31).

Extending ICC jurisdiction to incorporate TNC complicity in crimes against humanity may well enhance the ICC's reputation, which has suffered from criticism that it has unjustifiably targeted individuals from African States. The African States perceive that they are the victims of power politics, and believe that the ICC has shied away from matters that embroil the major western powers (Nowak 2015). Allied with this view, the ICC has also been criticized for failing to address the link between mass atrocities and economic activity. It is claimed that the ICC is considerably weakened by its inability to prosecute TNCs, which are the primary beneficiaries of the liberalized, global economy (Delmas-Marty 2013) and which are largely domiciled within the major western powers. An ICC investigation of a TNC accused of complicity in crimes against humanity would certainly be highly salient and therefore be a strong deterrent against business involvement in gross acts of oppression.

Rather than create a new broad based world court, expanding the ICC's jurisdiction would align with the UNGP's current emphasis on strengthening domestic legal systems and responses. The ICC is governed by the principle of complementarity. Its jurisdiction is only enlivened when States are unwilling or unable to carry out investigation and prosecution. Moreover, given that regional courts like the European Court of Human Rights, the African Court of Human and Peoples' Rights (as yet), and the Inter-American Court of Human Rights, do not entertain claims directly against TNCs there is little scope for overlap.

However, the hurdles for expanding the ICC's jurisdiction are high and have led some to regard attempts to do so as futile and even counter-productive given the ICC's current fragile state (de Jonge 2011, p. 78). Pursuant to Article 121 Rome Statute, the adoption of any amendment to jurisdiction will require at least 2/3 majority of State parties and must be ratified by at least 7/8 of State parties to enter into force. While it may be easier to expand the ICC's jurisdiction than to create a new World Court of Human Rights, the determination and resources required to convince a substantial majority of State parties to expand the ICC's jurisdiction should not be underestimated. As questions regarding the efficiency and effectiveness of the ICC's proceedings have been raised repeatedly in the international community (Ambach 2015; Mariniello 2015), State parties would have to be persuaded that adding to the ICC's jurisdiction would not exacerbate these problems.

Complementarity has also been raised as an objection on the basis that a number of States do not recognise the principle of corporate criminal responsibility (Kyriakakis 2008). According to de Jonge, governments in countries where corporate criminal liability is lacking would face significant opposition were they to accede to standards for TNCs in international law that diverged substantially from the law of their own jurisdictions (de Jonge 2011, p. 78). However, others argue that extending ICC jurisdiction to TNCs will not jeopardize the complementarity regime, but will actually enhance it by providing a mechanism to adjudicate upon corporate crimes against humanity where no such mechanism exists at State level (Kyriakakis 2008). Were the OHCHR report and guidance on means to improve corporate accountability and access to judicial remedy for business-related human rights abuse be adopted, particularly those sections dealing with recommendations for domestic law regimes to develop and apply principles for assessing corporate legal liability, then the complementarity concern should start to fall away.

Should there be momentum supportive of expanding the ICC's jurisdiction, Article 46C of the proposed *Protocol on Amendments to the Protocol to the Statute of the African Court of Justice and Human Rights* governing "Corporate Criminal Liability" provides a useful model that could be incorporated into the Rome Statute (Cassell and Ramasastry 2016, p. 36). The Article provides that: (1) the Court has jurisdiction over legal persons; (2) corporate intention to commit the crimes may be proven by showing that the corporation had a policy to undertake the acts; (3) a policy may be attributed to the corporation where it is the most reasonable explanation for its actions; (4) corporate knowledge can be proven by demonstrating that actual or constructive knowledge was possessed within the corporation; (5) corporate knowledge may be possessed even where it is shared by different corporate personnel; and (6) the criminal responsibility of legal persons shall not exclude the criminal responsibility of individuals who are perpetrators or accomplices in the same crime. Arguably this model and the ICC's restricted jurisdiction aligns well with the likely agency of TNCs and the scope of what they are able to directly affect through their own actions. The ability of a TNC to control and thus be responsible for a broader array of matters such as development, health and the environment is likely to be far more variable than that of a State (Alston 2014, p. 207).

Those in favour of a World Court argue that confining international jurisdiction to crimes against humanity is too restrictive. The ICC is only responsible for trying individuals for very specific egregious offences; it does not bring States to trial. It is also claimed that the ICC prosecutor's monopoly over the indictment process unduly restricts access to justice, and by definition does not incorporate access to private law remedies (although these might feasibly be addressed by the proposed international arbitration tribunal considered earlier). At this stage, the only judicial forums where citizens can initiate civil claims against States and TNCs for human rights violations are domestic courts, and where they operate, against States (but not TNCs) in regional human rights courts. For example, the African Court on Human and People's Rights is empowered to award the payment of fair compensation or reparation. As a result of the lack of an international mechanism for obtaining redress, a court with jurisdiction over a wide range of matters such as, environmental degradation, forced and child labour, displacement of indigenous peoples, corruption and fraud has been proposed (Pak and Nussbaumer 2009).

Despite the lack of strong support for a World Court, a considerable amount of preliminary work has already been undertaken. A World Court of Human Rights was first proposed in 1947, but because of the lack of experience with the UN's newly drafted human rights instruments and the advent of the Cold War the proposal was not pursued (Alston 2014, p. 197). In 2008, the Swiss Federal Department of Foreign Affairs established a panel of eminent persons known as the Panel on Human Dignity to implement its new Agenda for Human Rights, incorporating a proposal for a World Court. A group of scholars, Manfred Nowak, Martin Scheinin and Julia Kozma, produced a draft Consolidated Statute and Commentary in 2010 (Kozma et al. 2010), which was endorsed by the Panel on Human Dignity in 2011. One of the main features of the proposal was its application to 'entities,' defined to include 'any business corporation.' Pursuant to Article 5 of the draft: 'the Court shall have jurisdiction in respect of violations committed by any State Party or Entity of any human right enshrined' in a list of 21 human rights treaties. However, under Article 51 of the draft, that jurisdiction is constrained by whatever competency the relevant entity voluntarily accepts. Analogous with the role of State consent to the jurisdiction of the International Court of Justice, Article 51 of the draft permits the relevant entity to recognize the competence of the Court to receive and examine complaints in respect of all or just some of the human rights encapsulated within the treaties that form the Court's overall mandate. Assuming that the relevant TNC accepts the jurisdiction of the Court, then pursuant to Article 18 of the draft any rulings in relation to breach and reparation are legally binding. Subsequently, the draft Statute has been endorsed by the Association of Human Rights Institutes and the ICJ (Nowak 2014).

The project to establish a World Court of Human Rights received a further boost in 2014 when a proposed Statute of the World Court of Human Rights known as the Treaty of Lucknow was drafted by a global collaboration of judges, lawyers and scholars and endorsed by the World Judiciary Summit (World Court of Human Rights Development Project 2016). However the draft treaty does not address the responsibility of TNCs for human rights violations, and compared with the earlier Swiss sponsored draft the Lucknow draft is far more embryonic. Outside of the World Judiciary Summit, it has not garnered international support. Consequently, should a consensus develop in the OEIWG for a World Court of Human Rights incorporating jurisdiction over business related human rights violations, the Swiss draft provides the more mature model for implementation.

5 Conclusion: A Multi-pronged Approach

It seems likely that the UNCPs' emphasis on improving State level enforcement through capacity building, mutual legal assistance, provision of access to redress and assistance to victims, as well as the expansion of jurisdiction to incorporate TNC and subsidiary misconduct will continue to be the major means of improving enforcement and human rights compliance. In the longer term it may be possible to explore the creation of an arbitral tribunal with power to determine whether human rights breaches have occurred and to award reparations to victims. The use of collective redress techniques, litigation funding and contingency fees should provide enough entrepreneurial incentive for lawyers and financiers to assist victims to obtain redress. While a World Court on Human Rights adopting transparent formal court procedures and delivering consistent precedent may be preferable from a normative point of view, such a proposal seems unlikely to gain sufficient global support to make it a practical reality. Moreover, consistency in interpretation and the articulation of standards and guidance that might inform how binding obligations should be implemented can be undertaken by a treaty monitoring body, which can also undertake monitoring and supervision. Adding processes that facilitate individual communications, thematic rapporteurs and investigation of systemic abuse similar to those that operate under other human rights instruments will provide further incentive for State and business compliance.

With a very minor amendment it is possible to expand the ICC's jurisdiction to include a power to punish egregious human rights violations committed by TNCs. As a result of complaints that the ICC is biased against African nations, such an amendment which could be seen as tipping the scales more fairly against the corporate interests of western economies when those interests behave in a way that is simply unacceptable to humanity as a whole. This chapter therefore favours an hierarchical approach to enforcement of TNC human rights obligations: (1) consistent with OHCHR recommendations better alignment and strengthening of State regulation of corporate conduct with international human rights obligations; and (2) submission of human rights breaches that also comprise breaches of international criminal law to the ICC where host States are unwilling or unable to provide redress.

References

Aaronson, S. A., & Higham, I. (2013). "Re-righting business": John Ruggie and the struggle to develop international human rights standards for transnational firms. *Human Rights Quarterly, 35*(2), 333–364.

Abaclat v Argentina. (2011). ICSID Case No ARB/07/5, Decision on Jurisdiction and Admissibility.

Addo, M. K. (2014). The reality of the United Nations guiding principles on business and human rights. *Human Rights Law Review, 14*(1), 133–147.

African Union. (2014). *Protocol on amendments to the protocol on the statute of the African Court of justice and human rights*. s.l.:s.n.

Alston, P. (2014). Against a world court for human rights. *Ethics & International Affairs, 28*(2), 197–212.

Ambach, P. (2015). A look towards the future—The ICC and 'lessons learnt'. In C. Stahn (Ed.), *The law and practice of the international criminal court* (pp. 1277–1293). Oxford: Oxford University Press.

Amnesty International. (2016). *Island of despair: Australia's "processing" of Refugees on Nauru*. London: Amnesty International.

Anvil Mining Ltd. c. Association canadienne contre l'impunité. (2012). QCCA 117.

Australian Broadcasting Corporation. (2005). *The Kilwa Incident*. [Online] Available at: http://www.abc.net.au/4corners/content/2005/s1384238.htm. Accessed November 22, 2016.

Baughen, S. (2015). *Human rights and corporate wrongs: Closing the governance gap*. Cheltenham: Edward Elgar Publishing.

Blitt, R. C. (2012). Beyond Ruggie's guiding principles on business and human rights: Charting an embracive approach to corporate human rights compliance. *Texas International Law Journal, 48*(1), 33–62.

Border Force Act. (2015). (Cth).

Cassell, D., & Ramasastry, A. (2016). White paper: Options for a treaty on business and human rights. *Notre Dame Journal of International and Comparative Law, 6*, 1–50.

Cassidy, J. (2008). Watchdog or paper tiger: The enforcement of human rights in international forums. *University of Notre Dame Law Review, 10*, 37–59.

Childress, D. E., III. (2015). Is an international arbitral tribunal the answer to the challenges of litigating transnational human rights in a post-Kiobel world? *UCLA Journal of International Law and Foreign Affairs, 19*, 31–48.

Clapham, A. (2014). Non-state actors. In D. Moeckli, S. Shah, S. Sivakumaran, & D. Harris (Eds.), *International human rights law* (pp. 531–549). Oxford: Oxford University Press.

Cole, W. M. (2012). Human rights as myth and ceremony? Reevaluating the effectiveness of human rights treaties, 1981–2007. *American Journal of Sociology, 117*(4), 1131–1171.

Cole, W. M. (2015). Mind the gap: State capacity and the implementation of human rights treaties. *International Organization, 69*(2), 405–441.

Cotula, L. (2016). Rethinking investment treaties to advance human rights. *ILED Briefing, 2016* (September), 1–5.

Cronstedt, C., & Thompson, R. C. (2016). A proposal for an international arbitration tribunal on business and human rights. *Harvard International Law Journal, 2016*(Spring), 66–69.

Dai, X. (2013). The "compliance gap" and the efficacy of international human rights institutions. In T. Risse, S. C. Ropp, & K. Sikkink (Eds.), *The persistent power of human rights: From commitment to compliance* (pp. 85–102). Cambridge: Cambridge University Press.

de Jonge, A. (2011). Transnational corporations and international law: Bringing TNCs out of the accountability vacuum. *Critical Perspectives on International Business, 71*, 66–89.

Delmas-Marty, M. (2013). Ambiguities and lacunae: The international criminal court ten years on. *Journal of International Criminal Justice, 11*(3), 553–561.

Doe I v Cisco Systems, Inc. (2014). 66 F Supp 3d. 1239.

Donoho, D. (2006). Human rights enforcement in the twenty-first century. *Georgia Journal of International and Comparative Law, 35*(1), 1–52.

European Commission. (2015). *Implementing the UN guiding principles on business and human rights—State of play. Commission Staff Working Document*, Brussels: s.n.

Feeney, P. (2009). Business and human rights: The struggle for accountability in the un and the future direction of the advocacy agenda. *Sur. Revista internacional de direitos humanos [online], 6*(11), 161–175.

Frynas, J. G., & Pegg, S. (eds). (2003). *Transnational corporations and human rights*. Basingstoke, Hampshire; New York: Palgrave Macmillan.

Gallegos, L., & Uribe, D. (2016). The next step against corporate impunity: A world court on business and human rights? *Harvard Journal of International Law, 57*(Spring), 7–10.

Giannoulopoulos, D. (2016). *Britain must hold fast to the European convention on human rights as it leaves the EU.* [Online] Available at: http://blogs.lse.ac.uk/brexit/2016/11/24/britain-must-hold-fast-to-the-european-convention-on-human-rights-as-it-leaves-the-eu/. Accessed December 1, 2016.

Giroud, S., & Moss, S. (2015). Mass claims processes under public international law. In E. Lein, D. Fairgrieve, M. O. Crespo, & V. Smith (Eds.), *Collective redress in Europe: Why and how?* (pp. 481–503). London: British Institute of International and Comparative Law.

Grear, A., & Weston, B. H. (2015). The betrayal of human rights and the urgency of universal corporate accountability: Reflections on a post-Kiobel lawscape. *Human Rights Law Review, 15*(1), 21–44.

Hafner-Burton, E. M., & Ron, J. (2009). Seeing double: Human rights impact through qualitative and quantitative eyes. *World Politics, 61*(2), 360–401.

Hillebrecht, C. (2012). The domestic mechanisms of compliance with international human rights law: Case studies from the Inter-American human rights system. *Human Rights Quarterly, 34*(4), 959–985.

International Commission of Jurists. (2016). *Proposals for elements of a legally binding instrument on transnational corporations and other business enterprises.* Geneva: International Commission of Jurists.

International Organisation of Employers; International Chamber of Commerce, Business and Industry Advisory Committee & World Business Council for Sustainable Development. (2016). *UN treaty process on business and human rights: Further considerations by the international business community on a way forward.* [Online] Available at: https://business-humanrights.org/en/un-treaty-process-on-business-and-human-rights-further-considerations-by-the-international-business-community-on-a-way-forward. Accessed April 13, 2017.

JHA v Spain. (2008). CAT/C/41/D/323/2007.

Karavias, M. (2015). Shared responsibility and multinational enterprises. *Netherlands International Law Review, 62,* 91–117.

Kiobel v Royal Dutch Petroleum Co. (2013). 133 S. Ct 1659.

Knuckey, S., & Jenkin, E. (2015). Company-created remedy mechanisms for serious human rights abuses: A promising new frontier for the right to a remedy? *International Journal of Human Rights, 19*(6), 801–827.

Kozma, J., Nowak, M., & Scheinin, M. (2010). *A world court of human rights: Consolidated statute and commentary.* Vienna, Graz: Neuer Wissenschaftlicher Verlag.

Kyriakakis, J. (2008). Corporations and the international criminal court: The complementarity objection stripped bare. *Criminal Law Forum, 19,* 115–151.

M68/2015 v Mins for Immigration and Border Protection. (2016). 327 ALR 369.

Mariniello, T. (2015). 'One, no one and one hundred thousand' reflections on the multiple identities of the ICC. In T. Mariniello (Ed.), *The international criminal court in search of its identity and purpose* (pp. 1–14). Abingdon; New York: Routledge.

Martinez, J. S. (2012). *The slave trade and the origins of international human rights law.* New York: Oxford University Press.

McBeth, A. (2014). Crushed by an anvil: A case study on responsibility for human rights in the extractive sector. *Yale Human Rights and Development Law Journal, 11,* 127–166.

McConnell, L. J. (2017). *Extracting accountability from non-state actors in international law: Assessing the scope for direct regulation.* London; New York: Routledge.

Namah v Pato. (2016). [2016] PGSC 13.

No Business in Abuse. (2015). *Transfield's complicity in gross human rights abuses.* Sydney: No Business in Abuse.

Nowak, A. (2015). *The international criminal court: An introduction.* Cham; Heidelberg; New York; Dordrecht; London: Springer.

Nowak, M. (2014). The right of victims of human rights violations to a remedy: The need for a world court of human rights. *Nordic Journal of Human Rights, 32*(1), 3–17.

Nowak, M., & Januszewski, K. M. (2015). Non-state actors and human rights. In M. Noortmann, A. Reinish, & C. Ryngaert (Eds.), *Non-state actors in international law* (pp. 113–161). Oxford; Portland: Hart Publishing.

Office of the High Commissioner, United Nations Human Rights. (2016a). *State national action plans.* [Online] Available at: http://www.ohchr.org/EN/Issues/Business/Pages/NationalActionPlans.aspx. Accessed November 16, 2016.

Office of the High Commissioner, United Nations Human Rights. (2016b). *Improving accountability and access to remedy for victims.* Brussels: Office of the High Commissioner, United Nations Human Rights.

Office of the High Commissioner, United Nations Human Rights. (2016c). *The OHCHR accountability and remedy project: Illustrative examples for guidance to improve corporate accountability and access to judicial remedy for business-related human rights abuse.* Brussels: Office of the High Commissioner, United Nations Human Rights.

Oxford University Faculty of Law. (2016). *Results from "a public debate: 'a world court for human rights?'"*. [Online] Available at: https://www.law.ox.ac.uk/news/2016-06-15-results-%E2%80%9C-public-debate-world-court-human-rights. Accessed December 1, 2016.

Pak, N. S., & Nussbaumer, J. P. (2009). *Beyond impunity: Strengthening the legal accountability of transnational corporations for human rights abuses.* s.l.: Hertie School of Governance.

Pierre v Anvil Mining Management NL. (2008). WASC 30.

Prihandono, I. (2011). Barriers to transnational human rights litigation against transnational corporations (TNCS): The need for cooperation between home and host countries. *Journal of Law and Conflict Resolution, 3*(7), 89–103.

Ramcharan, B. G. (2011). *The fundamentals of international human rights treaty law.* Dordrecht: BRILL.

Rosenfeld, F. (2013). Mass claims in international law. *Journal of International Dispute Settlement, 4*(1), 159–174.

Ruggie, J. (2013). *Just business: Multinational corporations and human rights.* New York; London: WW Norton.

Ruggie, J. (2014). Global governance and 'new governance theory': Lessons from business and human rights. *Global Governance, 20*(1), 5–17.

Rott, P., & Ulfbeck, V. (2015). Supply chain liability of multinational corporations? *European Review of Private Law 23*(3), 415–436.

Russian Federation. (2015). *Law of the Russian Federation no. 7-KFZ (CDL-REF(2016)006.*

Sarfaty, G. A. (2015). Shining a light on global supply chains. *Harvard Journal of International Law 56*(2), 419–463.

SBS. (2014). *Dateline: The inside story.* [Online] Available at: http://www.sbs.com.au/news/dateline/story/inside-story. Accessed November 22, 2016.

Schabas, W. S. (2011). *An introduction to the international criminal court* (4th ed.). Cambridge: Cambridge University Press.

Shelton, D. (2013). Enforcement and remedies. In S. Sheeran & S. N. Rodley (Eds.), *Routledge handbook on international human rights law* (pp. 663–681). London and New York: Routledge.

Skinner, G., McCorquodale, R., De Schutter, O., & Lambe, A. (2013). *The third pillar: Access to judicial remedies for human rights violations by transnational business.* s.l.: International Corporate Accountability Roundtable, CORE and the European Coalition for Corporate Justice.

Social Service Agency, Global Policy Forum, Geneva Infant Feeding Association, Friends of the Earth Europe and CIDSE. (2015). *Written statement submitted to the human rights council open-ended intergovernmental working group on transnational corporations and other business enterprises with respect to human rights.* Geneva: United Nations, Human Rights Council.

Strong, S. (2013). *Class, mass and collective arbitration in national and international law.* New York: Oxford University Press.

Trechsel, S. (2004). A world court for human rights? *Northwestern Journal of International Human Rights, 1*(1), p. Art 3.

Tsakaridis, A. A. (2016). Corporate responsibility and human rights in the context of an international constitutional framework: The case of Angola. In L. Fielder & K. Topidi (Eds.), *Transnational legal processes and human rights* (pp. 245–265). Surrey; Burlington: Routledge.

United Kingdom, Border Agency. (2009). *Country of origin information report: The democratic republic of Congo*. London: United Kingdom Home Office.

United Nations Human Rights Council. (2007). *5/1 Institution-building of the United Nations Human Rights Council*.

United Nations Human Rights Council. (2014). *Resolution 26/9 elaboration of an international legally binding instrument on transnational corporations and other business enterprises with respect to human rights*. s.l.:United Nations Human Rights Council.

United Nations Human Rights Council (2016). *Open-ended intergovernmental working group on transnational corporations and other business enterprises with respect to human rights*. [Online] Available at: http://www.ohchr.org/EN/HRBodies/HRC/WGTransCorp/Pages/IGWGOnTNC.aspx. Accessed November 17, 2016.

United Nations Organization Mission in the Democratic Republic of Congo. (2005). *Report on the conclusions of the special investigation concerning allegations of summary executions and other human rights violations perpetrated by the Armed Forces of the Democratic Republic of Congo (FARDC) in Kilwa (Katanga Province) 15 October 2004*, s.l.: s.n.

United Nations, Committee on the Rights of the Child. (2016). *Concluding observations on the initial report of Nauru*. Geneva: United Nations, Committee on the Rights of the Child.

UR v Uruguay. (1983). UN Doc CCPRC/C/18/D/128/1982.

Whelan, G., Moon, J., & Orlitzky, M. (2009). Human rights, transnational corporations and embedded liberalism: What chance consensus. *Journal of Business Ethics, 97*, 367–383.

World Court of Human Rights Development Project. (2016). *The role and jurisdiction of the world court of human rights* [Online] Available at: http://www.worldcourtofhumanrights.net/home. Accessed December 1, 2016.

World Justice Project. (2016). *Rule of law index*. Washington, DC: The World Justice Project.

Zambrana-Tevar, N. (2015). *Can arbitration become the preferred grievance mechanism in conflicts related to business and human rights?* [Online] Available at: https://ssrn.com/abstract=2531890 or http://dx.doi.org/10.2139/ssrn.2531890. Accessed December 2, 2016.

Zerk, J. (2014). *Corporate liability for gross human rights abuses*. Geneva: OHCHR.

Professor Vicki Waye is currently the Chair of the University of South Australia Academic Board and a member of the UniSA University Council, a Foundation Professor of Law at the School of Law, and from 2010 to 2015 was the Dean of Teaching and Learning at the University of South Australia Business School (incorporating Business and Law). Professor Waye's teaching expertise includes Arbitration Law (both national and international), Evidence and Procedure, Corporate Law, Contract Law and Wine Law. Professor Waye's research focusses on two main fields—firstly, systems of justice, including ways that access to justice is affected by matters such as litigation funding and mechanisms of collective redress, and secondly, international trade law, particularly the global food trade.

Converged Approach in Regulation for Socializing Transnational Corporations

Mia Mahmudur Rahim

1 Introduction

The lengthy attempt to create a global code for TNCs was ultimately unsuccessful, yet the simultaneous rise of global frameworks and guidelines by various private bodies highlight the need for monitoring of the performance of TNCs in addition to evaluation of their accountability practice (Christmann and Taylor 2006; Rasche et al. 2013; Waddock 2008). As Chaps. 1 and 3 of this book describe, there are several global frameworks and guidelines that attempt to address this need. These frameworks are initiated by different groups of countries and international organisations whose objectives are not only divergent but also at times contradictory (Maon et al. 2009; O'Rourke 2003; Runhaar and Lafferty 2009; Schembera 2018). As such none of these frameworks and guidelines has been successful in laying down a clear way forward for the creation of an accepted global regulatory framework for TNCs. Indeed, it is hard to create such a framework in this era of globalisation. Globalisation has dramatically changed the architecture of global business and governance. It has provided ample opportunities for TNCs to spread their business operations, acquire and misuse resources, and grasp control over political decision-making processes. It has also given rise to a new political arrangement due to existing conflicts between TNCs and stakeholders (Monbiot 2013). The CSR movement is a reaction to these conflicts; it assists the shift of the market centred focus of global regulatory framework initiatives to 'people centred' (as opposed to country-centred) concerns (Gilpin 2018). Accordingly, the core CSR principles urge that TNCs must not only be compliant but also responsible to their wider stakeholders and the environment. Ultimately, this chapter argues that an

M. M. Rahim (✉)
School of Law, University of South Australia,
GPO Box 2471, Adelaide, SA 5001, Australia
e-mail: mia.rahim@unisa.edu.au

© Springer Nature Switzerland AG 2019
M. M. Rahim (ed.), *Code of Conduct on Transnational Corporations*,
CSR, Sustainability, Ethics & Governance,
https://doi.org/10.1007/978-3-030-10816-8_8

effective implementation of CSR principles by business corporations and their subsidiaries worldwide can serve the purpose of a global code of conduct for TNCs.

This is the final chapter of this book. Generally, the last chapter provides a synopsis of the key points of the preceding chapters; the design of this chapter, however, is an exception to the general convention. This chapter builds on the point built by the preceding chapter, namely that TNCs should be responsible for mitigating the loss accrued by their operations, and that the chance of creating a global framework to ensure this mitigation is difficult and highly obscure. This chapter presents how the implementation of CSR principles in corporations can be an alternative to a global code of conduct for socializing TNCs. It proceeds as follows. Firstly, it briefly defines CSR and its principles. Secondly, it assesses the arguments that underpin the debate surrounding the voluntary and mandatory approaches in implementing CSR principles. Thirdly, it presents the 'converged approach' and explains how this approach in regulation can assist regulators, stakeholders, and business corporations to raise corporate social responsibility performance. Finally, it concludes by providing a synopsis of this chapter.

2 Corporate Social Responsibility and Its Principles

2.1 Corporate Social Responsibility

Corporate Social Responsibility (CSR) is a fluid concept (Hopkins 2004; Marrewijk 2003). Its interchangeable and overlapping character is dominant in its various definitions. To some scholars, this concept is a source of competitive advantage; to others, it is 'an important response to the increasing demands of key stakeholders such as employees, investors, consumers and environmentalists' (Bagi et al. 2004). Again, the precepts of CSR change with each generation, and its criteria may change according to the society in question (Kakabadse et al. 2005). For instance, its meaning in Europe is different to its meaning in the USA or in developing or transitional societies. In the USA, companies consider philanthropy as a dominant factor of CSR; while in northern European economies companies bear their social responsibilities by paying taxes (ibid.: 280). In these circumstances, a consistent terminology for this concept is yet to be developed. It is currently described using a number of terms: corporate citizenship, the notion of an ethical corporation, CG, corporate sustainability, socially responsible investment, corporate accountability, and so on. There is as yet no overall agreement on its definition. The concepts underlying these terms are internally consistent and converge on certain common qualities and similar elements. In a broader sense, CSR is about the impact of business on a society or, in other words, the role of companies in the development of the society. In a narrower sense, it is a complex and multi-dimensional organisational phenomenon that may be defined as the extent to which, and the way in which, an organisation is consciously responsible for its actions (and non-actions) and the impact of these actions on its stakeholders.

CSR can be defined in various ways. Carroll (1999) provides an account of the evolution of the definition of CSR beginning from the 1950s and continuing through to the 1990s, focusing on specific features of each decade in terms of its development. Carroll (1999) notes that in the 1980s, some alternative theoretical issues were added to the concept itself, including corporate social performance, stakeholder theory, and business ethics theory (Freeman and McVea 2001). In the definitional development that occurred in the 1990s, these alternative themes took centre stage in the manifestation of CSR and all subsequent definitions were dominated by the stakeholder and societal approach, with the recognition of social, economic, and environmental issues as the basic components of responsibility. The best illustration of this is available in the definitions and views developed in the late 1990s and subsequently by different intergovernmental, government, and development organisations in addition to postmodern academics (Dahlsurd 2008).

The World Business Council for Sustainable Development defines CSR as 'the continuing commitment by business to behave ethically and contribute to economic development while improving the quality of life of the workforce and their families as well as of the local community and society at large' (Watts and Holme 1999: 3). According to this definition, business societies have responsibilities to contribute to the development of their employees, their families, the local community, and wider society to improve their quality of life and thus to try to ensure sustainable economic development (ibid.). The phrase 'continuing commitment' used in this definition indicates that CSR is not a temporary issue that a company considers only in certain situations. Rather, it is a permanent issue that should be placed strategically within the policies and programs of companies. Business for Social Responsibility defines CSR in a more holistic way. This organisation refers to CSR as a tool for 'achieving commercial success in ways that honour ethical values and respect people, communities, and the natural environment' (White 2006: 6). Thus, Business for Social Responsibility relates CSR to the idea of recognising and responding to a broader spectrum of stakeholder interests. The International Business Leaders Forum extends this idea and accepts it as a responsible business practice that could benefit business and society by maximising the positive impact business has on society while minimising the negative impact. In a similar fashion, a Green Paper published by the European Commission in 2001 defines CSR as 'a concept whereby companies integrate social and environmental concerns in their business operations and in their interactions with their stakeholders on a voluntary basis' (European Commission 2001). The World Economic Forum identifies the concerns for responsible business as follows:

> ...To do business in a manner that obeys the law, produces safe and cost-effective products and services, creates jobs and wealth, supports training and technology cooperation and reflects international standards and values in areas such as the environment, ethics, labour and human rights. To make every effort to enhance the positive multipliers of our activities and to minimise any negative impacts on people and the environment, everywhere we invest and operate. A key element of this is recognising that the frameworks we adopt for being a responsible business must move beyond philanthropy and be integrated into core business strategy and practice (World Economic Forum 2002).

Given these definitions, CSR appears to be a managing element that starts at the company level by its performance in a socially responsible manner, where the trade-offs between the needs and requirements of different stakeholders are balanced and acceptable to all.[1] In a recent publication, rather than giving any conclusive definition of CSR, the Australian Parliamentary Joint Committee on Corporations and Financial Services examined the concept of CSR from the following standpoints: (a) considering, managing and balancing the economic, social, and environmental impacts of companies' activities; (b) assessing and managing risks, pursuing opportunities, and creating corporate value beyond the traditional core business; and (c) taking an 'enlightened self-interest' approach to consider the legitimate interests of stakeholders in CG.[2]

Hopkins (2004) defines CSR as 'treating the stakeholders of the firm ethically or in a socially responsible manner'. Here, the words 'ethically' and 'responsible' emphasise the notion that the treatment of stakeholders must be deemed acceptable in civilised society for CSR to function effectively. According to Hopkins (2004), this treatment of stakeholders is an economic responsibility of companies (ibid.). Marsden (2001) perceives CSR as a core behavioural issue for companies. He states that 'CSR is not an optional add-on nor is it an act of philanthropy. A socially responsible corporation is one that runs a profitable business that takes account of all the positive and negative environmental, social and economic effects it has on society' (Marsden 2001). Andersen defines CSR as following a broader societal approach. He states that the broader meaning of CSR relates to the extension of 'the immediate interest from oneself to include one's fellow citizens and the society one is living in and is a part of today, acting with respect for the future generation and nature' (Dahlsrud 2008: 11).[3]

All of the definitions outlined above confirm that there is no conclusive definition of CSR and that it can have different meanings to different people and different organisations as an ever-growing, multifaceted concept. Nevertheless, it may be said that the concept of CSR is consistent and converges on certain common characteristics and elements. More precisely, if CSR as defined above is examined from a practical and operational point of view, it converges on two points.

---

[1]The definition offered by the European Commission mentioned in the text was made in 2001. However, the later definition made in 2002 speaks broadly of CSR, stating: 'Corporate responsibility is about companies having responsibilities and taking actions beyond their legal obligations and economic/business aims. These wider responsibilities cover a range of areas but as frequently summed up as social and environmental—where social means society broadly defined, rather than simply social policy issues. This can be summed up as the triple bottom line approach, that is, economic, social and environmental.'

[2]For details of this report, check this link: https://www.aph.gov.au/Parliamentary_Business/Committees/Joint/Corporations_and_Financial_Services/Completed_inquiries/2004-07/corporate_responsibility/report/index.

[3]While other scholars have studied CSR, to respect space constraints and retain the focus on the main theme of this chapter, only the works of these three recent and well-cited scholars are mentioned here. Some other prominent works are: Buhmann (2006), Carroll (1991, 1999), Conley and Williams (2005), Fox (2004), Lockett et al. (2006).

CSR requires companies: (a) to consider the social, environmental, and economic impacts of their operations; and (b) to be responsive to the needs and expectations of their stakeholders. These two points are also embedded in the meaning of the three words (i.e., 'corporate', 'social', and 'responsibility') of the phrase 'corporate social responsibility'. The word 'corporate' generally denotes business operations, 'social' covers all the stakeholders of business operations, and the word 'responsibility' generally refers to the relationship between business corporations and the societies within which they act. It also encompasses the innate responsibilities on both sides of this relationship. Accordingly, CSR is an integral element of business strategy: it is a way of delivering products or services to the market; it is a way of maintaining the legitimacy of corporate actions in wider society by bringing stakeholder concerns to the foreground; and a way to emphasise business concern for social needs and actions that go beyond philanthropy.

Despite the inconclusive definitions, different approaches and many dimensions of CSR, the principal notions of this concept have already been established. Although these notions are not conclusive, they are consistent and have converged on common characteristics and similar elements. These are related to the economic, social and environmental impacts of business operations and their responses to customers' expectations, employees, shareholders, and stakeholders in the context of these impacts. CSR is no longer confined to corporate philanthropy; rather, it has been established that accepting social responsibilities has a positive effect on companies' financial performance. Thus, CSR has established the core principles for furthering appropriate strategies for incorporating its various notions into corporate practice.

2.2 CSR Principles

The concept of corporate social responsibility can be traced back to the medieval ages; though on a contemporary note, it emerged in business related matters roughly 60 years ago. In one of the earlier models proposed, the concept of CSR was conceived as services rendered beyond economic and legal obligations, assuming it as a synonym to philanthropy. During the 1960s, such philanthropic notions were entwined with the improvement of relations between customers and employees of the firm. This application of CSR also enabled improvement in the management practices that could facilitate a firm's social impact and performance in relation to the society. The 1990s saw the unprecedented acceptance and growth of the concept and its relationship with a corporation's reputation and performance. As it is a scenario induced by globalization, it is also exposed to tightening regulations, intense competition, public scrutiny, and above all, towering expectations. CSR as of today is not only a significant part of huge financial deals but also a robust opportunity for business strategies. It has emerged as a fundamental management strategy of the twenty-first century.[4]

The 'triple bottom line' introduced by Elkington (1998) is one of the robust models that discuss the core of CSR. Within this model, the CSR concept emphasizes three responsibilities of a corporation, namely the social, economic, and environmental responsibilities, which promote economic prosperity, environmental quality, and social justice (ibid.).[5] Carroll (1979) identifies four responsibilities a business corporation should undertake to become socially responsible in a balanced way: 'the economic, legal, ethical and discretionary expectations that society has of organizations at a given point of time'. Another strong argument in the recent CSR practice scholarship is related to stakeholder engagement with corporate social responsibility performance. Freeman (1984) argues that the corporation has a responsibility to include stakeholders in corporate activities, as stakeholder engagement is a vital way for corporations to connect with their external environment effectively (Donaldson and Preston 1995; Freeman 1984). Considering these major sources of CSR practices, these practices could be grouped into four major orientations, which are: societal, environmental, economic, and stakeholder orientations.

Each of these orientations has different perspectives in their definitions and boundary of responsibilities in addition to their individual underlying principles (Marrewijk 2003). Briefly, the key principle of the societal orientation of CSR is that business corporations should contribute to building better societies and therefore they should include social concerns in their core strategies in addition to considering the full scope of their impact on societies. More particularly, this principle requires corporations to implement fair wage policy, uphold human rights, fair trade and ethical issues, produce safe products, and cooperate in the networks of corporations and communities (Garriga and Melé 2004; Konrad et al. 2006; Marrewijk 2003). The economic principle emphasises corporations' efficiencies in producing social goods without manipulating social and environmental values (Elkington 2001; Juholin 2004). This principle denotes that along with responses to the financial expectations of shareholders, business corporations should also address the economic wellbeing of the society as a whole (Konrad et al. 2006). The environmental principle, in short, is that corporations should not harm the environment in order to maximise their profits and should play a key role in repairing

---

[4]Nevertheless, the framework also received formidable opposition based upon evidence that the concept is not sufficiently firm to address the majority of the conflicts arising due to trade related issues among TNCs and developing countries. Some critics believe that CSR adds social and environmental clauses resulting in protectionism through the back door, and fosters disproportionate cultural standards and arbitrary bureaucratic monitoring demands on business corporations. Nonetheless, CSR movement has largely been successful in establishing that business corporations need to be socially responsible. The debate on the validity of CSR principles is therefore no longer at the centre of CSR discussion; instead, the debate is focused on how to incorporate these principles at the core of corporate self-regulation strategies. For details see Bakan (2012) and Peattie et al. (2002).

[5]For a discussion on the implementation of these precepts in corporations, see Thompson (2005).

the environmental damage made by their irresponsible usage of natural resources in the past (Matten and Moon 2007; McAdam and Leonard 2003). Finally, the key principle of the stakeholder orientation of CSR practices holds corporations responsible in considering the legitimate interests of their stakeholders (Freeman et al. 2006; Jamali 2008). These principles are the drivers of the sources of different CSR practices and hence important factors for initiating any strategies for developing CSR practices (Jamali et al. 2006; Windsor 2001). These principles cover the possible socio-political, environmental, and economic responsibilities of a corporation in a society. These principles are not prescriptive and do not go against the profit-making objective of a business corporation. Incorporating these principles into the self-regulation of business corporations would be a viable way to make large corporations, irrespective of their origin, responsible to social issues and accountable to stakeholders.

CSR is one of the most important frameworks for governing nonfinancial and environmental corporate performance. It is widely used by TNCs and has received acknowledgement by many key international actors and civil societies (De Bakker et al. 2005; Economist 2005; Margolis and Walsh 2003). Business society has accepted the CSR principles and has attempted to converge these principles with the precepts of corporate governance to enable business corporations and their operations to be more attuned to ethical and accountability norms. This convergence has already created a notable impact in corporate regulation practice: 'where there were once two separate sets of mechanisms, one dealing with 'hard core' corporate decision-making and the other with 'soft', people-friendly business strategies, scholars now point to a more hybridized, synthesized body of strategies and norms regulating corporate practices' (Gill 2008: 463). Many corporations have broadened the narrow scope of their governance, incorporated agency focus to address corporate ethics and accountability, and begun adding a broader stakeholder focus in their strategies.[6] By including issues such as human rights, workers' rights, and environmental protection with 'self-regulation', corporate directors gain opportunities to develop stakeholder engagement programs that could raise their competitiveness and to launch marketing campaigns that would emphasise their humanistic and democratic values as 'corporate citizens'.[7] Due to this increasing change in

---

[6]In many strong economies, for instance, many corporations have appropriate measures to internalise the costs externalised to the environment for their business operations. Their initiatives are not driven mainly by laws; rather, they are driven by the corporate conscience (along with business opportunities) to minimise costs as well as to contribute to environmental development. For some real-world instances, see Esty and Winston (2009), Pflum (2007), and Schmit (2010).

[7]Corporate citizenship is a contentious, but prominent idea in corporate management. The World Economic Forum in 2003 defined this citizenship as 'the contribution a corporation makes to society through its core business activities, its social investment and philanthropy programmes, and its engagement in public policy.' Many scholars argue that it is one of the outcomes of the impact of globalisation. Matten and Crane (2005) opine that 'globalisation has helped to shift some of the responsibility for protecting citizenship rights away from governments' and corporations have increasingly taken these responsibilities. They differentiate between the citizenship of a person in a country and corporate citizenship, as they describe this citizenship as 'the role of the

business society and corporate regulation practices, although the challenges in organizational implementation of these principles have been reduced, we have yet to create a conclusive strategy for an effective implementation of these principles in business corporations. Arguments for voluntary and mandatory strategies for this implementation are equally dominant; they contradict each other and have yet to converge through a suitable strategy.

3 Voluntary and Mandatory Modes for Implementing CSR Principles

This section discusses the core strategies related to the implementation of CSR principles. One of the key strategies involves relying on business corporations and other private bodies for this implementation. The second key strategy relies on the rule making power of the state for the inclusion of CSR principles in corporate 'due diligence'.[8] These two strategies are commonly known as the voluntary and mandatory modes for implementing CSR principles.

The voluntary mode refers to a CSR-implementation process that is dependent on the will of a corporate entity. It denotes that corporate entities may or may not add CSR principles to the core of their internal strategies, and there is no external force to bind them to add these principles in a particular way. This mode is predominant in the CSR literature; it is typically used by corporations in their CSR practices and has many advantages that can improve the outcomes of traditional policy dimensions (Peters and Turner 2004).[9] Through this mode, corporate bodies can: (a) achieve better flexibility in terms of the ways and means of reaching targets; (b) increase the scope of discussion amongst stakeholders; (c) enhance public

---

corporations in administering citizenship rights for individuals'. In the same vein, Gardberg and Fombrun (2006) claim that programs for corporate citizenship 'are strategic investments comparable to R&D and advertising. The can create intangible assets that help corporations overcome nationalistic barriers, facilitate globalization, and outcompete local rivals....citizenship profiles therefore enable the sociocognitive integration that global corporations require to operate effectively across diverse local markets.' I find this idea dominated by the notion of corporate social responsibility; it holds the broader objectives of the CSR movement. As such I find the discussion on the implementation of the CSR principles more plausible than evaluating the contentions around this idea.

[8]Black's US Law Dictionary defines due diligence as follows: 'the diligence, [that is such a measure of prudence, activity, or assiduity, as is] reasonably expected from, and ordinarily exercised by, a person who seeks to satisfy a legal requirement or discharge an obligation' (8th edition, 2006). John Ruggie's definition of this concept is based on this definition; he denotes due diligence as 'a process whereby corporations not only ensure compliance with national laws but also manage the risk of human rights harm with a view to avoiding it' (para 55, UNHRC GA, Report of 7 April 2008; UN Doc. A/HRC/8/5).

[9]For more discussion of the merits of the voluntary mode of CSR practices, see Kolk et al. (1999) and Schrage (2004) cited in Rowe (2005: 3).

image; (d) promote innovations; and (e) reduce enforcement costs, among others (Cavaliere 2000; Peters and Turner 2004; OECD 1997). The most important benefit of this mode is its focus on co-operation and compromise rather than confrontation (Peter and Turner 2004). This mode helps to create consensus-building strategies and provides flexibility that enables participants to take action according to their needs and corporation type (Bizer and Julich 1999; Brau and Carraro 1999; Carraro and Siniscalco 1996; OECD 1997). From an economic perspective, this mode can also benefit corporations in a way that is relevant to their own situations (Arora and Cason 1995). In their work, Peter and Turner (2004) describes how 'unpriced' economic return is obtainable from the voluntary mode of CSR in corporate management, which generates the same type of efficiency advantages as priced incentives (e.g., via emission taxes and permits).

Nevertheless, the voluntary mode of CSR is not flawless.[10] Rather, it is continuously stressed in the empirical literature that this mode on its own is not a panacea for the CSR and corporate regulation nexus; it has many intrinsic limitations likely to hinder its effectiveness (UNEP 1998).[11] The flux of this mode largely depends on the potential participants who believe that there are sufficient benefits to these types of practices. Where there is no such business self-interest, this mode may not be effective, and this may be interpreted as a weakness of CSR (Sairinen and Teittinen 1999). At this point, to propose new corporate regulations that go beyond CSR and touch on concrete and enforceable legal rules, several scholars have developed a body of scholarship frequently entitled 'Progressive Corporate Law'. They reject the voluntary nature of CSR, with its focus on self-regulatory ethics, and suggest far more comprehensive, mandatory changes to the fundamental legal structure of corporations (Greenfield 2000; Mitchell 2001; Testy 2004), advocating for the mandatory mode of implementing CSR principles in corporate regulation. This mode refers to the implementation of these principles in corporate entities through regulation. In other words, it is based on legal regulation that binds a regulatee to adhere to a certain act following a given prescription. Legal regulation is buttressed by the political will of the sovereign power of a state, and hence, the regulatee is bound to implement the prescription of the regulator.

The voluntary mode requires a minimum of existing trust and co-operation between governmental agencies and industry to foster public confidence (Midttun 2008; White 2005). Without a satisfactory level of trust, it is not likely that a voluntary effort will form an effective partnership between corporate bodies and their stakeholders. Particularly for corporations, the creation of this trust is important, because limited trust amongst stakeholders makes it difficult to offset the costs of monitoring and verification by the potential efficiency gained from their voluntary CSR performance (Cavaliere 1998). Peter and Turner (2004: 10) note that 'unless the community can be convinced that offering regulatory relief to industry

---

[10]For a detailed discussion against the voluntary mode of CSR practices, see Matten et al. (2004), OECD (2003), and Zarsky (2002) in Rowe (2005).

[11]For a detailed discussion, see Peters and Turner (2004).

in exchange for voluntary action is a reasonable way ahead, it is likely that the corporations will find it difficult to get political acceptance' to implement their large-scale voluntary schemes successfully 'even where efficiency gains are felt to be certain'.

Voluntarily performing corporate social responsibilities requires both resources and skills (e.g., organizational strength, expertise, and considerable investment) without any definite gain in the short term (Bianchi and Noci 1998). It requires that business corporations incorporate CSR principles according to a detailed plan that can also add value to an organisation's economic performance. It is worth mentioning here that the requirement of incorporating CSR principles varies with corporation size. Whereas there may be incentives for large corporations to embrace CSR (e.g., increased consumer loyalty), this may not be the case for smaller corporations. In particular, from a financial and competitive-risk standpoint, it is more difficult to justify small corporations' CSR performance efforts than those of large corporations. Hence, incorporating CSR practices on a voluntary basis may be inappropriate for small corporations (Russell and Powell 1999).

The implementation of any holistic approach for incorporating CSR principles in corporate self-regulation through legal regulation could create an ideological imbalance in corporate governance. In the era of globalization in which 'deregulation' is a key principle, corporate societies as a whole may not prefer state-promulgated laws. Corporations perceive regulatory intervention in the market as opposing innovation and the free flow of market forces, and hence, turning from a voluntary mode of practice to a binding responsibility may be unwelcomed. At this point, there would be significant barriers to incorporating CSR principles in business laws and imposing sanctions upon corporations for their social and environmental irresponsibility. The proceeding section delves deeply into these contradicting modes of CSR implementation and discusses the arguments that underpin these two modes.

4 Pro-business and Pro-regulation Arguments for Including CSR Principles in Corporate Self-regulation

The contesting positions of the pro-business and pro-regulation arguments are the main source of disagreement on the mode of implementing CSR principles in corporate self-regulation. Again, the ideological contest between these two sets of arguments can be traced back to the broader debate on the issue of legislating versus not legislating. Philosophically, this debate is not new; it is the result of a longstanding political debate between the advocates of the neo-liberal school and those of the state-led school. Drawing on both schools' stands regarding the CSR implementation scholarship, the following part of this section explicates the gist of pro-business and pro-regulation arguments related to the inclusions of CSR principles at the core of corporate self-regulation.

4.1 Pro-business Arguments

The core of the pro-business arguments regarding the objective of corporate regulation is that the laws for regulating business activities should not interfere with internal business strategies, as this hampers innovation and obstructs businesses from reaching an optimal point in the market competition. The conceptual basis of this argument is the precept of the neo-liberal school.

The core precept of neo-liberalism is associated with the notions of individualism, market freedom, and deregulation. Taken together, these notions posit a minimalist, or non-interventionist, government. Individualism is an emphasis upon the importance of one's own freedom to choose strategies to fulfill self-interest. In this school, this notion is apparent in the separate legal personality doctrine. A business entity is a separate artificial person, and hence, it has the right to take its own course without following any prescriptions imposed from the government (Hanrahan et al. 2002). The market freedom notion in this school recommends reliance on market forces to allocate resources. According to this notion, an unregulated market is more efficient than a regulated one. It holds that if regulation is absent—though there could be tariffs and other artificial restrictions imposed upon businesses—there would still be scope for their own process for reaching business judgments in terms of financial cost and benefit, and profit and loss. Deregulation is closely related with this notion; indeed, this notion maintains that business in society is more likely to be encouraged if the existing rules regulating business are progressively relaxed or abolished.

This school, as a style of corporate regulation, relies more upon ideological commitment by the subject than direct coercion by the state. It demands that the regulation and resources of a state should be focused on the collective interest of the ruled rather than the interest of the ruler: 'it demands the recognition of a new kind of political subjectivity: the juridical subject in the administrative state obeys a different logic to that of the economic subject within civil society' (James 2008: 192).

Within the conceptual framework of this school, pro-business advocates argue that rather than regulations, market incentives drive CSR and business case relationships forward. According to this school, CSR is a tool used to gain advantages for the business. The neo-liberal school discourages regulation, as this may simply lead to competitive disadvantages. This school argues that corporations—whether performing social responsibilities or not—depend upon the market advantages or disadvantages of these responsibilities. According to the followers of this school, leaving these practices up to corporations could help them to develop a more profitable situation that helps them to accommodate their stakeholders and meet the demands of stakeholders through market incentives (González and Martinez 2004). In a broader sense, these incentives are the outcome of the market rationalities that aim to maximize market players' performance. The Coase theorem asserts that to achieve the social optimum, it is not necessary for government to set the standards of the market (Coase 1960: 44 cited in Peter and Turner 2004: 451). Moreover, Coase (1960) argues that private economic actors can solve the problems of externalities automatically among themselves when property rights over the assets are clearly defined and bargaining amongst the parties is allowed (Mankiw 2004: 201).

Friedman (1970) affirms this argument, rejecting any strategies that bind corporations to perform any responsibilities other than engaging themselves to generate more profits for their stockholders (Friedman 1970 in Windsor 2006: 96). In societies, every group has a specific function, and a corporation's main function is to do business to generate returns for investors. Adopting the agency theory framework, Friedman (2007) emphasises the commercial activities of corporations and contends that performing social responsibilities ends in decreased profit margins for business. To him, 'the alleged social responsibilities of business people are nothing but agents acting inappropriately as 'civil servants' (Kakabadse et al. 2005: 278) and hence 'business people eventually do more of a disservice than good to society' (Kakabadse et al. 2005: 279). Those arguing in this line also claim that corporations that incur costs for performing social responsibilities are at an economic disadvantage compared with other less socially responsible business corporations, which in turn hampers the effectiveness of the market (Bradgon and Marlin 1972; Vance 1975).

4.2 Pro-regulation Arguments

At the core of the pro-regulation arguments is the notion that government holds the political mandate to ensure the welfare of all and the proper allocation of assets in society. Hence, it should implement regulations to ensure that the gains generated in the market—a component of the society—are distributed to maximize the public interest. The conceptual basis of this argument is the precept of 'realism', a broad concept with different meanings in different disciplines. This concept denotes the present need, statement, and intricacies of a subject in a given circumstance. It is a dominant school of thought concerned with fact or reality and against impractical and visionary precepts. The precepts of realism that support the implementation of CSR principles in corporate self-regulation assume that reality inheres in the here and now, in the everyday, unlike Platonism and philosophical realism (or idealism).[12]

Proponents of this school contend that the 'states perform essential political, social and economic functions, and no other organization rivals them in these respects' (Burchill 2001: 96). States are understood as rational actors that pursue their national interest (ibid.: 93). Moreover, realists assume that states are

---

[12]For details on 'realism', see Garth and Sterling (1998), Sayer (2000), and Williamson (1996).

functionally similar and unitary actors (Hobson 2000: 20; Viotti and Kauppi 1999: 53–56). In other words, any differences of view among political leaders or domestic actors within the state are ultimately resolved so that the state speaks with one voice (Viotti and Kauppi 1999: 20). Accordingly, realists argue that the state should play a role in corporate regulation to: (1) respond to the public demand for correction of inefficient or inequitable market practices; (2) ensure that there are mechanisms guaranteeing benefit to the society as a whole rather than allowing any vested interest; and (3) assure the society that resources are directed to productive use.

Against the arguments of the neo-liberal school, pro-regulation advocates argue that a state needs to intervene in the market to drive CSR forward. To them, performance of these liabilities should not be totally vested upon the will of corporations, since market actors do not act rationally all the time and economies are not always self-balancing, even in an active welfare state (Stiglitz 2001: 345).[13] Despite the appealing logic of the Coase theorem, as Mankiw (2004: 211) contends, private actors on their own frequently fail to resolve the problems created by externalities.[14] This theorem applies only when the interested parties have no problem reaching and enforcing an agreement. However, it is not possible to confirm that bargaining will always work; even in the scope of a mutually beneficial agreement, there could be inappropriate bargaining. According to this theorem, desirable outcomes may not be achieved as a matter of routine, for example, in the issues of environmental development if the majority of businesses in the real world do not keenly seek to develop their environmental performance (Peter and Turner 2004: 451).

Corporations usually tend to use an imbalanced, rather than a balanced, economy, as this type of economy helps them to concentrate more on business outcomes.[15] In this economy, though there could be tough competition amongst corporations to maximize their individual market share, the average return of business generally remains higher than that in a balanced economy. Moreover, in this economy, corporations have increased scope to create monopolies vis-à-vis a guarantee of the highest return for a long period. In these circumstances, according to the followers of this school, governments need to intervene to ensure equal opportunity for all and to address large-scale misuse of natural resources. At this point, the role of government, particularly for the promotion of CSR practices, is to incorporate the principles of CSR through moderate regulations without placing corporations in disadvantageous positions. It is important to note that government intervention in CSR issues does not mean tilting the market rationality; rather,

---

[13]For details of this Nobel laureate economist's arguments on this point, see generally Bank (1997) and Stiglitz (1991, 2003).

[14]See generally Chang (2003) and Stiglitz (1996).

[15]Generally a balanced economy denotes a condition of finances in a country in which both its imports and its exports are of an equal proportion. It also denotes the equal proportion of business activities in rural and urban areas, equal gross ability of income and expenditure in all areas of a country, and minimum differences amongst the health and education services within all sectors of a country. An imbalanced economy is the opposite of a balanced economy.

it means ensuring corporations perform duties they are obliged to perform in return for the benefits they receive from government policy, social protection, and a broader scope of business. The US Supreme Court settled that corporations are 'presumed to be incorporated for the benefit of the public' (ibid.), and since they 'receive certain special privileges and franchises' (ibid.), they are subject to 'proper government supervision' (ibid.). Regulation, therefore, may not necessarily be a disadvantage; it can create incentives by ensuring a level playing field, by creating obstacles to free riders, and by ensuring the security of business transactions (Porter and Van der Linde 1995: 3).

The principles of neo-liberal and state-led schools do not assist in the search for the manner in which CSR principles can be incorporated into the activities of corporations. Whereas the neo-liberal school intends to ensure the maximum benefits of business through market rationalities, the state-led school aims to ensure the maximum good for all through necessary regulations. Taking the core of these Schools, we can summarise the position of corporations and corporate regulation for social responsibility as follows:

(1) The position of corporations pursuing mere profit is no longer the sole aim of corporate governance. The scholarship of corporate governance is under growing pressure to consider changes in the values and circumstances of the surrounding society—even if it means giving up profit in the short run. As business activity is closely interrelated with social, environmental, and political systems, these activities have a whole array of consequences—such as pollution or unemployment—on individuals, communities, nations, and the entire species (Gray et al. 1996: 1–2). The notion of CSR conceptualizes this development in corporate governance and regulation, suggesting that corporations are responsible for contributing to this development.
(2) Corporate performance is now judged by social policies rather than products and services (Juholin 2004: 21), as the impact of irresponsible business behavior may result in social and environmental crises and cause suffering to shareholders, customers, and employees alike.
(3) Corporations have become the major institutions of business in society, and they are vital to both economic and social development. They exercise more power than ever; for example, they are the most powerful and competent actors in society for assisting social and environmental programs (Juholin 2004). Laws can compel corporations to respond to social demands, but should not command or prescribe the way a corporation should fulfill its responsibility to the society; legal regulation can set social responsibility performance goals, but it should be the corporations who design suitable strategies to reach these goals.

5 The Converged Approach: Convergence of Pro-business and Pro-regulation Arguments

In the corporate regulation landscape, while some legal regulation reformers have argued that the prescriptive mode of regulation has failed to facilitate, reward, or encourage companies to go beyond their profit-centred behaviour, others have argued that relying only on corporate self-regulation is not a viable approach to enable the incorporation of social values in corporate behaviour in the absence of non-legal social drivers. In the context of this dilemma, we need a regulatory approach—different from the conventional approaches in regulatory framework—that effectively encourages corporations to transcend their social responsibilities. In this section I conceptualise such an approach, which I term the 'converged approach'. It draws upon regulatory scholarship that rejects the dichotomisation of regulation and deregulation. Rather, it conceptualises a pragmatic view of the power that companies wield, the need for companies to internalise public policy goals, and the limitations of traditional prescriptive regulation to achieve this internalisation, and, in consequence, change corporate culture.

5.1 Conceptualisation of the 'Converged Approach'

Within the discursive field of corporate regulation, numerous discourses interact and compete for dominance, with varying degrees of success. However, none of these concepts (e.g., consumerism, realism, neo-liberalism, environmentalism, or Marxism) dominates corporate regulation scholarship and practice. Though the neo-liberalism precept is considerably more practiced, it is always contested. Indeed, the discursive field of corporate regulation does not consist of a simple competition between a dominant discourse—neo-liberalism—and a resistant discourse—anti-neo-liberalism. At this point, Foucault (1998: 100) insists, '[W]e must not imagine a world of discourse divided between the accepted discourse and excluded discourse, or between the dominant discourse and the dominated one; but as a multiplicity of discursive elements that may come into play in various strategies'.[16] Scholars and practitioners are skeptical of the role of law in regulation framework as an abstract, monolithic, and apolitical system of regulation. In this perspective, it is plausible that scholars and practitioners search for a different regulatory approach that considers legal regulation as a pluralistic and fragmented system. The converged approach reflects on this search. This approach would utilise laws 'not as a vertically autonomous source of authority which arbitrates down

---

[16]For some studies on Foucauldian theory pertinent to an analysis of law, see Baxter (1996), Litowitz (1995), and Wickham and Pavlich (2001). A comment by Joseph Stiglitz is worth mentioning here: 'there is a need to learn from theory and history, from best practices, and from what has worked. But care must be taken in extracting the appropriate lessons' (Stiglitz 2001).

among human beings, but as a horizontal collage of disjointed agencies of regulation' (Carty and Mair 1990 in James 2008: 185). Its precepts would not be based on apolitical notions either; they would rather be based on an 'ideologically empty' system in which numerous discourses compete to deploy the regulatory strategy in order to be recognized and accepted as a framework for fulfilling a given objective (Hunt and Wickham 1994: 57; Hunt 1992).

The normative basis of the converged approach can be traced back to the theoretical ingredients of the Third Way.[17] The Third Way is the term loosely used to describe the emergence of new social democracy throughout the world. Though it is easy to explain this term in this way, it is by no means a simple matter to analyze coherently. It is a socio-political concept mostly conceptualized in Europe. The principal architect of this theory has been Anthony Giddens; his two recent seminal books, *The Third Way* and *The Third Way and its Critics,* expand on this theory.[18] Though this term frequently refers to a means of social democratic variety between free market capitalism and centrally planned socialism, this study, however, extends its focus to classical social democracy and neo-liberalism. Giddens narrates this notion as follows:

> Classical social democracy thought of wealth creation as almost incidental to its basic concerns with economic security and redistribution. The neoliberals placed competitiveness and the generating of wealth much more to the forefront. Third way also gives very strong emphasis to these qualities, which have an urgent importance given the nature of the global market place. They will not be developed, however, if individuals are abandoned to sink or swim in an economic whirlpool. Government has an essential role to play in investing in the human resources and infrastructure needed to develop an entrepreneurial culture (Giddens 1998: 99).

Hombach (2000) describes the Third Way in a more simplistic way, as a type of policy that could steer 'a third course, a path between competing ideologies, a system that represents a realistic response to the changes that have taken place in the world'. Hombach (2000) argues that this perspective has superseded 'the extremes of free market economies on the one hand and centralized welfare state economies on the other'. It interprets 'market failure' within neo-classical economics as a basis of regulatory intervention of the internal regulation of corporations when the effect of such failure is widespread, although there are various

---

[17]The concept of Joseph Stiglitz's 'New Perspective' is also close to my concept of the converged approach. The New Perspective considers government and market as complements rather than substitutes. In this perspective, the role of government is to create the institutional infrastructure that the market requires; its role is to create laws to define property rights, to enforce contracts, to ensure effective competition, and to minimize fraud. This perspective allows regulatory intervention into the market to implement these laws to check market failure. It is more related with economic issues and advocates co-operation between the government and private ordering to develop the market. The third-perspective is more related with regulatory strategies to help the convergence of the public and private policy goals. For details of the New Perspective, see Stiglitz (2001).

[18]Anthony Giddens is one of the world's leading social scientists (Giddens 1981, 1984, 1990, 1996).

Converged Approach in Regulation ... 171

instances of 'regulatory failure' (Arestis and Sawyer 2001: 2). Thus, the precepts of the Third Way can also be understood as an intervention into the new classical economics.[19] Giddens (1998) considers globalization vital to his conceptualization of the Third Way:

> Globalization, in sum, is a complex range of processes, driven by a mixture of political and economic influences. It is changing everyday life, particularly in the developed countries, at the same time as it is creating new transnational systems and forces. It is more than just the backdrop to contemporary policies: taken as a whole, globalization is transforming the institutions of the societies in which we live.[20]

In the circumstances transformed due to the impact of 'globalization', the roles of government and regulation are seen to shift towards creating a favorable environment, as Giddens argues, for transnational investment. He relates the impact of these circumstances with state policy perspectives in terms of a shift from industrial policy and the globalization demand measures favored by the demands of social democracy, deregulation, and market liberalization (Giddens 2000: 73). Giddens notes that the economic notion of the Third Way needs to 'concern itself with different priorities—with education, incentives, entrepreneurial cultural flexibility, devolution, and cultivation of social capital' (ibid.). At the same time, he emphasizes economic development in society and argues that the policies for such development should not be based on 'old-style interventionism' (ibid.). Accordingly, Blair and Schroder (1999: 163) argue for the creation of 'conditions in which existing businesses can prosper and adapt and new businesses can establish and grow'. The Third Way encourages the corporate sector to collaborate at the local level to create wealth, jobs, and responsible risk-taking in the pursuit of entrepreneurial activity; it highlights the need for such collaboration amongst the public and private sectors to maximize shared benefits (Wheeler 2002: 27). It is a socio-political argument to ensure 'productivity…profitability… [and] the bottom line.'[21]

The precepts of the Third Way argue for the strong role of the state in corporate regulation, and on the other hand, they limit the role of the state in regulation. Giddens mentions that the goal of the regulatory politics of this Way would be to develop a new mixed economy. He divides this economy into two: one aims to

---

[19]Arestis and Sawyer (2001: 3–5) postulate that the economic notion in the Third Way should be based on seven principles.

[20]According to Giddens (1998, 2000), globalization is an umbrella term that has different meanings to different subjects. In general, it refers to the increasing unification of the world's economic order through reduction of the possible barriers to increase material wealth, goods, and services; it describes the process by which regional economies, societies, and cultures could be integrated through communication, transportation, and trade. Hence, it could also be referred to as a process driven by a combination of economic, technological, socio-cultural, political, and biological factors. Giddens does not define globalization differently; he emphasises the effect of globalization on a nation's socio-economic policy perspective. For a robust discussion of globalisation, see Bhagwati (2007) and Croucher (2004: 10).

[21]Speech by Stephen Byers, Secretary of State for Trade and Industry at the *New Ways to Work Conference* on 9 May 2000, mentioned in Wheeler (2002: 27).

separate the roles of state and private sectors and the other is the social market. The objective of the Third Way is to develop such regulatory policies that could help the development of a mixed economy where there exists a synergy between the public and private sectors, 'utilizing the dynamism of markets but with the public interest in mind' (Giddens 2000: 100). This regulatory approach advocates a balance between regulation and deregulation to maintain a balance between the economic and non-economic life of the society (ibid.). It is not all about the debate between the political positions of right and left. Rather, it is a new approach to map out the strategy necessary for a renewal of social democracy (Wheeler 2002).[22]

The changed social democracy landscape greatly contributed to the evolution of the 'modern regulation' which has also laid the basis of the conceptual core of the 'converged approach' in regulation. The 'renew deal scholars'[23] describe this evolution through three legal paradigms: first, a system that merely facilitates private ordering; second, a regulatory model; and third, progression from the regulatory model towards the governance approach. In the first paradigm, though the set of formal laws is prominent, economic actors consider the rules a 'thin regulatory framework for freedom of contract and property security' (Lobel 2004: 282). At this stage, private parties are free to carry out their own transactions within a minimal set of rules. This paradigm shifted towards the development of substantive laws within which the regulatory state was formed. Of particular importance to this paradigm is the perception of the centralised authority that social subsystems are incapable of self-adjustment; hence, this paradigm deems it logical to intervene in diverse areas through goal-oriented regulatory policies. However, this regulatory model often fails to improve compliance, because it is fated to be either under-effective or over-effective or distort other social values. Parker (2006) notes that enforcement of these types of regulation often fails to improve compliance, as they insufficiently deter. Specifically, the laws that aim to deter for business offences are limited in their effectiveness, because it is difficult to detect the type of offence committed by business actors, and therefore, it is difficult to enforce punishment. These circumstances, if not addressed, create a trap in which the penalties for non-compliance, as Parker (2006) describes, are either too weak or too strong. Due to this trap, the object of regulation usually becomes frustrated, as it fails to obtain required reflection from the regulatee (Braithwaite 2002: 108).

The third transformation in the legal regulation paradigm is based on re-constitutive legal strategies that aim to 'restructure subsystems rather than simply

---

[22]There are differences and similarities between the notions of the Third Way advanced by Giddens and Blair. However, they are not identical. For details, see Driver and Martell (2000: 156–157).

[23]Amongst the regulatory reformers, there is a growing trend of stepping outside of a litigation and rule enforcement regulatory focus to explore an alternative conception of law and law-making scholarship. Lobel (2004: 262–390) has attempted to draw together such scholarship under an umbrella that she labels the 'Renew Deal'. Many scholars who are active in a wide variety of fields are considered as Renew Deal Scholars, including Dorf and Sabel (1998), Freeman (1997), Karkkainen (2003: 943), and Sturm (2001:458).

prescribe substantive orders' (GunterTeubner 1986; Stewart 1986: 90). Laws and public policies at this stage are more related to market mechanisms, less related with discretionary provisions, more focused on the rationale for regulation, and more related with the development of institutions (Stiglitz 2001: 348). Jänicke and Weidner (1997) identify references relevant to this line of regulatory transformation. They studied the evolution of environmental regulation in thirteen countries and found that most countries first opted for formal market-based laws as the core of the regulatory framework; second, direct control through substantive laws; and third, approaches for the reflexive mode of laws that facilitate coordination with the private actors (Jänicke and Weidner 1997: 310–312).

With this move in 'new governance'[24] type regulatory scholarship, Teubner (1988: 1–11) emphasizes breaking the taboo circulating in legal thinking and embracing the facts. Different schools of thought within legal academia are breaking this taboo and moving out of the conventional models of regulation, administration, and adjudication (Charnovitz 1996: 282–283). '[P]ointing to the false dilemma between centralized regulation and deregulatory devolution', Lobel (2005: 343) argues that there is a growing consensus on the necessity of innovative approaches of law and lawmaking to incorporate social policy goals with self-regulated corporate responsibility. Renew deal scholars argue for more governance approaches in legal regulation, as 'a myriad of policy initiatives in different fields are employing new regulatory approaches in legal practice that reflect this theoretical vision' (ibid.). Sturm (2006) has summarized the common elements of this type of regulatory governance as follows:

> [T]his approach places a focus on regulation through centrally coordinated local problem solving. Public agencies encourage local institutions to solve problems by examining their own practices in relation to common metrics and by comparing themselves to their most successful peers. Problem solving operates through direct involvement of affected and responsible individuals. Information about performance drives this process. Its production and disclosure enable problems to be identified, performance to be compared, pressure for change to mount, and the rules themselves to be revised. Public bodies coordinate, encourage, and hold accountable these participatory, data-driven problem solving processes (Sturm 2006: 247).

This mode of governance in modern regulation could be contentious due to the need to synergize two contradictory circumstances (in most instances) in the contemporary regulation landscape. On the one hand, this landscape needs to respond to the increasing public demand and NGO advocacy to include more enforceable tools to monitor and evaluate corporate strategies to meet their environmental

---

[24]New governance comes from a conceptual background which examines how decision-making and people-friendly strategies have begun to converge. The core of this governance is the convergence of the rulemaking power of the government and the strength of stakeholders as well as the private ordering system. Rubin (2005) finds the NG approach preferable where the regulator 'knows the result it is trying to achieve but does not know the means for achieving it, when circumstances are likely to change in ways that the [regulator] cannot predict, or when the [regulator] does not even know the precise result that she desires' (p. 2131).

accountability and social responsibilities. On the other hand, it needs to ensure that public policies do not hinder the development of economic efficiency but maintain the principles of property rights. In this flux, the converged approach opts for the decentralization of legal power, the pluralization of public actors, and economic incentives. Within this approach, therefore, the role of the state in the trend of incorporating the core principles of CSR has been juxtaposed with new governance where state-promulgated laws, civil regulation, and market rationale coexist in various interdependent configurations (Levi-Faur 2006: 521; Shearing and Wood 2003: 405). This approach allows regulatory intervention in business so long as this intervention helps to create a better business case for corporations in general. This is because legal intervention in the market generally tries to relate with the stance chosen by the involved parties in response to a public policy goal. In respect of this growing consensus and akin to converging the concurrent arguments of pro-business and pro-regulation advocates, the modern regulation implies that the regulatory mechanism or legal strategies should rely on a mix of different styles to improve compliance rather than on any single strategy.[25] According to this regulation concept, the state has roles as well as limitations in corporate regulation; in other words, the state should not 'row, but steer: not so much control, as challenge.'

5.2 Application of the Converged Approach

The application of this approach does not focus on either deregulation or hard regulation but on regulatory redesign to provide scope to the private ordering system to develop their own strategies to respond to public policy goals. In other words, it suggests changing 'the regulatory structure in ways that promote competition' (Stiglitz 2001: 347). In order to develop a regulatory framework, this approach includes an assessment of all available options at the policy level of a country. The most common instruments would be high public-private interaction, low public-private interaction, obligatory measures, voluntary measures in regulation, and so on. The proportion of these options in the preparation of the regulatory framework would be unequal. From this perspective, businesses are given adequate opportunities to produce their own plans to maximize their profits within the boundaries of the law and minimal ethical constraints, and at the same time, obligatory regulation is used to ensure corporations' liabilities to society. The strength of this approach is its ability to provide scope to fix the proportion of different policy instruments. For instance, the proportion of command-and-control type regulation and regulation by consensus or negotiated rule making would be lower in developed economies than in weak economies, while the aim is to incorporate CSR principles in corporate self-regulation. Simultaneously, the proportion

---

[25]For a general discussion on meta-regulation, see Gilad (2010) and Rahim (2011).

of self-regulation would be preferred in developed societies. Such variation may exist along with variations in types of corporations and strengths of regulatory agencies.

At the core of this approach is the fusion of different strategies to suit the corporate culture of a certain type of corporation in a unique context as well as its acknowledgment of the main arguments of pro-business and pro-regulation advocates in corporate regulation. Relating it to the implementation of the core principles of CSR, holistically, the strategic fusion in this perspective is a combination of the regulatory and voluntary mode of CSR to meet the social responsibility of a business that 'encompasses the economic, legal, ethical, and discretionary expectations that society has of organizations at a given point of time' (Carroll 1979: 500 in Schwartz and Carroll 2003). This approach helps the regulation scholarship to shift from its traditional framework to this new framework understood as a policy option through which policymakers could try to balance the drive of corporations for profits and the needs of the society in which businesses can make a meaningful impact.

The debate between pro-business and pro-regulation advocates over the value of CSR practice and its political effects is no longer dominant in corporate regulation scholarship. Rather, their nexus in the face of changes in regulatory strategies, corporate self-regulation, and social policies has minimised this controversy over both the potential and limitations of corporate-accountability mechanisms. The converged approach in regulation further contributes in minimising the contradicting arguments in CSR implementation, as this approach implicates that the regulatory strategy to implement CSR principles in corporate self-regulation should consider corporations' need for social responsibility performance and the scope to produce internal regulation according to their individual needs and circumstances. It also implies that corporate self-regulation should not be solely dependent on corporate governance. Rather, this regulation could be based on the 'relationships among the many players involved (the stakeholders) and the goals for which the corporation is governed.'[26] Given that this concept is vital for socialising corporations, there are two potential core strategies in a regulatory framework based on the converged approach for incorporating the CSR principles at the core of corporate self-regulation:

(1) Regulatory strategies for implementing CSR principles do not depend on any single system; rather, it should be a fusion of the precepts of different systems that could facilitate business case development as well as the rights of the stakeholders of business operations;

---

[26]Corporate Governance Systems and Processes: The Key for Uncompromising Growth and Development http://ivythesis.typepad.com/term_paper_topics/2009/07/corporate-governance-systems-and-processes.html (Accessed 22 November 2010).

(2) Laws related to the incorporation of CSR principles at the core of corporate self-regulation avoid direct interference into the internal management of corporations. Unlike the prescriptive laws, the legal strategies for this incorporation should ensure ample scope for corporations to develop their own strategies in response to public policy goals.

I believe that the scope of this converged regulatory approach is wider than the scope of a traditional command-and-control and prescriptive legal regulation. This approach allows the regulatee to contribute in developing the regulatory framework. As such, it provides governments with more chances to evaluate corporate self-regulation intensively, to connect corporate self-regulation to the public justice debate and dialogue, and to move private justice of the internal management system to the public justice of legal accountability.

5.3 Progress of the Converged Approach

The converged approach is not novel in regulation scholarship and practice. To some extent, however, it has attained a wider and more enthusiastic acceptance in the practice than legal academic literature. The progress of this regulation approach therefore relies on stakeholders' aims related to the application of this approach in a regulatory framework. Its progress will be halted if they fail to support this application by at least one substantive social policy goal or responsibility values.

It is undeniable that businesses affect the manner in which values in society are created, and without businesses, innovation, better consumption, and restoration of the environment could be hampered. Akin to this perspective, the converged approach asserts that the distortion in the usual ways of doing business could lead society towards a less productive, labor-consuming, and innovative way of transforming natural resources for human needs. It allows legal intervention in business so long as this intervention helps to create a better business case for corporations in general. According to this approach, therefore, regulatory intervention in the market should try to relate with the stance on which the involved parties choose to respond, and the issues in developing regulations should hold the broader perspective of a specific point of time and the underlying objective of a given subject. This is clearly demonstrated in the EU strategies for regulating CO_2 emissions from cars. In the beginning, the EU was reluctant to impose any regulations for controlling these emissions. During the initial stages of developing their CO_2 emission-control policies, without imposing any regulatory directives, they determined that the car industries must take measures to keep CO_2 emissions below 130 g CO_2/km. After a few years, it was found that the emissions had not been significantly lowered, and the EU was obliged to lower the emission levels according to the Kyoto protocol. Ultimately, they will need to shift their stand to regulate the concerned industries to meet the Kyoto and SDS goals they have planned to meet by 2012 and 2020, respectively (Ballebye 2008: 1). The Commission is not yet in favor of formally incorporating CSR principles in business regulations; however, they are gradually indicating that they do not oppose this approach entirely. They have mentioned that the public authorities need to promote CSR practices, because: (a) these practices are useful instruments to promote community policies; and (b) necessary 'to ensure a proper functioning of the internal market and the preservation of a level playing field.'[27] This has been achieved in the background of the recent proliferation of strategies that source different CSR instruments for implementing CSR principles.[28]

From a societal perspective, there is a need for corporations to be socially responsible. Hence, the laws and regulations that bind social actors to behave in an accepted way should also bind corporations. Moreover, like all good citizens, corporations in this regard should take responsibility for the externalities they are creating. CSR helps to minimise these externalities; it helps to hold a moral dimension in business strategies. Furthermore, where the market system is the sub-system to the social system, and where the idea of 'the good life' is the basis of economic growth, business corporations also have, besides a legal and economic responsibility, a social responsibility to be at level with the state of development of a society at any given point.

But this does not mean that laws and public policies undermine the capacity and objectives of corporations (i.e., the delegated rights of corporate directors to gain the maximum return of investments of the shareholders). This approach is not a way of carving rights out of existing frameworks by undermining the property rights of others but a way of overcoming the problems caused by the issues of property rights of such a subject that might create negative externalities to others who do not possess any right on the subject. It argues that stakeholder engagement in corporate responsibility issues could create additional, primarily 'opportunity' interests, for corporations.[29] Active stakeholders of corporations drive CSR forward; stakeholders can influence policy formation without being attached to either government or business and can place pressure on corporations to perform their social responsibilities. Taking consumers and other constituencies of the business, stakeholder groups can even directly contribute to business development. Hence, corporations as well as corporate regulators, as this approach argues, should create scope for the systematic interference of stakeholders in corporate self-regulation.

---

[27]European Commission, Communication from the Commission concerning Corporate Social Responsibility: A business contribution to sustainable development (COM 2002: 347 in Conzelmann 2008: 136).

[28]A comprehensive discussion can be found in Papadakis K, Participatory governance and discourses of socially sustainable development: Lessons from south Africa and European Union, *international Labour Studies,* September 2005, 38.

[29]Stake-holding in this perspective has an articulated voice depending upon the Kantian style imperatives such as 'no stakeholder should be used as a means to an ends.' For details, see Sternberg (1997: 70); for a discussion on Kant's expression of 'End-in-Itself', see generally Slote (1997: 138–9).

6 Conclusion

The basis of corporate responsibility has transitioned from why companies must be socially responsible to how they can become socially responsible. CSR is now a major component of new business and corporate management models for long-term sustainability. It has converged with the new trend of corporate management and contributed to the shift of the traditional notion of corporate governance to a vehicle for pushing corporate management to consider broader social issues. CSR defines corporate responsibilities to society as follows: firstly, that companies have a responsibility for their impact on society and the natural environment, which on occasion goes beyond legal compliance and the liability of individuals; secondly, that companies have a responsibility for the behaviour of others with whom they do business; and thirdly, that business needs to manage its relationship with the wider society, whether for reasons of commercial viability or to add value to society.

With the rise of sensitive consumerism, as well as increasing competition for market share, this convergence has made companies more attuned to public, environmental, and social needs. Many TNCs have integrated the ethos of this convergence into their core policy objectives. They are increasingly trying to ensure that CSR principles are implemented within their supply chains, as they have acknowledged that a demonstrated commitment to CSR helps them to secure their long-term profits, brand images, and managerial efficiencies.[30] They are now more willing to develop their self-regulation strategies in such a way that will assist them to adequately respond to the needs of the society within which they operate. At the national level, CSR has also attracted considerable attention. The number of countries that have either incorporated CSR principles into their corporate regulation framework or are trying to do so is increasing day by day.

However, we are yet to achieve a common and sound regulatory concept for implementing CSR principles worldwide. At present, regulatory strategies for this implementation in most of the developed countries are not authoritative. Rather, they are advisory and focused on bringing a broader perspective to the necessity of environmental responsibility in corporate self-regulation. Broadly speaking, incorporation of CSR notions in corporate self-regulation in these economies appears to focus on 'process-oriented regulation' where system-based strategies, enforced self-regulation, management-based strategies, meta-regulation approaches, and principle-based strategies coexist to ensure greater flexibility for the regulators where an objective needs to be incorporated in the era of deregulation (Harlow 2016; Hutter 2006; May 2005). Suitable implementation strategies in developing countries remain unclear too. In these countries, public interest advocacy groups to

---

[30]This concept may be described by a number of terms, such as 'corporate citizenship', 'The Ethical Corporation', 'corporate governance', 'corporate sustainability', 'social responsible investment', and 'corporate accountability' etc. Regardless of the terminology, the core principles remain the same. In this chapter, the term 'CSR' is used not because it carries any special meaning, but simply to be consistent.

oversee corporate social responsibility performance are absent, civil groups are not organised, the media does not have a specific focus on corporate issues, and the corruption rate in general is high. Hence, the incorporation of CSR principles in corporate regulation to date has not been noteworthy.

The world needs at minimum a regulatory standard for socialising business corporations, if it is not possible to have an international framework for this purpose. Countries may have their own internal regulatory arrangements that effectively increase social responsibility performance of corporations within their jurisdiction, but without sufficient legal prescriptions, the corporate capacity to recreate and increase efficiencies is undermined. This chapter conceptualises the 'converged approach'—a regulation approach that every country can adopt in their corporate regulation framework for corporate social responsibility performance.

Based on the normative core of the Third Way, this approach aims to merge the ethos of the contesting positions of the pro-business and pro-regulation advocates. It contends that performing social responsibilities has positive externalities, and state intervention through this regulatory approach in market policies could create incentives for businesses to engage in CSR practices. For application, this regulatory approach does not depend on any single source, strategy or actor; rather, it relies on a fusion of different factors and actors that facilitate business case development as well as the rights of stakeholders of corporate operations. It avoids direct interference in the internal management of corporations; unlike the prescriptive mode in legal regulation, this approach ensures ample scope for corporations to develop their own strategies to reflect on social needs and values. In the absence of an effective and agreed upon global framework for regulating TNCs, it would be worth exploring the application of this regulatory approach for raising social responsibility and accountability performance of TNCs, regardless of their country of origin, size, and ownership structure.

References

Arestis, P., & Sawyer, M. (2001). *Economics of the 'Third Way': Introduction*. Glos: Edward Elgar Publishing Limited.

Arora, S., & Cason, T. N. (1995). An experiment in voluntary environmental regulation: Participation in EPA's 33/50 Program. *Journal of Economics and Management, 28*, 271–286.

Bagi, A., Krabalo, M., & Narani, L. (2004). *An overview of corporate social responsibility in Croatia*. Zagreb: AED.

Bakan, J. (2012). *The corporation: The pathological pursuit of profit and power*. Hachette UK.

Ballebye, M. (2008). *CSR as a tool to reduce CO_2- Is intervention necessary?* (Masters), Aalborg University.

Bank, T. W. (1997). *World development report 1997—The state in a changing world*. Retrieved from https://openknowledge.worldbank.org/handle/10986/5980.

Baxter, H. (1996). Bringing Foucault into law and law into Foucault. *Stanford Law Review*, 449–479.

Bhagwati, J. (2007). *In defense of globalization*. Oxford: Oxford University Press, USA.

Bianchi, R., & Noci, G. (1998). Greening' SMEs' competitiveness. *Small Business Economics, 11,* 269–281.
Bizer, K., & Julich, R. (1999). Voluntary agreements-trick or treat? *European Environment, 9*(2), 59–67.
Blair, T., & Schroder, G. (1999). *Europe: The third way/Die Neue Mitte.*
Bradgon, J. H., & Marlin, J. (1972). Is pollution profitable? *Risk Management, 19*(4), 9–18.
Braithwaite, J. (2002). *Restorative justice and responsive regulation.* Oxford: Oxford University Press, USA.
Brau, R., & Carraro, C. (1999). *Voluntary approaches, market structure and competition.* Retrieved from http://www.ensmp.fr/Fr/CERNA/CERNA/Progeuropeens/CAVA/index.html.
Buhmann, K. (2006). Corporate social responsibility: What role for law? Some aspects of law and CSR. *Corporate Governance, 6*(2), 188–202.
Burchill, S. (2001). *Realism and neo-realism.* Basingstoke: Palgrave.
Carraro, C., & Siniscalco, D. (1996). Voluntary agreements in environmental policy: A theoretical appraisal. In A. Xepapadeas (Ed.), *Economic policy for the environment and natural resources.* Cheltenham: Edward Elgar.
Carroll, A. B. (1979). A three-dimensional conceptual model of corporate performance. *Academy of Management Review,* 497–505.
Carroll, A. B. (1991). The pyramid of corporate social responsibility: Toward the moral management of organizational stakeholders. *Business Horizons, 34*(4), 39–48.
Carroll, A. B. (1999). Corporate social responsibility. *Business and Society, 38*(3), 268.
Carty, A., & Mair, J. (1990). Some post-modern perspectives on law and society. *Journal of Law and Society, 17*(4), 395–410.
Cavaliere, A. (1998). *Voluntary agreements, over-compliance and environmental reputation.* Milan: FEEM Fondazione Eni Enrico Mattei.
Cavaliere, A. (2000). Over-compliance and voluntary agreements: A note about environmental reputation. *Environmental & Resource Economics, 17*(2), 195–202.
Chang, H.-J. (2003). *Globalisation, economic development, and the role of the state.* London: Zed Books.
Charnovitz, S. (1996). Two centuries of participation: NGOs and international governance. *Michigan Journal of International Law, 18*(1).
Christmann, P., & Taylor, G. (2006). Firm self-regulation through international certifiable standards: Determinants of symbolic versus substantive implementation. *Journal of International Business Studies, 37,* 863–878.
Coase, R. (1960). The problem of social cost. *The Journal of Law and Economics, 3*(October), 1–44.
Conley, J. M., & Williams, C. A. (2005). Engage, embed, and embellish: Theory versus practice in the corporate social responsibility movement. *Journal of Corporation Law, 31,* 1.
Conzelmann, T. (2008). A new public-private divide? Co-and self-regulation in the EU. In F. Larat (Ed.), *Efficient and democratic governance in the european union.* Connex: European Union.
Croucher, S. L. (2004). *Globalization and belonging: The politics of identity in a changing world.* Oxford: Rowman & Littlefield Publishers Inc.
Dahlsrud, A. (2008) How corporate social responsibility is defined: An analysis of 37 definitions. *Corporate Social Responsibility and Environmental Management, 15*(1).
De Bakker, F. G., Groenewegen, P., & Den Hond, F. (2005). A bibliometric analysis of 30 years of research and theory on corporate social responsibility and corporate social performance. *Business & society, 44*(3), 283–317.
Donaldson, T., & Preston, L. E. (1995). The stakeholder theory of the corporation: Concepts, evidence, and implications. *Academy of Management Review, 20*(1), 65–91.
Dorf, M. C., & Sabel, C. F. (1998). A constitution of democratic experimentalism. *Colombia Law Review, 98*(2), 267–473.
Driver, S., & Martell, L. (2000). Left, right and the third way. *Policy & Politics, 28*(2), 147–161.
Elkington, J. (1998). Partnerships from cannibals with forks: The triple bottom line of 21st century business. *Environmental Quality Management, 8*(1), 37–51.

Elkington, J. (2001). *The triple bottom line for 21 st-century business.* London: Sterling.
Esty, D. C., & Winston, A. S. (2009). *Green-to-gold-plays.* Retrieved from http://www.positivearticles.com/Article/Green-to-Gold–Plays/47943.
European Commission. (2001). Promoting a European framework for corporate social responsibility: Green paper. Retrieved from http://europa.eu/rapid/press-release_DOC-01-9_en.pdf
Foucault, M. (1998). *The will to knowledge.* Penguin Books: London.
Forum, W. E. (2002). Global corporate citizen: The leadership challenge for CEOs and boards. Retrieved from http://www.weforum.org/pdf/GCCI/GCC_CEOstatement.pdf
Fox, T. (2004). Corporate social responsibility and development. *Quest of an Agenda. Development, 47*(3), 29–36.
Freeman, E. (1984). Strategic management: A stakeholder approach (Vol. 1). Pitman.
Freeman, J. (1997). Collaborative governance in the administrative state. *UCLA Law. Review, 45.*
Freeman, E. R., & McVea, J. (2001). A stakeholder approach to strategic management. The Blackwell handbook of strategic management, pp. 189–207.
Freeman, R. E., Velamuri, S. R., & Moriarty, B. (2006). Company stakeholder responsibility: A new approach to CSR. *Business Roundtable Institute for Corporate Ethics, 19.*
Friedman, M. (1970). A Friedman doctrine: The social responsibility of business is to increase its profits. *New York Times Magazine, 13,* 33.
Friedman, M. (2007). The social responsibility of business is to increase its profits. *Corporate Ethics and Corporate Governance,* 173–178.
Garth, B., & Sterling, J. (1998). From legal realism to law and society: reshaping law for the last stages of the social activist state. *Law and Society Review,* 409–472.
Giddens, A. (1981). *A contemporary critique of historical materialism.* London: Macmillan.
Giddens, A. (1984). *The constitution of society: Outline of a theory of structuration.* Cambridge: Polity Press.
Giddens, A. (1990). *The consequences of modernity.* Cambridge: Polity Press.
Giddens, A. (1996). *Beyond the left and right.* Cambridge: Polity Press.
Giddens, A. (1998). *The third way: The renewal of social democracy.* Oxford: Polity Press.
Giddens, A. (2000). *The third way and its critics.* Oxford: Polity Press.
Gilad, S. (2010). It runs in the family: Meta regulation and its siblings. *Regulation & Governance, 4*(4), 485–506.
Gill, A. (2008). Corporate governance as social responsibility: A research Agenda. *Berkeley Journal of International Law, 26,* 452–462.
Gilpin, R. (2018). *The challenge of global capitalism: The world economy in the 21st century.* Princeton: Princeton University Press.
González, M. d. l., & Martinez, C. V. (2004). Fostering corporate social responsibility through public initiative: From the EU to the Spanish Case. *Journal of Business Ethics, 55,* 277.
Gray, R., Owen, D., & Carol, A. (1996). *Accounting and accountability: Changes and challenges in corporate social and environmental reporting.* London: Prentice Hall.
Greenfield, K. (2000). Corporate social responsibility: There's a forest in those trees: Teaching about corporate social responsibility. *Georgia Law Review, 34,* 1011.
Hanrahan, P., Ramsay, I., & Stapledon, G. (2002). *Commercial applications of company law.* Melbourne: CCH Australia.
Harlow, C. (2010). Law and public administration: Convergence and symbiosis. *International Review of Administrative Sciences, 71* (2), 279–294.
Hobson, J. M. (2000). *The state and international relations.* Cambridge: Cambridge University Press.
Hombach, B. (2000). *The politics of the new centre.* Oxford: Polity Press.
Hopkins, M. (2004). *Corporate social responsibility: An issue paper.* Working Paper No. 27, Policy Integration Department, World Commission on Social Dimension of Globalisation.
Hunt, A. (1992). Foucault's expulsion of law: Toward a retrieval. *Law & Social Inquiry, 17*(1), 1–38.
Hunt, A., & Wickham, G. (1994). *Foucault and law: Towards a sociology of law as governance.* Pluto Press.

Hutter, B. M. (2006). The role of non-state actors in regulation. Retrieved from http://eprints.lse.ac.uk/36118/1/Disspaper37.pdf

Jamali, D. (2008). A stakeholder approach to corporate social responsibility: A fresh perspective into theory and practice. *Journal of Business Ethics, 82*(1), 213–231.

Jamali, D., Mezher, T., & Bitar, H. (2006). Corporate social responsibility and the challenge of triple bottom line integration: Insights from the Lebanese context. *International Journal of Environment and Sustainable Development, 5*(4), 395–414.

James, N. (2008). Distracting the message: Corporate convictions and the legitimation of neo-liberalism. *Macquarie Law Journal, 8,* 179.

Jänicke, M., & Weidner, H. (1997). Summary: Global environmental policy learning. *National environmental policies: A comparative study of capacity-building.* Berlin: Springer.

Juholin, E. (2004). For business or the good of all? A Finnish approach to corporate social responsibility. *Corporate Governance, 4*(3), 20–31.

Kakabadse, N. K., Rozuel, C., & Lee-Davies, L. (2005). Corporate social responsibility and stakeholder approach: A conceptual review. *International Journal of Business Governance and Ethics, 1*(4), 277–302.

Karkkainen, B. C. (2003). Adaptive ecosystem management and regulatory penalty defaults: Toward a bounded pragmatism. *Minosota Law Review, 87.*

Kolk, A., Van Tulder, R., & Welters, C. (1999). International codes of conduct and corporate social responsibility: Can transnational corporations regulate themselves? *Avril, 8,* 143–180.

Konrad, A., Steurer, R., Langer, M. E., & Martinuzzi, A. (2006). Empirical findings on business–society relations in Europe. *Journal of Business Ethics, 63*(1), 89–105.

Levi-Faur, D. (2006). Regulatory capitalism: The dynamics of change beyond telecoms and electricity. *Governance, 19*(3).

Litowitz, D. (1995). Foucault on law: Modernity as negative Utopia. *Queen's Law Journal, 21,* 1.

Lobel, O. (2004). The renew deal: The fall of regulation and the rise of governance in contemporary legal thought. *Minnesota Law Review, 89.*

Lobel, O. (2005). Interlocking regulatory and industrial relations: The governance of workplace safety. *Administrative Law Review, 57,* 1071.

Lockett, A., Moon, J., & Visser, W. (2006). Corporate social responsibility in management research: Focus, nature, alliance and sources of influence. *Journal of Management Studies, 43*(1), 115.

Mankiw, N. G. (2004). *Principles of economics.* Thomson.

Maon, F., Lindgreen, A., & Swaen, V. (2009). Designing and implementing corporate social responsibility: An integrative framework grounded in theory and practice. *Journal of Business Ethics, 87*(1), 71–89.

Margolis, J., & Walsh, J. (2003). Misery loves companies: Rethinking social initiatives by business. *Administrative Science Quarterly, 48*(2), 268–305.

Marrewijk, M. V. (2003). Concepts and definitions of CSR and corporate sustainability: Between agency and communion. *Journal of Business Ethics, 44*(2–3), 95–105.

Marsden C. (2001). *The role of public authorities in corporate social responsibility.* http://www.alter.be/socialresponsibility/people/marchri/en/displayPerson [23 June 2003].

Matten, D., & Moon, J. (2007). Pan-European approach. A conceptual framework for understanding CSR. Corporate ethics and corporate governance, pp. 179–199.

Matten, D., Crane, A., & Chapple, W. (2004). Behind the mask: The real face of corporate social responsibility. *Journal of Business Ethics, 45*(1), 109–120.

McAdam, R., & Leonard, D. (2003). Corporate social responsibility in a total quality management context: Opportunities for sustainable growth. *Corporate Governance, 3*(4), 36–45.

Midttun, A. (2008). Partnered governance: Aligning corporate responsibility and public policy in the global economy. *Corporate Governance, 8*(4), 406–418.

Mitchell, L. E. (2001). *Corporate irresponsibility: America's newest export.* New Haven: Yale University Press.

Monbiot, G. (2013). *Captive state: The corporate takeover of Britain.* Pan Macmillan.

OECD. (1997). *Reforming environmental regulation in OECD Countries.* Paris: OECD.

OECD. (2003). *Voluntary approaches for environmental policy: Effectiveness, efficiency and usage in policy mixes*. Paris: OECD.
O'Rourke, D. (2003) Outsourcing regulation: Analyzing nongovernmental systems of labor standards and monitoring. *Policy Studies Journal 31*(1):1–29
Parker, C. (2006). The" compliance" trap: The moral message in responsive regulatory enforcement. *Law & Society Review, 40*(3), 591–622.
Peattie, K. J., Solomon, J., Hunt, J., & Solomon, A. (2002). Research insights into corporate social responsibility. *New Academy Review, 1*(3), 39–54.
Peters, M., & Turner, R. K. (2004). SME environmental attitudes and participation in local-scale voluntary initiatives: Some practical applications. *Journal of Environmental Planning and Management, 47*(3), 449–473.
Pflum, M. (2007). Wal-Mart commits to going green. *ABC News*. Retrieved from http://abcnews.go.com/GMA/TenWays/story?id=3602643&page=1.
Porter, M., & Van der Linde, C. (1995). Toward a new conception of the environment-competitiveness relationship. *The Journal of Economic Perspectives, 9*(4), 97–118.
Rahim, M. M. (2011). Meta-regulation approach of law: A potential legal strategy to develop socially responsible business selfregulation in least developed common law countries. *Common Law World Review, 42*(2), 174.
Rasche, A., Waddock, S., & McIntosh, M. (2013) The united nations global compact: Retrospect and prospect. *Business & Society, 52*(1), 6–30.
Rowe, J. K. (2005). Corporate social responsibility as business strategy. In: *Globalization, governmentality and global politics*. Abingdon: Routledge.
Runhaar, H., & Lafferty, H. (2009). Governing corporate social responsibility: An assessment of the contribution of the UN Global Compact to CSR strategies in the telecommunications industry. *Journal of Business Ethics, 84*(4), 479–495.
Russell, C. S., & Powell, P. T. (1999). Practical considerations and comparison of instruments of environmental policy. In J. v. d. Bergh (Ed.), *Handbook of environmental and resource economics*. Cheltenham: Edward Elgar.
Sairinen, R., & Teittinen, O. (1999). Voluntary agreements as an environmental policy instrument in Finland. *European Environment, March-April*, 67–75.
Sayer, A. R. (2000). *Realism and social science*. London: Sage Publications Ltd.
Schembera, S. (2018). Implementing corporate social responsibility: Empirical insights on the impact of the UN Global Compact on its business participants. *Business and Society, 57*(5), 783–825.
Schmit, J. (2010). Going greener: Wal-Mart plans new solar power initiative. *USA Today*.
Schrage, E. (2004). Promoting international worker rights through private voluntary initiatives: Public relations or public policy. *Report presented to the US Department of State by the University of Iowa Centre for Human Rights*.
Schwartz, M. S., & Carroll, A. B. (2003). Corporate social responsibility: A three-domain approach. *Business Ethics Quarterly, 13*(4), 503–530.
Shearing, C., & Wood, J. (2003). Nodal governance, democracy, and the new 'Denizens'. *Journal of Law and Society, 30*(3).
Slote, M. (1997). *From morality to virtue*. Edinburgh: Edinburgh University Press.
Sternberg, E. (1997). *Stakeholder theory: The defective state it's in*. London: IEA.
Stewart, R. B. (1986). Reconstitutive law. *Maryland Law Review, 46*.
Stiglitz, J. (1991). The economic role of the state: Efficiency and effectiveness in the public domain. In T. P. Hardiman & M. Mulreany (Eds.), *Efficiency and effectiveness in the public domain*. Dublin: IPA.
Stiglitz, J. (1996). *Some lessons from the East Asian miracle* (Vol. 11). Washington: World Bank.
Stiglitz, J. (2001). *An agenda for development for the twenty-first century*. Cambridge: Polity Press.
Stiglitz, J. (2003). Globalization and the economic role of the state in the new millennium. *Industrial and Corporate Change, 12*(1), 3.

Sturm, S. (2001). Second generation employment discrimination: A structural approach. *Columbia Law Review, 101*.

Sturm, S. (2006). The architecture of inclusion: Advancing workplace equity in higher education. *Harvard Journal of Law and Gender, 29*.

Testy, Y. K. (2004). Capitalism and freedom: For whom? Feminist legal theory and progressive corporate law. *Law and Contemporary Problems, 67*(4), 87–108.

Teubner, G. (1986). After legal instrumentalism? Strategic models of post-regulatory law. *Dilemmas of Law in the Welfare State, 299*.

Teubner, G. (1988). Introduction to autopoietic law. *Autopoietic law: A new approach to law and society, 1*(3).

Thompson, G. (2005). Global corporate citizenship: What does it mean? *Competition and Change, 9*(2), 131–152.

UNEP. (1998). *Voluntary initiatives, Industry and Environment, 21*(1–2): UNEP.

Vance, S. (1975). Are socially responsible firms good investment risk? *Management Review, 64,* 18–24.

Viotti, P. R., & Kauppi, M. V. (1999). *International relations theory: Realism, pluralism globalism and beyond*. Boston: Allyn and Bacon.

Waddock, S. (2008). Building a new institutional infrastructure for corporate responsibility. *Academy of Management Perspectives, 22,* 87–108.

Watts, P., & Holme, R. (1999). *Corporate social responsibility*. Geneva: World Business Council for Sustainable Development.

Wheeler, S. (2002). *Corporations and the third way*. Portland: Hart Publishing.

White, A. (2005). Fade, integrate or transform? The future of CSR. *Business for social responsibility, issue paper, www. bsr. org*.

White, A. L. (2006). Business brief: Intangibles and CSR. *Business for social responsibility, 6*.

Wickham, G., & Pavlich, G. (2001). *Rethinking law, society and governance: Foucault's bequest*. Oregon: Hart Publishing.

Williamson, O. E. (1996). Revisiting legal realism: The law, economics, and organization perspective. *Industrial and Corporate Change, 5,* 383–420.

Windsor, D. (2001). The future of corporate social responsibility. *The International Journal of Organizational Analysis, 9*(3), 225–256.

Windsor, D. (2006). Corporate social responsibility: Three key approaches. *Journal of Management Studies, 43*(1), 93–114.

Zarsky, L. (2002). Beyond good deeds: For multinational corporations to adopt socially responsible practices, voluntary measures are not enough.

Dr. Mia Mahmudur Rahim is a Senior Lecturer in Law at the University of South Australia. Previously he worked at the Queensland University of Technology and the Bangladesh Judiciary. He completed a Bachelor of Laws with Honours and Masters of Laws from Dhaka University, a Masters in International Economic Law from Warwick University, a Masters in Public Administration from the National University of Singapore and a Ph.D. from the School of Law at Macquarie University. His research interests lie in different forms of regulation and how this relates to legal structures that encourage social responsibility and accountability practice of regulatees. One of his recent books *Legal Regulation of Corporate Social Responsibility* has explained how a meta-regulation mode in laws can effectively raise social responsibility performance of corporations. He is one of the authors of *Corporate Social Responsibility in Private Enterprises* and the lead editor of *Social Audit Regulation*.

Correction to: The UN Global Compact for Transnational Business and Peace: A Need for Orchestration?

Mariko Shoji

Correction to:
Chapter "The UN Global Compact for Transnational Business and Peace: A Need for Orchestration?"
in: M. M. Rahim (ed.), *Code of Conduct on Transnational Corporations*, CSR, Sustainability, Ethics & Governance, https://doi.org/10.1007/978-3-030-10816-8_5

The original version of the book was inadvertently published with incorrect information in chapter "The UN Global Compact for Transnational Business and Peace: A Need for Orchestration?"; the corrections are given below.

Page 92, Table 1, the text 'PRI(Delet)' in Case 3 has been deleted.
Page 94, Table 3, the word 'Contribution' has been added after 'Profit Led'.

The chapter has now been corrected.

The updated version of this chapter can be found at
https://doi.org/10.1007/978-3-030-10816-8_5

© Springer Nature Switzerland AG 2019
M. M. Rahim (ed.), *Code of Conduct on Transnational Corporations*,
CSR, Sustainability, Ethics & Governance,
https://doi.org/10.1007/978-3-030-10816-8_9

Printed in the United States
By Bookmasters